KU-582-125

REGIONS, NATIONS AND EUROPEAN INTEGRATION

Remaking the Celtic Periphery

SWANSEA UNIVERSITY COLLEGE
LIBRARY

Classmark: HC256.7 REG
Location: Bannen Library
Accession No

1004239445

This book must be returned immediately it is asked for by the Librarian,
and in any case by the last date
stamped below.

1 - MAR 1995

- 1 APR 1997
U.C.S. LIBRARY

DATE DUE FOR RETURN
1 8 JAN 1995
U.C.S. LIBRARY

DATE DUE FOR RETURN
1 6 FEB 1995
U.C.S. LIBRARY

DATE DUE FOR RETURN
1 7 MAR 1995
U.C.S. LIBRARY

0 1 JUN 2000

SWANSEA UNIVERSITY COLLEGE LIBRARY

REGIONS, NATIONS AND EUROPEAN INTEGRATION

Remaking the Celtic Periphery

Edited by

GRAHAM DAY AND GARETH REES

Published on behalf of the
Board of Celtic Studies
of the University of Wales

CARDIFF
UNIVERSITY OF WALES PRESS
1991

© the University of Wales, 1991

British Library Cataloguing in Publication Data

Regions, nations and European integration:
remaking the Celtic periphery.
I. Day, Graham II. Rees, Gareth
337.142

ISBN 0708311199

All rights reserved. No part of this book may be reproduced, stored in a retrieval system, or transmitted, in any form or by any means, electronic, mechanical, photocopying, recording or otherwise, without clearance from the University of Wales Press, 6 Gwennyth Street, Cardiff, CF2 4YD.

Jacket design by Pica Design, Cardiff
Typeset by Megaron, Cardiff
Printed in Great Britain by Billings Book Plan Limited, Worcester

LIBRARY

Contents

Preface

The University of Wales's Board of Celtic Studies provided generous financial support both for the conference – 'The Periphery into the 1990s' – from which the papers collected here are derived and for the publication of these proceedings. It is, of course, a pleasure to acknowledge this assistance.

We have been greatly helped in the production of this book by the staff of the University of Wales Press, who have shown their usual forbearance in the face of our unerring ability to miss deadlines. Special mention must also be made of Martin Read of the University of Wales College of Cardiff for his willingness to sort out problems deriving from our inexperience in the use of information technology; and of Henry Maas of Four Crosses, Powys who has made a major contribution in improving the quality and presentation of the text through his expert editing. Most of all, however, our thanks are due to the contributors. Not only did they create an extremely stimulating conference, but also they have — for the most part — responded speedily to the demands of the publishing process.

One of the clear conclusions to emerge from the conference was that there is a need to extend the kind of multi-disciplinary social science research which is represented in the contributions to this book. Certainly, what follows is presented as a contribution to what will hopefully be a continuing process of deepening our understanding of societal change in the 'periphery'. Sadly, the social and economic problems which the regions and nations of the latter will continue to confront demand no less.

Graham Day, Bangor
Gareth Rees, Cardiff

Contributors

David Adamson, Department of Behavioural and Communication Studies, Polytechnic of Wales, Pontypridd

Philip Cooke, Department of City and Regional Planning, University of Wales College of Cardiff

Raymond Crotty, Trinity College, Dublin

Graham Day, School of Sociology and Social Policy, University College of North Wales, Bangor

Goio Etxebarria, Department of Applied Economics, University of the Basque Country, Bilbao

Neil Evans, Coleg Harlech, Harlech

John Lovering, School for Advanced Urban Studies, University of Bristol

Charlotte Lythe, Department of Economics, University of Dundee

David McCrone, Department of Sociology, University of Edinburgh

Lynn Mainwaring, Department of Economics, University College of Swansea

Kevin Morgan, Department of City and Regional Planning, University of Wales College of Cardiff

Angela Morris, Department of Sociology, University of Edinburgh

Jonathan Morris, Cardiff Business School, University of Wales College of Cardiff

Liam O'Dowd, Department of Social Studies, Queen's University, Belfast

Gareth Rees, School of Social and Administrative Studies, University of Wales College of Cardiff

Arantxa Rodrigues, Department of Applied Economics, University of the Basque Country, Bilbao

Colm Ryan, Department of Social Studies, Queen's University, Belfast

Dennis Thomas, Department of Economics and Agricultural Economics, University College of Wales, Aberystwyth

Introduction

GRAHAM DAY AND GARETH REES

The 'Celtic periphery'

The essays brought together in this book were originally presented at a conference held at Gregynog Hall, Powys, in the spring of 1990. The aim of the meeting was to make progress toward overcoming some of the divisions that impede our understanding of social and economic development as it affects the more outlying parts of the British Isles. In convening the meeting, we were guided by our experience of editing the inter-disciplinary year book, *Contemporary Wales*; and we were motivated by our view that beneath the everyday circumstances and current problems of Wales, Scotland and the two parts of Ireland, there is much common analytical ground, whose exploration is hindered by spatial and disciplinary barriers. We therefore invited a number of academics with varying disciplinary and geographical affiliations to address the theme of 'The periphery in the 1990s'.

The very choice of a title for the conference (and for this book) reflects the difficulties of stating precisely just what is the common point of reference. The term 'periphery' has an admittedly somewhat ill-defined and not uncontentious meaning. This is compounded by the fact that the inclusion of the whole of Ireland means that we are dealing with issues affecting more than one state. Neither is the use of the designation 'Celtic' definitive, as not all of the areas in question may be labelled accurately in this way. Moreover it is clear that not only do these areas share features with other parts of the British Isles which are not considered here (for example, parts of the north of England), but also that they themselves exhibit a considerable diversity of economic, political and cultural characteristics.

Nevertheless, we would continue to argue that there are important commonalities; indeed, we believe that the proceedings of the conference strongly confirm this view. Perhaps above all, what is shared in these areas and, in turn, ultimately marks them off from elsewhere, is the *intensely problematic* nature of the interrelationships between four analytically distinguishable dimensions of contemporary social change: economic restructuring; political mobilization; the construction of cultural identities; and the reorganization of state activities.

Wales, Scotland and both parts of Ireland have each been undergoing substantial economic restructuring during the 1980s, which reflects their characteristic roles in wider, international patterns of economic change. However, of common significance have been the impacts of the increasing integration of economic forces at the European level. And, of course, these are certainly going to continue to exert a powerful influence through the 1990s. These impacts will not only be felt in shifting patterns of prosperity and employment, but also within the political arena. Changes in the economic situation lead to, and are accommodated by, shifts in political organization, identification and action. In the areas under consideration, the structures of political mobilization are shaped by access to characteristic cultural and ethnic resources, frequently embodying the reconstruction of 'national' identities of various kinds. Here, a crucial role is played by the state, which necessarily both reflects the political specificities of these areas in its agencies, as well as attempting to regulate and manage the impacts of wider economic shifts.

Accordingly these four dimensions provide an organizing framework for the essays which follow. However, we do not wish to suggest that the *interrelationships* between them are exhaustively explored. In part, this is due to the underdevelopment of analysis in some areas. In particular, less attention than we would have wished is devoted to what is currently a particularly striking feature of social processes at the 'periphery': the struggles over the construction and reconstruction of cultural identities. More generally, of course, the contributions reflect the ways in which intellectual frameworks have developed, and they continue to bear a clear *disciplinary* imprint.

The contributions

The opening chapter by John Lovering sets the experience of the 'periphery' in the context of a wide-ranging review of the recent economic fortunes of Britain as a whole. Contrary to those who would argue that spatial differentiation is on the decline, he presents a convincing case that 'core–periphery' distinctions have sharpened, within an overall process of British peripheralization. In his view, despite radical policy shifts, little has changed in the long-term path whereby Britain has slipped further and further down the international league table of economic performance, seemingly incapable of halting a pattern of deindustrialization which has decimated manufacturing industry and generated substantial levels of unemployment and economic distress, especially in the outlying regions. At the same time as this general decline has taken place, 'growth'-orientated activities have become increasingly concentrated in southern England. Although during the last decade the 'peripheral' areas have suffered rather less drastically than the north of England, they have also undergone marginalization. There has been no recovery even to the levels of activity which prevailed a decade ago; rather, there has been a drift of financial services, 'elite' occupations and skilled labour towards the south. These economic developments are shown to have inevitable consequences for incomes, opportunities for advancement and class composition in the 'peripheral' areas; the emergent 'service class' is, for example, a predominantly southern English class. This restructuring, already fundamental, has been aided rather than checked by the state, and is now likely to be heightened by European integration.

The one exception in Lovering's generally dismal account of the plight of the 'periphery' appears to be Wales, which has suffered less during the 1980s than Scotland and Northern Ireland, and even witnessed some recent manufacturing recovery. In his discussion of the current economic circumstances of Wales, Dennis Thomas begins with this issue. The more bullish assertions of those who believe Wales has succeeded in 'migrating' from 'periphery' to 'core', are questioned in the light of evidence that Wales remains a low-earnings economy, whose employment recovery has not yet made good the losses of the early 1980s. Furthermore, there has been a replacement of relatively well-paid male manual jobs in manufacturing by low-paid female jobs in branch-plant and service activities. Wales's standing as an 'economic role model' for the break-out from 'peripheralization' looks a lot less promising than the surface gloss might suggest. On this basis, it becomes conceivable that the gains made in recent years may prove to be overspill developments, conditional upon the continued good fortune of the south. Rather than lasting regeneration of the Welsh economy, there appears to be an alternative vision of a low-tech, low-quality future dependent on inward investment, with an increased level of uncertainty arising from the widening horizons for economic calculation within enterprises, provided by European integration and the lowering of east–west barriers.

The two contributions by Charlotte Lythe and Lynn Mainwaring focus specifically on the likely effects of increasing integration within the European Community (EC) on Scotland and Wales respectively. Both argue that the strengthening of the Single Market after 1992 and monetary union in the longer term will worsen the regional situation unless there is compensatory intervention from both Westminster and Brussels. While, as Mainwaring contends, this would be a reasonable quid pro quo for the benefits accruing to the British economy as a whole, nothing in recent government policy suggests that it will be forthcoming. Rather, there is all too clearly a readiness to sacrifice the less prosperous regions in order to maintain the growth of the south. As Lythe shows, the enlargement of the EC has meant that there are now many other regions with a better case for support than those in Britain (the Republic of Ireland among them). With growing European disparities and a declining role for Britain, there is a risk that the 'peripheries' will be driven into deepening dependence on low-wage, routine assembly and production operations.

David McCrone's examination of Scottish politics situates the growing sense of disaffection and national awareness in terms of the impact these economic changes are having. The alacrity with which Conservative governments since 1979 have pursued a strategy of opening up the economy to market forces, abandoning as far as possible their regulatory role, has put an enormous strain on the unity of the British state. McCrone agrees with others in suggesting that Thatcherism combines economic *laissez-faire* with strong assertions of national identity, but notes that these are peculiarly *English* in their resonance. Accordingly they merely serve to accentuate Scottish feelings of difference: the upsurge in the nationalism of the 'core' inspires a counteractive nationalism of the 'periphery'. McCrone presents this latter nationalism as a complex formation, with political, social and cultural dimensions. He emphasizes that there is no simple alignment between nationalist aspiration and political affiliation; currently it is the Scottish Labour Party, rather than the explicitly nationalist SNP, which is benefiting. The adjustments required to match political structures to the kind of 'multi-level sovereignty' compatible with Britain's new role in Europe may yet, he suggests, produce the break-up of Britain forecast some years ago by Tom Nairn (1977).

According to David Adamson, nationalism (with or without a capital letter) has not made such headway in Wales during the 1980s. The transformations that have taken place in the workplace and the labour market, especially the relative decline of traditional manufacturing employment, have instead undermined the hold of

Labourism, in South Wales in particular, and created considerable ideological confusion and fluidity. A 'new working class' has appeared, and its formation is greatly influenced by new modes of consumption and 'lifestyle' patterns. With the weakening hold of conventional politics upon its allegiance, there is scope for the development of new social movements and a potential for radical consumer politics; but there is also fragmentation and privatization which might erode any kind of collective response. Adamson's argument suggests a number of lines for future research, including the investigation of the ways these developments are specifically Welsh.

The importance of the multiple possibilities for 'identity' consequent upon recent restructuring is also indicated in Liam O'Dowd's discussion of Irish politics, in which he pinpoints the significance of intellectuals in harnessing such possibilities. The responses of the two parts of Ireland to the challenges of economic integration have been profoundly different; and the social role of intellectuals has been one factor accounting for this. In the South, modernizing intellectuals were able to embrace a European identity and use the machinery of the state to underwrite it, replacing the previous ideology of Catholic ruralism with a conception of a capitalist Ireland available for multinational investment within a 'Europe of Nations'. In the North, by contrast, the lack of any coherent intellectual tradition which could articulate successfully with the popular culture of Protestant Loyalism has resulted in an impasse which blocks any possibility of an all-Ireland political discourse that might resolve the divisions between the Protestant and Catholic communities. For the present, it would seem, the best that can be done is to isolate the conflicts of the North and seek to contain them there.

Angela Morris takes issue with recent analyses of the 'heritage industry' in Britain. Although agreeing that its success owes much to the need for something which will displace the sense of national decline, she seeks to remind commentators that history and heritage look different when viewed from the 'periphery'. The unfinished business which Scottish history represents means that there is no agreed and settled image which can be projected as *the* national heritage. Instead, historical claims are bound to be contested. The same could be said of Wales (Williams 1985); and in view of O'Dowd's essay is patently the case for Ireland as well. Clearly, then, important further work needs to be done in tracing out the interrelationships between the construction of national histories and contemporary cultural and political identities; and the heritage industry constitutes an important arena for such explorations.

The role of the state is to the fore in the next set of contributions. In their different ways, they all highlight the continuing importance of state management of the restructuring process in places which have become exceptionally reliant on state support as a consequence of previous policies. Despite the rhetoric of neo-liberalism, state agencies remain very active in trying to counteract the effects of economic decline in manufacturing and heavy industry.

Gareth Rees and Kevin Morgan return to the question of the Welsh 'economic miracle'. However, they do so in order to explore the extent to which the institutional infrastructure of state agencies in Wales has generated a 'regional innovation system', upon which a more general model of decentralized economic management could be based. While allowing that in certain respects Wales has benefited more from recent restructuring than some of the more jaundiced accounts might suggest, they argue that so far the 'miracle' is a highly qualified one, despite the slickness of packaging and presentation. Certainly, whilst there are currently signs of new initiatives, Rees and Morgan conclude that a great deal remains to be done if Wales's capacity to innovate is to be improved sufficiently to meet the challenges of emergent European integration.

Jonathan Morris and his co-authors also address the role of regional state agencies in setting a direction for economic restructuring. They describe a Welsh 'model', in which the agencies have gone all out to attract inward investment and can claim some success in doing so. The equivalent organizations in the Spanish Basque country have aimed instead at the development of an indigenous small- and medium-sized firm sector, capable of competing effectively within the European market. This has resulted in the creation of what they describe as an 'industrial district', with a complex of machine tools firms capable of achieving a good export record. Comparison of the two models of development suggests, however, that there is a difficult trade-off between advanced technology and economic self-sufficiency, on the one hand, and jobs on the other.

As Colm Ryan and Liam O'Dowd show, the problems of state involvement are obviously far greater in Northern Ireland. As in other 'peripheral' regions, the state plays a critical role in managing economic restructuring. However, in Northern Ireland, any intervention becomes caught up with the legacy not only of past state strategies, but also of sectarian divisions. This illustrates especially clearly the contradictions between a neo-liberal state agenda and the continuing need to control local development and the potentially divisive and disruptive forces in which it is embroiled. Drawing on their research into the experience of two particular localities, Newry and Craigavon, Ryan and O'Dowd show that the current policy goal of stimulating local enterprise meets very different responses within what is a highly fragmented situation. Moreover, this is especially problematic in view of the simultaneous need of the state to maintain centralized control.

Economic restructuring in the rural context is the topic of Graham Day's paper. He deals with recent change in rural Wales in the context of the major transformations witnessed in the British countryside during the 1980s. These have brought about a much greater diversity of circumstances than was previously the case, which he illustrates by a discussion of the economic variations between different rural localities. Day assesses the role of various interventionist agencies, including 'grassroots' organizations, in managing rural change, and concludes that they are contributing towards significant shifts in the meaning of social and cultural life in rural Wales.

The remaining papers address themselves squarely to the issue of the extent to which the 'Celtic' peoples share a common 'peripheral' situation. In a fine-grained historical examination of the development paths taken by Wales, Scotland and Ireland, Neil Evans revisits the work of Michael Hechter and lays to rest the ghost of 'internal colonialism'. Drawing upon an enormous range of recent historical research, Evans demonstrates the very different connotations and applicability of concepts of 'colonization' to the three countries. He then describes the course of their economic development, making the important point that industrialization served to fix pre-existing disparities in their relative fortunes. The differences in the manner in which each nation became linked into the wider British context were extremely consequential for the types of political mobilization which ensued and for the construction of the various national identities. Evans shows how each has its distinctive positioning with respect to 'Britishness' and to the British state.

In a brief but incisive final note, Raymond Crotty questions the whole idea of a 'periphery' which would encompass Ireland alongside the outer regions of Britain. In his view, Ireland is a unique example, in European terms, of a country that is retrogressing, as measured by its capacity to support its population. This he attributes to a history of capitalist colonization shared by the Third World, but not by the other nations of Europe. This would imply that capitalist colonization has not been the fate of either Wales or Scotland, a claim borne out by Neil Evans's analysis. To sustain his argument that the Irish nation has undergone an exceptional experience, Crotty is compelled to regard those Irish people who have participated willingly in this process as 'agents and collaborators', who are not part of 'the nation'. This is a reminder that national identity and membership continue to be a negotiable status in the areas with which we have been concerned; it also presents some of the same difficulties which faced Hechter (1975) in his attempt to explain uneven development as the consequence of ethnic discrimination and the 'cultural division of labour'.

Apart from some minor stylistic changes, we have left the essays much as they were when they were delivered to the conference. Consequently, there are shifts of academic register, which obviously owe something to the authors, but at the same time represent the contrasting kinds of discourse which prevail in the disciplines represented. This undoubtedly makes for some problems of communication, as any multi-disciplinary gathering quickly shows, but there is also much illumination to be derived from the interplay between the various angles of approach and levels of analysis adopted by economists, political scientists and sociologists. Certainly, those who participated in the Gregynog meeting enjoyed the rare opportunity for a cross-disciplinary exchange which was not intended to contest the merits of different disciplinary stances, but which allowed a genuine chance to throw light on some questions of common interest. Perhaps most crucially, however, the gaps and relative silences in the contributions imply an entire agenda of research questions which we hope to see taken up and explored in future work, in the course of which co-operation across the disciplines can be strengthened.

Bibliography

Hechter, M. 1975. *Internal Colonialism: the Celtic Fringe in British National Development*, 1536–1966. Routledge & Kegan Paul
Nairn, T. 1977. *The Break-up of Britain: Crisis and Neo-nationalism.* New Left Books.
Williams, G. A. 1985. *When Was Wales?* Blackraven Press.

Part 1
Economic Change, Peripheral Development and European Integration

Chapter 1

Southbound Again: The Peripheralization of Britain

JOHN LOVERING

Introduction: Britain in the 1990s: regional integration or peripheralization?

Many commentators have pointed out that the rapid deindustrialization of the early 1980s gave rise to a deepening of the 'north–south divide' in England. At the same time it widened many of the differentials between southern England and the periphery of Wales, Scotland and Northern Ireland. [1] In the late 1980s, however, a new orthodoxy could be heard, especially in government circles and amongst sympathetic academics. According to these optimists, the day is in sight when 'the problem of the regions' will be a thing of the past. The UK, nudged along by a radical Conservative government, is adapting to a changing international environment, and its internal economic geography is undergoing a transformation. The painful upheavals of the early 1980s were but temporary shock effects, preconditions for a new kind of regional economic recovery in the 1990s, as part of a wider transition to a new and more competitive national economy.

Advocates of this view point out that the recovery from the mid 1980s soon began to push prosperity northwards and westwards from the south of England. They see the development of new industries and services as laying the foundations for the re-creation of regional economies. According to one particularly cheerful account:

> Provincial areas are booming . . . the core prosperity, the extended London area, now reaches beyond Bristol to the West, and through

---

1 The term 'periphery' is used here in a broad geographical sense, taking a European perspective, without any implicit theoretical claims. It is explicitly not meant to endorse the notion of 'internal colonialism'.

the Midlands well into Lancashire and Yorkshire. Northern Ireland is a special case. Scotland is obviously furthest away from the South East, but has been showing signs of relative prosperity. Perhaps the most difficult of the English regions is the North East, but even this is showing some benefits. (Lomax 1990, pp. 61–2)

Scotland and Wales, in particular, are held to contain significant examples of successful modernization. Evidence that the recession in 1990 affected industries in the south more heavily than elsewhere has been seen as a further indication that the 'periphery' and the north are beginning to improve their economic status (see, for example, Fazey 1990; Norman 1990).

The new breed of optimists base their case on faith in the efficacy of the reformed market. They assert that the restructuring brought about by a government committed to liberating market forces has created a new integrated economy, a single British Market, prefiguring the much less definite prospect of a single European Market. Freed of the distortions and government interference of the past, the 'hidden hand of the market' is now beginning to exhibit its more benign aspects (hitherto confined to the imaginary world of economics textbooks). Inequalities in incomes and costs will generate spontaneous flows of capital and labour which will tend to equalize the opportunities open to residents, and to firms, right across the nation. At long last, the north could be poised to regain the relative prosperity it enjoyed before the interwar period (Martin 1989a), when monopolistic practices and government intervention began seriously to distort the market.

This theory has been endorsed in the highest circles; in 1987 Lord Young declared that 'the workings of the market mean that industries are forced further and further north to take business opportunities' (*Business* 1987). It is said that companies are increasingly seeking out cheaper labour away from the 'hothouse' of the south-east. They will continue to be encouraged to do so by a migration of younger skilled people away from the south-east in search of cheaper houses and a better environment; 'a favourable trend is on the way, all government has to do is to acknowledge it, give it a helping hand, and then claim the political benefits' (Lomax 1990, p. 60).

The following pages summarize some statistics regarding the changing economic position of Northern Ireland, Scotland, Wales and northern and southern England. The available evidence indicates that the future foreseen by the optimists has yet to manifest itself in a general improvement in the balance of advantages between the south and the rest of Britain. In fact it suggests the opposite; the economic centrality of the south of England has increased, while other parts are becoming more marginal to the performance of the UK as a whole, even though certain areas within northern and western Britain are becoming more closely integrated into corporate networks which range across and beyond the UK. For example, Scotland and Wales contain important sites in the electronics industry (see Morgan 1987). But these examples of reintegration do not imply that the UK economy as a whole is becoming more spatially uniform. Indeed, on a number of indicators there is a clear distinction between the southern English 'core' and the remainder of the UK. There has been a general 'dilution of the separate identities of the standard regions, and the emergence of a simpler but deeper distinction between North and South' (Stewart 1990, p. 38). This broad economic differentiation is likely to be reflected in disparities in the range of opportunities open to residents.

The optimists could still assert that the evidence in the following section is beside the point, since it refers to the past, and the new economy of the future is only beginning to emerge. Later sections address this possibility by examining the influences which have shaped the development of the UK economy in the last decade and those that are likely to condition it in the foreseeable future. They suggest that Britain's recent economic development has not been anywhere near as transformative as the optimists suggest, and the forces which predominated in the 1980s are likely to remain in place well into the 1990s. Correspondingly, the dominant spatial tendencies are unlikely to be radically different from those of the recent past. The most likely prospect for the 1990s is either 'more of the same', or a more severe version, the continued marginalization of most of the geographical periphery and northern England, alongside the selective development of some favoured zones within those areas.

Indicators of economic change

A number of recent studies at the level of small areas, such as local labour markets, have generally confirmed the existence of a 'north–south divide' (Champion and Green 1989; Cooke 1989). A wider focus is adopted here in order to draw out the broader balance of economic activity between three zones: southern England, northern England, and Wales with Scotland and Northern Ireland. No attempt is made to establish a sophisticated definition of these three zones. This section merely builds on readily available data relating to the familiar Standard Regions. The 'periphery' is defined as

Wales, Scotland and Northern Ireland. 'Northern England' is composed of the north, north-west, north-east and the West Midlands.[2] 'Southern England' is made up of the south-east, south-west, East Anglia and the East Midlands.

Contribution to national output

Southern England is the core of the UK economy, and it has become more so in the 1980s. It contains half of the population, and the main drivers of British industry. This is the only zone to produce a share of output greater than its share of the population (table 1.1).[3]

In the 1980s the output of the south grew far more rapidly than that of the rest of the UK. The next-highest increase in GDP was in Wales, followed by Northern Ireland and Scotland. Growth was weakest in northern England table 1.2).

Between 1979 and 1988 the workforce of southern England expanded at six times the rate of the periphery (despite high growth in Northern Ireland) and ten times that of northern England (table 1.3). The south accounted for 48 per cent of the UK workforce in 1979, but 87 per cent of the increase over the following nine years.

Table 1.1   Shares of population and GDP, 1988

	% of population	% of GDP
Scotland	8.9	8.4
N. Ireland	2.8	2.1
Wales	5.0	4.2
Periphery	*16.7*	*14.7*
Northern England	34.3	31.3
Southern England	49.0	54.0
UK	100.0	100.0

The increasing concentration of economic activity and workers in the south of England resulted in a growing southern share of

2   This grouping has been adopted by others; see, for example, Lewis and Townsend (1989), p. 5.
3   Tables are from *Regional Trends* unless otherwise stated.

employment, rising by three percentage points. At the same time the south's share of UK unemployment declined (table 1.4).

Table 1.2   Increase in GDP, 1979–88 (current prices)

Scotland	124.0
N. Ireland	131.1
Wales	131.5
Periphery	*127.2*
Northern England	120.9
Southern England	143.7

Table 1.3   Increase in workforce, 1979–88

	000s	%
Scotland	14	(1.1)
N. Ireland	38	(5.8)
Wales	32	(1.3)
Periphery	*84*	*(1.9)*
Northern England	100	(1.1)
Southern England	1,445	(11.1)
UK	1,652	(6.3)

Table 1.4   Shares of employment and unemployment

	% share of Employment		% share of Unemployment	
	1979	1988	1979	1988
Scotland	9.1	8.6	12.9	13.1
N. Ireland	2.3	2.3	4.8	6.0
Wales	4.4	4.3	6.2	5.3
Periphery	*15.8*	*15.2*	*23.9*	*24.4*
Northern England	35.3	32.9	41.3	42.1
Southern England	48.9	51.9	34.8	33.6
Total	100	100	100	100

The 'two geographies of restructuring': declining and emergent regimes

The south has gained most of the new jobs, in both absolute and relative terms. Tables 1.5 and 1.6 separate the earlier period of net job loss from the later growth phase (leading into the 'Lawson boom'). They show that the turnaround affected the south differently from the rest of the UK. The periphery and northern England gained only a quarter as many jobs in 1986–8 as they lost earlier in the decade. In sharp contrast, the south gained nearly twice as many as it had lost.

Table 1.5   Employment loss, 1979–86, and gain, 1986–8 (000s)

	1979–86		1986–8		Ratio of gain/loss
	Loss	% of UK	Gain	% of UK	
Scotland	−223	12.5	37	4.2	16%
N. Ireland	−33	1.8	10	1.1	30%
Wales	−146	8.2	63	7.1	43%
Periphery	*−402*	*22.5*	*110*	*12.5*	*27%*
Northern England	−1094	61.3	256	29.0	23%
Southern England	−288	16.1	517	58.6	180%
Total	−1784	100	883	100	49%

Table 1.6   The turnaround in employment (000s)

	1979–86	1986–8
Scotland	183	−123
N. Ireland	64	−22
Wales	94	−81
Periphery	*341*	*−226*
Northern England	794	−597
Southern England	797	−1486
Total	1932	−2309

During the 1980s, the history of unemployment in the three zones was more similar than that of employment. Job gains after 1986 did not make inroads upon recorded unemployment in the south to the degree that they did in Scotland, Northern Ireland and northern England (as table 1.7 shows, in this respect Wales once again turns out to be more like southern England). These disparities may reflect the fact that unemployed people outside southern England are more likely to leave the register, or to migrate out of the region (mainly to the south); while the south has attracted and retained a hard core of unemployed claimants. In terms of its attraction to job-seekers, and its simultaneous inability to provide the jobs they seek, Britain's capital echoes the pattern of other world urban centres, including those in the Third World.

Table 1.7   Change in jobs and in recorded unemployment 1986–8

	Increase in jobs	Decline in unemployment	Ratio
Scotland	37	123	3.3
N. Ireland	10	22	2.2
Wales	63	81	1.3
Periphery	*110*	*226*	*2.0*
Northern England	256	597	2.3
Southern England	517	663	1.2
UK	883	1486	1.7

The Conservative government has placed considerable emphasis on self-employment, which accounted for twice as many new jobs created between 1981 and 1988 as did employment in a job working for others. Self-employment is a predominantly southern English phenomenon (it is also a predominantly male one, see Lovering 1990, p. 12) (table 1.8). This is despite the fact that the self-employed proportion of the workforce in the periphery has traditionally been high, largely through the influence of farming. If these forms of self-employment were excluded, the bias towards the south would be even greater. In 1986–8 the south accounted for three-quarters of the increase in self-employment (which actually declined in Northern Ireland). Again, northern England emerges as the 'least successful' of the three zones.

Table 1.8   Self-employment, 1988

	Number (000s)	% of UK total
Scotland	215	7.2
N. Ireland	60	2.0
Wales	146	4.9
Periphery	*422*	*14.1*
Northern England	876	29.4
Southern England	1,688	56.5
UK	2,986	100

The peripheralization of Britain: underlying processes

These spatial patterns are intimately bound up with Britain's position in the world economy (Massey 1984). Internationally the UK has retained its importance for a range of financial services and an increasingly modest range of industrial activities. These developments represent the continuation of longer-term trends which became particularly marked after 1975 (Wells 1989). During the late 1980s, they have been overlaid by a consumption-led expansion. This increased imports (expenditure on manufacturing began to exceed domestic output in 1982), but it also to some extent sustained domestic-orientated industries and services (two-thirds of manufacturing output is still sold domestically, Cutler *et al.* 1989). After 1988 expansion gave way to a slow-down induced by high interest rates. The overall decline in both the service and the manufacturing trade balance through the 1980s was financed by earnings from primary industries, especially oil, and accumulating deficits (Wells 1989).

These parameters of restructuring have influenced the location of activity. It is well known that the south has secured the lion's share of the growth in financial services (Breheny and Congdon 1989), thanks to the City and the 'London factor' (Martin 1989a, p. 94). Table 1.9 shows that the south increased its share of financial activities very significantly in the 1980s.

Because it is the centre of the finance and other service industries, and only a fifth of its employees work in manufacturing, it is sometimes suggested that southern England is the epitome of a 'post-industrial region' (for example, Martin 1989b, p. 87). However, it should not be forgotten that the south has retained its share of industry, and is actually the centre of UK manufacturing, accounting for nearly half of national manufacturing GDP. Manufacturing output contracted especially severely during the 1980s in northern England and Scotland. Once again, the distinctiveness of Wales is apparent, its share of manufacturing GDP rising significantly (table 1.10).

Table 1.9   Financial and business services

	Shares of GDP (%)		Change	% of employment 1988
	1979	1988		
Scotland	7.1	6.5	− 0.6	6.5
N. Ireland	1.7	1.3	− 0.4	1.9
Wales	2.7	2.4	− 0.3	1.8
Periphery	*11.5*	*10.1*	*− 1.4*	*10.2*
Northern England	24.9	22.0	− 2.9	23.7
Southern England	63.6	67.8	4.2	66.1
Total	100	100	−	100

The south actually increased its share of manufacturing investment, at the cost of northern England rather than of the periphery (table 1.11). The extent to which 'reindustrialization' is a southern English affair is perhaps not widely appreciated.

Table 1.10   Manufacturing: shares of GDP, 1979–88, and employment, 1988

	% of UK GDP		% of UK employment 1988
	1979	1988	
Scotland	8.4	8.1	8.0
N. Ireland	1.6	1.7	2.6
Wales	3.9	5.1	4.0
Periphery	*13.9*	*14.0*	*14.6*
Northern England	40.6	39.4	40.4
Southern England	45.4	45.7	45.0
Total	100	100	100

Table 1.11 Shares of manufacturing investment (gross domestic fixed capital formation in manufacturing) (percentages)

	1979	1987	Change
Scotland	8.6	7.4	− 1.2
N. Ireland	2.4	2.3	− 0.1
Wales	6.8	6.6	− 0.2
Periphery	*17.8*	*16.3*	*− 1.5*
Northern England	43.3	40.3	− 3.0
Southern England	38.9	43.4	4.4

Table 1.12 Distribution, hotels, catering and repair industries, 1988

	% share of GDP	% share of employment
Scotland	8.0	8.4
N. Ireland	2.0	2.8
Wales	3.7	2.9
Periphery	*13.7*	*14.1*
Northern England	31.0	31.9
Southern England	55.3	54.0

Consumption-driven, domestic-orientated industry and services have also been focused on the south, since it is the dominant consumer market. Table 1.12 shows that the south accounts for 55 per cent of GDP, and 54 per cent of employment in the distribution, hotels, catering and repair industries, a slight rise in both during the 1980s.

Summary

The macro-economic developments and forms of restructuring adopted in the 1980s resulted in a marked centripetal tendency. In terms of output, workforce, employment (including self-employment) and the location of growth industries, southern England has indisputably become more central to the UK economy. The peripheralization of Britain has involved above all the draining of activity from the northern third of England. The periphery of Wales, Scotland and Northern Ireland has in general fared less badly. Wales, in particular, on some indicators bears affinities with southern England. However, this disguises the emergence of a marked 'east–west' divide within Wales (Thomas 1989, p. 203), as most of the reindustrialization and service sector growth has occurred in south-east Wales and Clwyd.

The relative economic decline of northern England and the periphery has been expressed in human terms in the most vivid way by the physical movement of people. The balance of movement between the regions between 1976 and 1986 resulted in a net loss in Wales and Scotland of 2,000 (out of around a quarter of a million in- and out-migrants), a net loss in the north of 101,000 (out of around three-quarters of a million), and a net gain in the south of 103,000 (out of one and a third million). A large part of British migration takes place within southern England (Stilwell, Boden and Rees 1990; Doogan and Court 1990). Population loss through migration in northern England has created opportunities for the remaining unemployed people. In Northern Ireland, on the other hand, this effect has been minimal because of high population growth rates (CENIERC 1990, p. 9).

These aggregate figures obscure the different kinds of migration. It appears that much of the work-related migration to the south draws away more highly qualified labour. For example, the demand for engineers in southern England probably results in a steady drain of graduates and valuable experienced employees from the north and periphery, especially Scotland (see Lovering 1991).

Incomes and standards of living

Although the relative decline of output in the periphery and the north has been accompanied by a fall in their share of UK workers, these flows have not balanced each other out. Incomes have not risen to equality with southern England. However an 'optimistic' account could stress that lower incomes outside southern England are compensated by lower prices, so that the disparities are less than they appear at first sight. Table 1.13 shows a recent estimate of indices of real disposable income (incorporating estimates of variations in the cost of living in different regions). To some degree it would be correct to infer from this table that the different zones and regions are indeed roughly equal in terms of real incomes.

However, once again there is something different about the south of England. On top of a population the bulk of which, in income terms, is broadly like that anywhere else in the UK, lies a stratum of people who are unusually affluent by British standards. Southern England contains half the UK population, but receives two-thirds of its rentier income, and two-thirds of incomes over £30,000 per annum (tables 1.14 and 1.15). Britain's yuppies and capitalists live primarily in southern England.

Table 1.13   Indices of household income

	'Regional Affluence'
Scotland	99
N. Ireland	120
Wales	88
Northern England:	
North	99
Yorkshire and Humberside	95
North-west	98
West Midlands	96
Southern England:	
East Anglia	94
South-east	102
South-west	100
East Midlands	98

Source: Regional Trends, National Westminster Bank 1990

Table 1.14   Taxable income earnings

	% of population	% of tax units earning (£000s)			
		< 10	10–20	20–30	30 +
Scotland	8.6	8.9	8.6	7.2	7.3
N. Ireland	2.1	2.4	1.6	2.4	1.4
Wales	4.6	4.8	4.1	3.3	2.4
Periphery	*15.3*	*16.0*	*14.4*	*12.8*	*11.2*
Northern England	33.9	33.8	35.6	30.2	24.1
Southern England	50.8	50.1	50.1	57.0	64.7
Total	100	100	100	100	100

Table 1.15   Share of investment incomes to UK households

	%
Scotland	7.3
N. Ireland	1.0
Wales	3.6
Periphery	*12.0*
Northern England	24.4
Southern England	63.7
UK	100.0

Regional variations in income and welfare indicators are dwarfed by intra-regional variations between individuals and households (Stark 1989). They also obscure important inequalities between localities. Southern England certainly contains some 'losers', such as Deal, the Isle of Sheppey, and the inner cities of London and other urban areas (Champion and Green 1989). Conversely, there is an archipelago of advantaged places stretching to the north and west (Champion and Green 1989; Lewis and Townsend 1989). Nevertheless, the impact of prosperous localities in the north and periphery and poor ones in the south on the broader regional pattern 'is likely to be only small' (see Champion and Green 1989, p. 95). The statistics summarized above indicate quite clearly that on the aggregate level there is a major distinction between northern England and the south (Stewart 1990).

Moreover, the 'north–south divide' within England is part of a widening UK core–periphery divide. In economic terms, the north and the geographical periphery are shrinking relative to southern England. The decline has been most pronounced in northern England, which spread southwards in the 1980s to capture the West Midlands (Lewis and Townsend 1989). The core of activity has increasingly been concentrated in a segment of southern England stretching from Exeter to Cambridge.

The political economy of restructuring

The economic restructuring of the 1980s has been influenced by some relatively novel features of economic management. The policies of the Thatcher government have combined elements of liberal anti-corporatism, centralization and British state nationalism (Overbeek 1989). The early 1980s saw an attempt to 'shock the economy' into a new trajectory (Martin 1989b; Jessop *et al.* 1988) which must now be judged to have been unsuccessful even in its own terms (Costello, Michie and Milne 1989; Wells 1989). This was followed by a return to more orthodox methods of macroeconomic recession management, alongside a relative decline in government expenditure on most items except defence (until 1985) and transfer payments. The suppression of demand turned into a credit-fuelled expansion, followed from 1988 by a recession induced by interest rate policy. The collapse of many industries, rising employment and legislative changes, meant that until the closing years of the decade, most managements enjoyed increased bargaining power over labour (MacInnes 1987).

One important economic effect of government economic management was a massive redistribution of income (Lovering 1990). Widening differentials in wages and salaries, and growing self-employment and investment income, meant that the lowest 50 per cent of households were worse off in the late 1980s than in 1979 (Stark 1989, p. 181). In addition, a shift in the taxation system towards indirect taxation reduced the degree of redistribution.

The restructuring of the labour market

One important aspect of economic restructuring has been the demise of the 'Fordist' labour market. During the 1980s, many industries which were formerly characterized by 'wide and broad' internal labour markets ceased to be so. Large-scale manufacturing units have declined, and the average size of establishments has fallen. Many surviving companies have reorganized their employment practices. Analogous processes have been at work in the service industries and are currently under way in the public sector, partly through the influence of the move to agency status. The more dynamic surviving and new firms have tended to modify their technical and social divisions of labour, moving towards more individualized terms of employment and pay. There seems to be evidence that while employment of high-level research and development personnel is expanding or consolidating, employment on more routine tasks continues to decline. Meanwhile, self-employment and elite 'external labour markets' are becoming more important as channels for advancement for the more marketable workers (for a discussion see Lovering 1990).

The impact of this restructuring varies across the UK. Industrial trends suggest that the decline of traditional internal labour markets is likely to have been most severe in the north and the periphery, since large-scale manufacturing industries were often disproportionately important in local labour markets in these zones (Lever 1979), as was the public sector. As we have seen, the growth of self-employment is concentrated in the south. There are also signs that companies are increasingly, locating their 'career jobs' in the south. For example, most research and development work is undertaken there, while northern England the periphery are relatively specialized in routine work (Massey 1984; Lovering 1991).

The spatial redistribution of different kinds of jobs around a 'south–rest of the UK' divide is likely to mean that the character of the local labour market is becoming increasingly different on either side of that divide. The 'sandwich' formed by internal labour markets, and 'elite' and 'secondary' external labour markets, is likely to be fatter and better filled in the south. Elsewhere, avenues for upward advancement through internal labour markets are more likely to have disappeared without being replaced by new opportunities in external markets. It seems reasonable to infer that the worker who is valued for his or her skills, experience and adaptability — the 'post-Fordist' worker — is increasingly concentrated in the south. Conversely, the basis on which workers are required in the north and periphery is more likely to be their competitive low cost.

These developments, unravelling the social organization of employment built up since the war, are giving rise to a geographically uneven recomposition of class (Overbeek 1989; Adamson 1988). The 'service class' is overwhelmingly a southern English creation: there are 5,000,000 professional and managerial workers and self-employed in the prosperous arc of southern England. Meanwhile, the periphery and northern England are characterized by a relatively high proportion of 'working-class' occupations (tables 1.16 and 1.17).

Table 1.16   The 'new' working class and the 'old' (% of total)

	Clerical and non-manual workers	Craftspeople and labourers
	%	%
Scotland	8.1	9.4
N. Ireland	2.1	2.3
Wales	3.8	4.9
Periphery	*14.0*	*16.6*
Northern England	30.5	36.1
Southern England	55.5	47.3

Table 1.17 The service class is southern: professional and managerial workers (% of total)

	%
Scotland	8.1
N. Ireland	1.9
Wales	3.9
Periphery	13.9
Northern England	30.8
Southern England	55.3

The bases of the centripetal pressures

Economic restructuring in the UK in the 1980s has resulted in the 'evacuation' of the north and (to a lesser extent) the periphery. This is because declining older industries were especially important in those latter zones, while newer growing activities were biased towards southern England (Martin 1989a). But the question arises, why should the location of surviving or expanding sectors differ from that of expiring sectors?

In order to begin to answer this question it is necessary to place the events of the past decade in a longer historical perspective. Here it is only possible to sketch the outlines of an analysis.[4] An economic crisis emerged in the early 1970s which has been characterized by political economists as the demise of the previous 'Fordist' regime of accumulation, or the end of the fourth Kondratieff long-wave (see, for example, Marshall 1987; Hall 1981). But a new hegemonic regime, or a new long-wave, has yet to establish itself. In terms of investment and employment patterns, the 1980s did not see a significant shift towards a new economy, despite the predictions of government spokespeople and academic enthusiasts for 'post-Fordism'. The UK economy has been characterized by 'business as usual' (facilitated by lower real wage costs and enhanced management power), continued decline in international rankings, and a number of genuine but usually small innovations in technology and employment patterns (Costello *et al.* 1989; Green 1989; Lovering 1990; MacInnes 1987). In this perspective, the 1980s was primarily a period of 'hiatus' in the development of the British economy, suspended between a certain past and an unknown future.

4 This interpretation is developed a little in Lovering 1990. It draws on Overbeek (1990), Jessop *et al.* (1988), Costello *et al.* (1989), and various contributors to Green (1989), especially Wells and Nolan.

Government policy has done little to transform the economy, although it has added a few local difficulties. Governments since the mid 1970s have failed to re-establish a basis for capital accumulation on a national level, and also failed to integrate the UK economy as a whole into more advantageous international circuits of capital (Overbeek 1990), although some individual capitals may have made this leap successfully. The UK as a whole is still on its long-term slide from being the workshop of the world towards a residual status based on low-skill, low-technology activities. Nor has the impact of successive governments been positive from the point of view of the economic and social welfare of many, perhaps most, UK citizens.

The relative stagnation of the UK economy

The failure to re-establish national accumulation is manifested in the relative stagnation of the UK economy, compared to the recent past and to other economies. The result, as Kevin Morgan has pointed out, is that the UK as a whole remains a 'problem region' by international standards (Morgan 1987, p. 48). The restructuring of the 1980s has not prevented further decline in the UK's international ranking. In terms of growth, the UK has slipped further below European neighbours, the US and Japan (table 1.18). Despite the much publicized recovery of the late 1980s, investment per head is even further behind than in 1979 (table 1.19). Productivity growth has been based more on intensification of labour than a radically new wave of investment (Nolan 1989, p. 118). There is little evidence that the British economy as a whole has become more competitive internationally, earnings from oil having been used to finance imports rather than investment (Wells 1989). The decline of the UK is indicated by record trade deficits and the behaviour of capital, which is still 'haemorrhaging into overseas assets' (Healey 1990, p. 92). In short, restructuring has not changed Britain's international role so much as narrowed it down. Meanwhile, although the consumption-based boom of the late 1980s helped some domestic-orientated sectors, the growth of the domestic market remained slower than that of France or Italy over the last twenty years (Cutler *et al.* 1989, p. 29). The UK as a whole has become more industrially backward, and employment has become more dependent on the service sector.

The redistribution of income to the better-off may have disguised the fact that the real income of the average UK citizen has fallen relative to other First World countries (table 1.20).

Table 1.18   Rate of growth of GDP during 1980s (%)

Japan	29.4
USA	19.6
Denmark	16.4
Italy	15.7
France	11.7
W. Germany	10.3
UK	10.3

Table 1.19   Capital formation in manufacturing per head

UK level as compared to	1979	1986
Japan	32%	21%
W. Germany	41%	45%
USA	62%	51%

Table 1.20   British 'standard of living'

UK level as compared to	1979	1986
Japan	105%	93%
W. Germany	92%	90%
USA	68%	66%

The processes whereby these broad economic tendencies resulted in peripheralization can be described in terms of Myrdal's account of 'cumulative causation'. Britain's model of (faltering) growth has been such that the 'spread effects', which diffuse activity away from the centre of growth, have generally been overwhelmed by the countervailing 'backwash effects', which tend to redirect growth back to the core zone (see Lewis and Townsend 1989).

A number of factors explain the limited diffusion of activity from the southern English 'core'. The centralization of UK activity on southern England is driven by the demand-pull exerted in domestic consumer markets by the spending of the well-off; by the relative availability of certain kinds of scarce labour in the south; and by the many influences which lead companies to wish to retain higher-level activities near the capital and near points of international access (especially Heathrow). The inflow of foreign firms has generally reflected the same pressures. Half of the 130,000 new jobs created by incoming firms between 1983 and 1988 were in southern England and Wales (CENIERC 1990, p. 5).

The limited sectoral range of UK 'reindustrialization', and its generally 'jobless' character, meant that the expansion of the mid 1980s was insufficient to exhaust existing industrial capacity, and occupy sites left vacant by the sharp collapse of the early 1980s. There was consequently little pressure on industry to disperse significantly, except in special cases where cheaper labour or new sites were required. The dominant role of services in the expansion meant that the pressures for relocation were stronger in office work than in factory work. But here the biggest gains have been made by cities and towns lying in or near the south, such as Bristol, Bournemouth, Southampton, Swindon, Gloucester, Cheltenham and Coventry. The periphery and northern England do not offer equivalent combinations of pools of routine workers and the ability to attract high-level labour, and the level of demand is in any case limited.

The scarce labour required by some key industries is already to be found mainly in the south (Massey 1984; Morgan 1987; Lovering 1991). This is partly attributable to the apparent attractions of southern lifestyles and to housing market traps (Hall *et al.* 1987). But the importance of the pre-existing supply of skilled labour, and thereby the importance of the locations in which such labour can be found, is enhanced because the supply is so inelastic. This is in turn largely an effect of the general decline of training. As Cutler *et al.* note: 'Skill training has hardly been a necessity in an economy whose failure in manufacturing trade has meant that employment is increasingly generated in a services sector which has a low skill requirement' (1989, p. 85).

Overall, the UK offers no examples of major new Marshallian industrial districts, which have been identified elsewhere, and are allegedly the basis of new regional economies (Scott 1989). The restructuring of the 1980s has not, therefore, created the basis of a qualitatively new spatial pattern in the UK.

The state and geographical redistribution

If the British state has proved incapable of improving the supply side of the UK economy (Nolan 1989; Jessop *et al.* 1988), it has nevertheless been able to effect marginal changes in the social impact of Britain's sustained economic crisis. Traditionally the public sector has provided a number of influences which have compensated for the peripheralization of areas beyond the south.

But public intervention has become less effective in moderating the inequalities arising from the workings of the economy. The weakening of these countervailing influences is evident in many areas, not least in the severe run-down of regional assistance since the 1970s (CENIERC 1990; Lewis and Townsend 1989). Table 1.21 shows the broadly redistributive impact of social security spending. Most benefits redistribute to the north and periphery, except retirement and war pensions, which act to transfer resources from north to south, especially to the south-west and the south-east coast. Child benefit reverses the flow, especially benefiting Northern Ireland. Widows' benefit also transfers income towards the periphery. The main redistribution, however, is through gains outside the south on unemployment, sickness and invalidity, and disablement benefits (Walker and Huby 1989). Northern England and the periphery made some relative gains through the 1980s through the increased targeting of payments on clients, benefiting poorer areas. But the overall impact may be expected to decline if welfare spending continues to occupy its present place in government priorities.

Table 1.21   Redistributive bias of social security spending

	% share
Scotland	9.7
N. Ireland	3.0
Wales	5.4
Periphery	*18.1*
Northern England	36.3
Southern England	45.6
Total	100

While the welfare state tended to compensate for the advantages of southern England, the warfare state tended to work in the opposite direction (table 1.22). The southern bias of defence spending seems likely to intensify in the 1990s, with the impending contraction of the UK defence sector and its integration into European defence and high-technology industry (Lovering 1991).

Although it has failed to reinvigorate the UK economy as a whole (Overbeek 1990), the British state has directly and indirectly sustained the economic domination of London and southern England (Martin 1989a). Britain remains much more highly centralized than, for example, Germany (TCPA 1987). This is not incompatible with a modicum of economic development outside the south. In particular, as we have seen, parts of Wales echo the patterns of the English 'south' (more so than most of northern England, or even the remote English south-west). The peripheralization of Britain has been deeply influenced by the British state, testimony to the key role the nation-state continues to play in structuring the workings of the capitalist economy (Callinicos 1989).

Table 1.22 Southern bias of military procurement

	Shares of MOD procurement spending, 1987–8
	%
Scotland	7.5
N. Ireland	1.5
Wales	0.5
Periphery	*9.5*
Northern England	28.5
Southern England	62.0
Total	100

Source: Statement on the Defence Estimates, 1990, p. 61

Peripheralization in the 1990s

The periphery and northern England have been 'peripheralized' in the 1980s. Such genuine growth as has occurred has been concentrated in a segment of central southern England, lying parallel to the coast of Europe, stretching from Exeter to Cambridge. As Lomax points out, this area is no bigger than Maine (Lomax 1990).

It is appropriate to end by speculating on the prospects for the 1990s. The scenario that suggests itself is very different from that offered by the 'optimists'. Recent forecasts have predicted that recent geographical trends will broadly continue (see CENIERC 1990). Cambridge Econometrics predicts that East Anglia and the south-west will continue to grow fastest in the 1990s, capturing most of the growth and population spilling over from the south-east, and keeping southern England as the economic heartland of the UK economy. The gains recently made by the north will diminish. Regional divergence will persist, although it may grow less rapidly than it did in the 1980s (CRER 1990).

The short-term: the recession of 1990–1

The UK economy entered a 'technical recession' in 1990 when real GDP fell for two successive quarters (National Westminster Bank 1990). This poses new threats to manufacturing industry, which generally slimmed down during the 1980s. Many British companies 'now only have their cores, they have little else to lose' (Leadbetter 1990a). Companies in the south were at first hit hardest by the recession, since they had gained most from previous consumption-led expansion. It has been suggested that industry is more export-orientated outside the south, and consequently it has been less severely affected by the domestic contraction. In a CBI survey in summer 1990, output was expected to increase only in the north and the periphery (except Wales) and the East Midlands (Norman 1990). In Scotland the Scottish Development Agency claimed that 'many Scottish plants are now part of a larger European corporate strategy which will not be put at risk by a localised downturn in the UK' (cited in Leadbetter 1990a).

However, entry to the European Exchange Rate Mechanism (ERM) in October 1990 was expected to create a climate for manufacturing 'harder than at any time since 1979–81' (Leadbetter 1990b). The new pressure on exporters, which will continue until they are as competitive as their German counterparts (Leadbetter 1990a), suggests that the north will be hit harder than the south. From a regional perspective, entry to the ERM at a target rate of DM2.95 may have unpromising parallels with Churchill's restoration of the Gold Standard.

The longer term

The generally undynamic nature of the economic restructuring has meant that the motors which are driving the UK economy in the 1990s are likely to be much the same as in the 1980s. The southern English finance industry, and the small high-technology sectors clustered in 'ROSEland' (rest of the south-east), and the cluster of more widely distributed foreign-owned companies producing for the European market, will remain key influences. The lack of dynamism in the UK economy is leading many leading UK companies to look for markets and linkages on the European scale, or wider, rather than domestically, for example, in aerospace and electronics (Lovering 1991). This seems unlikely to change, unless, that is, the growing demand by industrialists for a neo-corporatist national industrial strategy finds support.

In general the impact of the European market would seem likely to continue, as in the past, to benefit existing large capital (Cutler *et al.* 1989). If the main thrust of European Community (EC) practice continues to be, as Cutler *et al.* argue, the assertion of market priorities, we may expect further concentration of control, research and development and other high-level activities around the German core. Lower-paid functions will be fought over by a growing band of supplicants, now including in addition to southern Europe, most of the former eastern bloc. This trend is unlikely to be seriously affected by EC regional policy. In any case, transfer payments are likely in future to be redirected towards poorer members, especially the Mediterranean countries, and away from the UK, except perhaps Northern Ireland (Cutler *et al.* 1989, p. 95).

The longer-term impact of moves towards European monetary union will depend on the terms on which monetary policy is conducted. If European policy is deflationary, disadvantaged areas, unable to adjust exchange rates to compensate for deficits, will be forced to adjust through costs and employment. It remains to be seen how far the EC will impose 'IMF-type' regimes amongst its constituents, but unless an unexpected and unprecedented improvement occurs on the UK supply side, the prospect is for further peripheral decline.

Although the UK has gained a disproportionate share of foreign investment in Europe (especially from Japan) the aggregate impact has been very modest. Moreover, it is by no means certain that this source of reindustrialization will not dry up. Two-thirds of Japanese investment is in Asia (Cutler *et al.* 1989). If, as some expect, the development of the EC is marked by introversion, non-European investors may look elsewhere. Much has changed since Toyota announced its intention to set up in Clwyd.

Conclusion

The British economy has become more integrated into a European economy without at the same time regenerating itself. If this trend continues, it is improbable that Britain will be much more than a peripheral partner in European economic development (Cutler *et al.* 1989). This is likely to have internal implications. For, divided though it is, nevertheless Britain has been much *less* geographically unequal than other European countries (Lewis and Townsend 1989, p. 7). Integrating in a fragmented manner to a Europe that is itself in upheaval, Britain would seem to be vulnerable to new pressures towards disintegration.

Wales, Scotland and Northern Ireland are becoming increasingly 'a periphery within a periphery', a status now shared by northern England. This is not a promising position to be in, unless the current pressure for an industrial strategy and the revival of regionalism (Goddard and Coombes 1987; Stewart 1990) result in a major change of UK policy, or the European Community takes a new course (Amin and Gillespie 1990). The 'prosperity zone' of the 1990s will continue to lie within southern England. The relative economic weight of the periphery and the north are likely to continue to decline.[5] Britain may fail to become like its European neighbours in many ways, but it is on course to emulate the division between a relatively privileged core-zone and a marginalized remainder.

Bibliography

Adamson, David 1988. 'The New Working Class and Political Change in Wales', *Contemporary Wales*, 2

Amin, Ash and Andy Gillespie 1990. 'Salvation in Europe', *Business* (April), pp. 120–4

Breheny, Mike and P. Congdon (eds.) 1989. *Growth and Change in a Core Region*. Pion.

Business, September 1987

Callinicos, Alex 1989. *Against Post-modernism*. Verso

CENIERC 1990. *Regional Economic Prospects*. Cambridge Econometrics and the Northern Ireland Economic Research Centre

Champion, Tony and Anne Green 1989. 'Local Economic Differentials and the "North–South" Divide' in Lewis and Townsend (eds.)

5 Stewart foresees a continuation of present trends, rather than a 'regional rebirth' or a radical transformation of the 'strong south' into a dynamic self-sustaining economy which could diffuse benefits to the north and periphery (Stewart 1990).

Cooke, Phil (ed.) 1988. *Localities*. Unwin Hyman

Costello, Nicholas, Jonathan Michie and Seumas Milne (eds.) 1989. *Beyond the Casino Economy*. Verso

CRER 1990. 'Cambridge Regional Economic Review – The Economic Outlook for the Regions and Counties of the UK in the 1990s'. Department of Land Economy

Cutler, Tony, Colin Haslam, John Williams and Karel Williams 1989. *1992 – The Struggle for Europe*. Berg.

Doogan, Kevin and Gill Court 1990. *The South West in the 1990s*. Paper contributed to 'Sector Futures and Regional Prospects' Conference, SAUS–KPMG, Peat Marwick McLintock–National Westminster Bank, 28–9 September, School for Advanced Urban Studies, Bristol

Fazey, Ian Hamilton 1990. 'The North–South Divide Begins to Close', *Financial Times* (10 September)

Goddard, John and Mike Coombes 1990. 'North–South: Mind the Gap', *Business* (April), pp. 112–13

Green, Francis (ed.) 1989. *Restructuring the UK Economy*. Harvester Wheatsheaf

Hall, Peter 1981. 'The Geography of the Fifth Kondtratieff Cycle', *New Society* (26 March)

Hall, Peter *et al.* 1987. *Western Sunrise*. Allen & Unwin

Healey, Nigel 1990. 'Prisoners of the Past', *Business* (October), pp. 88–92

Jessop, Bob, Kevin Bonnett, Simon Bromley and Tom Ling 1988. *Thatcherism: a Tale of Two Nations*. Verso

Johnston, R. J., C. J. Pattie and J. G. Allsopp 1988. *A Nation Dividing?* Longman

Keeble, David 1989. 'High-technology Industry and Regional Development in Britain', *Environment and Planning C: Government and Policy*, pp. 153–72

Leadbetter, Charles 1990a. 'Why 1990 is not 1979', *Financial Times* (4 October)

Leadbetter, Charles 1990b. 'Exporters Likely to Feel the Squeeze', *Financial Times* (6 October)

Lever, W. F. 1979. 'Industry and Labour Markets in Great Britain' in F. Hamilton and G. Linge (eds.), *Spatial Analysis, Industry and the Industrial Environment*. Wiley

Lewis, Jim and Alan Townsend (eds.) 1989. Introduction in *The North-South Divide*. Paul Chapman Publishing

Lomax, David 1990. 'The British Economy and Current Weaknesses' in *The State of the Economy*. Institute of Economic Affairs

Lovering, John, 1990. 'A Perfunctory PostFordism, Economic

Restructuring and Labour Market Segmentation in the 1980s', *Work, Employment and Society* (Special Issue, May)

Lovering, John 1991. 'The Changing Geography of High-technology Military Industry in Britain', *Regional Studies*, 25 (4)

MacInnes, John 1987. *Thatcherism at Work*. Open University Press

Marshall, Michael 1987. *Long Waves of Regional Development*. Macmillan

Martin, Ron 1989a. 'The Political Economy of Britain's North–South Divide' in Lewis and Townsend (eds.)

Martin, Ron 1989b. 'Regional Imbalance as a Consequence and Constraint in National Economic Renewal' in Green (ed.)

Massey, Doreen 1984. *Spatial Divisions of Labour*. Macmillan

Morgan, Kevin 1987. 'High Technology Industry and Regional Development', *Contemporary Wales*, 1, pp. 39–52

National Westminster Bank 1990. *UK Regional Review* (September)

Nolan, Peter 1989. 'The Productivity Miracle?' in Green (ed.)

Norman, Peter 1990. 'Slowdown Hits West Midlands and the South Hardest', *Financial Times* (16 August 1990), p. 9 (CBI/BSL Regional Trends Survey)

Overbeek, Henk 1989. *Global Capitalism and National Decline*. Unwin Hyman

Peck, Jamie 1990. 'The State and the Regulation of Local Labour Markets: Observations on the Geography of the Youth Training Scheme', *Area*, 22, pp. 17–27

Scott, A. J. 1989. 'Flexible Production Systems and Regional Development', *International Journal of Urban and Regional Research*, 12, pp. 171–85

Stark, Thomas 1989. 'The Changing Distribution of Income under Mrs Thatcher' in Green (ed.)

Stewart, Murray 1990. *Regional Development Prospects*. SAUS Working Paper 89. School for Advanced Urban Studies, Bristol University

Stilwell, John, Peter Boden and Philip Rees 1990. 'Trends in Internal Net Migration in the UK: 1975 to 1986', *Area*, 22 (1)

TCPA 1987. *North–South Divide: a New Deal for Britain's Regions*. Town and Country Planning Association

Thomas, Dennis 1989. 'Wales in 1988: an Economic Survey', *Contemporary Wales*, 3.

Walker, R. and M. Huby 1989. 'Social Security Spending in the UK: Bridging the North–South Divide', *Environment and Planning C: Government and Policy*, 7, pp. 321–40

Wells, John 1989. 'Uneven Development and De-industrialisation in the UK since 1979' in Green (ed.)

Sources of official statistics

Eurostat
Regional Trends 1990
Social Trends 1990
Statement on the Defence Estimates 1990

Chapter 2

The Welsh Economy: Current Circumstances and Future Prospects

DENNIS THOMAS

Introduction

According to the Cambridge Econometrics report *Regional Economic Prospects* it would now seem that, in economic terms, Wales is no longer a 'peripheral' region. The report divides the eleven Standard Planning Regions in the United Kingdom into four groups on the basis of economic performance during the recovery phase of the 1980s. Wales is shown to have grown distinctly faster in terms of employment and GDP than any northern or peripheral region over the period 1983 to 1989, and on this basis is classified along with the two Midlands regions of England.

The report states that 'Wales now performs more like a midlands region than a northern region' and that 'the boundary of the north–south divide now clearly lies at the northern edge of the midlands'. The 'periphery' is reduced to only Scotland and Northern Ireland, whose 'remoteness ... from the south of England has been a common factor in their slow growth'. In contrast Wales is 'beginning to gain the full economic benefit of a geographical position in which its major cities are as close to London as those of the midlands', with investors seeming to regard Wales 'as an integral part of the southern half of Great Britain'.

The purpose of this chapter is not to indulge in a semantic discussion of the meaning of 'periphery', but to place the current circumstances of the Welsh economy in context. As such the chapter will, hopefully, provide a background for others which follow, and identify some key issues which may be developed when considering the future prospects of the Welsh economy. The reference to the statements made in the *Regional Economic Prospects* report should serve to indicate the problems involved in categorizing or viewing regions in broad, aggregative terms.

The Welsh economy in the 1980s

The economic changes which have taken place in Wales during the 1980s have been well documented.[1] The period has been one of particularly rapid socio-economic change. At the heart of the transformation have been the collapse of the traditional industries of coalmining and steel, and developments in light manufacturing and engineering, many of which involve foreign ownership. Rural areas have witnessed a continuing decline in agriculture characterized by falling incomes, increasing costs, and the problems associated with a variety of EC policy measures.

The traditional industrial sectors have experienced severe job losses. The remorseless decline in coalmining has left a workforce of some 3,800 miners in six working deep pits in South Wales, compared with 22,000 in 1983–4. In steel, following the disappearance of half the jobs in the industry between 1977 and 1980, output and employment stabilized during the 1980s with major investments being made at Welsh plants. However, the recent reorganization of tinplate operations in South Wales has produced further job-shedding, and employment, at around 25,000, is now only one-third of the 1979 level. Together coal and steel currently account for a little over 3 per cent of total employment in Wales.

Manufacturing employment fell by almost a quarter over the period 1980–3. Since then, however, the manufacturing sector has experienced a steady recovery which has seen output and employment rising faster than the national average. Manufacturing employment increased by 5.2 per cent per annum during the period 1986–9, compared with 0.4 per cent annum for the United Kingdom, while manufacturing production in 1989 was some 33 per cent higher compared with 1985. The recent slow-down in manufacturing growth has not been as great as that experienced in the UK as a whole.

The most significant growth in manufacturing employment over the period 1986–9 was that experienced by the engineering sector, exceeding 33 per cent. Particular note may be made of more than 19,000 workers now variously employed in the motor vehicle and

1   Annual surveys of the Welsh economy are published in *Contemporary Wales*. These contain detailed information on the principal economic indicators as well as recent developments. The performance of the Welsh economy is analysed in relation to the British economy and also in terms of its various regional and sectoral components; see George and Mainwaring (1987), Thomas (1988, 1989). See also George and Mainwaring (1988), Mackay (1988), Morris and Mansfield (1988) and the *Welsh Economic Review* (1988–9).

components sector, accounting for some 8 per cent of total manufacturing output in Wales (compared with 5 per cent in the UK). Recent project announcements by Ford and Bosch in South Wales, and by Toyota in North Wales, however, need to be balanced by the run-down in the indigenous motor vehicle industry, for example, the Rover Group at Llanelli.

The multiplier effect associated with the expansion of manufacturing employment might have been expected to increase demand for local services, but the expansion in the Welsh private service sector has not been faster than experienced by the UK as a whole. Furthermore, despite the fact that Wales, and in particular its south-eastern corner, has gained from the relocation of business services from southern England, the growth of this sector has also lagged. Although the growth in service sector employment has been insufficient to compensate for the extensive deindustrialization of the Welsh economy, there has been a significant change in sectoral composition. In 1989 the service sector accounted for 65 per cent of total employees in employment in Wales, compared with 55 per cent in 1979. The share of manufacturing sector employment has fallen from some 30 per cent in 1979 to around one-quarter in 1989.

This broad-brush account of economic change in the Welsh economy suggests that the recession of 1980–3 has been followed by considerably heightened activity during the second half of the 1980s. Several features are regularly quoted as evidence of a renascent economy, namely: record levels of factory building; increased levels of new business formation; and considerable amounts of inward investment which accounted for over 20 per cent of the UK total in 1988 and 1989. To these features may be added a number of specific programmes which include:

The Valleys Initiative in South Wales, hailed by the Secretary of State for Wales as 'perhaps the most exciting transformation of any economy being seen this century'.

The A55 North Wales Expressway, or the 'Road of Opportunity' for Gwynedd and Clywd, designed to carry economic development and prosperity across North Wales and to the rural north-west.

New initiatives in rural Wales by the major development agencies including the Welsh Development Agency's Rural Affairs Division and Mid Wales Development's Special Rural Action Programme, which includes a Western Initiative; and

Last, but not least, is the Wales Tourist Board's five-year strategy aimed at improving quality, professionalism and value for money without being detrimental to the main assets of scenery, culture, heritage and language.

All these developments, it has been claimed, contribute to Wales's emergence as an 'economic role model', combining interventionism and free enterprise, for the rest of Great Britain to follow. The economy is seen as having experienced an economic regeneration and a total transformation into a healthy, diversified and growing economy. Having shed most of its dependence on the declining basic industries, it is argued, the Welsh economy is now better placed to share in national growth and much less vulnerable to long-term decline.

An assessment of the various initiatives listed above must await another occasion, but one possible, albeit cynical view, would suggest that if the list were extended to include:

the proposed Parc Dyffryn development in the Vale of Glamorgan, complete with racecourse and private school
the success of the Cardiff Devils' ice hockey team in winning the Heineken National League
the naming of Pwllheli as the venue for the sailing events if Manchester were to be successful in its bid to host the 1996 Summer Olympics,
the reappointment of Terry Yorath as manager of Swansea City FC, and, of course, the appearance of Ron Waldron as Welsh rugby's saviour

then all the pieces in the jigsaw would be complete and in place at the start of the 1990s! All's well in Wales and it is not only the Director of CBI Wales who can talk of a new 'golden age'.

Seriously, however, even independent observers from outside produce a caricatured, aggregative view of the Welsh economy and its prospects. A report by the Henley Centre for Forecasting (1989) states that Wales is perhaps the best example of the role that confidence plays in the economic assessment of a region. 'That this concept is essentially unquantifiable is immaterial and does not detract from its relevance.' Indeed, it is claimed, this is 'precisely what economists mean whey they refer to the "animal spirits" of business investment decisions'. Whilst accepting that differences exist within Wales, the report states that 'there can be little doubt that new defining characteristics of the Welsh economy are coming to the fore — inward investment, Japanese, American and German companies, high development skills, the development of Cardiff Bay . . . ' The report detects a significant change in the image which Wales is displaying to the world and highlights confidence as a key factor in the economy's growth and in the anticipation of further growth.

Obviously it is as inappropriate to be cynical or dismissive of recent developments in Wales as it is to view them through rose-tinted spectacles. Nevertheless the picture of an economic regeneration and the emergence of a growing and stronger economy must be tempered and placed in historical and regional context.

Current circumstances of the Welsh economy

During the late 1970s and early 1980s the market forces that tended to work to the disadvantage of those regional economies of the UK like Wales were strengthened by a weakening of regional policy and the severe UK deflation engineered by the Government after 1979. These developments had consequences for society, industry structure and the labour market reflected in falling output, dramatic increases in unemployment and the continuing relative deprivation of Wales as a region within the UK. To begin with, then, the current circumstances of the Welsh economy must be placed in historical perspective and related to the very low base to which the economy had been reduced. This leads on to a consideration of Wales's position relative to other regions and of the differences which exist within Wales. Finally we need to appreciate that there are doubts whether there has been a real shift towards a basically stronger economy.

Historical context

Between 1980 and 1983 Welsh industrial output plummeted so dramatically that it took four years of steady growth to 1987 for output to be restored to the 1980 level. Unemployment peaked at over 170,000 in the first quarter of 1986. In the second half of the 1980s considerable output growth was accompanied by a steady fall in unemployment, even allowing for the regular revision of the count, but this fall has been slower than that experienced by much of Great Britain. The latest unemployment figures show seasonally adjusted unemployment in February 1990 standing at 84,200, well above the figure of 70,000 recorded in the first quarter of 1980.

Although the fall in unemployment has been insufficient fully to reverse the employment losses suffered between 1979 and 1983, new official data, produced following publication of the 1987 Census of Employment, indicate that Wales performed significantly better in employment terms during the period of national recovery than hitherto thought. Latest figures show an increase in the number of employees in employment between June 1983 and June 1989 of some 10 per cent, compared with an 8 per cent increase for Great Britain. This increase, however, was only in part compensation for the employment reduction experienced during the early part of the 1980s, and was largely due to an increase in the number of female employees, particularly part-time, whose numbers grew faster than in Great Britain as a whole. Part-time female employees now account for over 20 per cent of the total number in employment, compared with the 15–16 per cent in 1979. The male–female split of 55–45 compares with 60–40 in 1979 and reflects the absolute decline in male employment during the 1980s.

The developing mismatch between employment increase and the fall in unemployment was accompanied by a steady deterioration in earnings relative to Great Britain figures. Table 2.1 compares average gross weekly earnings for the years 1979 and 1989. The figures show that average earnings have fallen behind the Great Britain average in all categories. In particular, male manual wages, formerly above the national average when boosted by steel workers' and coalminers' pay, have now fallen below the national figure.

Regional comparisons

Wales continues to lag behind other regions in terms of several key indicators, even experiencing a decline in some. The latest figures for regional GDP per head, reported for 1988 in table 2.2, show that Wales records a value of £5,707, which is 84 per cent of the UK figure. Only Northern Ireland has a lower figure, leaving Wales in relatively the same position as in 1979.[2] Figures for average weekly household incomes again show Wales recording a figure of about 84 per cent of that for the UK, with only Northern Ireland and the north registering lower figures. The last column in the table shows that 17.5 per cent of household income in Wales is accounted for by social security benefits compared with 11.6 per cent for the UK.

2   Gross Domestic Product (GDP) is defined as the total sum of all incomes earned from productive activity at factor cost:current prices. The definitions of regional and county GDP should be the sum of incomes earned from productive activity in the region and county respectively, with the income of commuters included in the region or county where they work. The county GDP figures are compiled on this basis as far as possible but regional estimates are not. Comparing profits and trading surpluses of public enterprises can contribute a substantial proportion of a county's GDP, particularly where there are one or two large establishments sited in a small county. GDP figures do not indicate where the profits of companies operating in a region/county end up. GDP per head figures are calculated using the resident population as the denominator.

Table 2.1 **Average gross weekly earnings: full-time employees on adult rates, Wales and GB, all industries and services, April 1979 and April 1989**

	Wales	GB	Wales as % of GB
	£	£	
Manual male			
1979	94.1	93.0	101.2
1989	209.8	217.8	96.3
Non-manual male			
1979	104.6	113.0	92.6
1989	280.9	323.6	86.8
All males			
1979	97.6	101.4	96.3
1989	238.6	269.5	88.5
Manual female			
1979	56.4	55.2	102.2
1989	131.8	134.9	97.7
Non-manual female			
1979	63.5	66.0	96.2
1989	180.5	195.0	92.6
All females			
1979	61.4	63.0	97.5
1989	168.0	182.3	92.2

Source: New Earnings Survey, 1989; Welsh Economic Trends

Figures for average gross weekly earnings reported in table 2.3 show Wales as generally possessing the lowest earnings amongst the regions of Great Britain.[3] Earnings for all full-time males at £238.6, or

3   The figures are based on survey data and relate only to those full-time employees on adult rates whose pay for the survey period was not affected by absence. Variations in figures between regions reflect differences in occupational structure rather than rates for a given job.

Dennis Thomas

Table 2.2 Regional GDP, income and expenditure

| | GDP per head | | | Average weekly household income (1987–8) | | Average weekly household expenditure (1987–8) | | % of household income from social security benefits |
| | 1988 | | 1979 | | | | | |
	£	% of UK	% of UK	£	% of UK	£	% of UK	
South-east	8,112	119.4	116.3	388.62	125.4	232.74	118.5	7.8
East Anglia	6,601	97.1	94.1	256.78	95.1	200.22	101.9	11.7
South-west	6,374	93.8	91.1	273.74	101.4	203.11	103.4	11.0
West Midlands	6,188	91.9	96.1	241.65	89.5	177.55	89.5	14.1
East Midlands	6,428	94.6	96.2	241.33	89.4	179.46	91.4	12.5
Yorkshire and Humberside	6,190	91.1	92.9	232.84	86.3	172.34	87.7	14.4
North-west	6,341	93.3	96.2	245.77	91.0	186.26	94.8	13.4
North	6,000	88.3	90.9	220.13	81.5	164.38	83.7	16.1
England	6,954	102.3	102.2	–	–	–	–	–
Scotland	6,382	93.9	94.6	234.23	86.8	172.78	88.0	14.1
Northern Ireland	5,301	78.0	78.3	224.81	83.3	199.68	101.6	19.4
Wales	5,707	84.0	85.0	227.48	84.3	177.17	90.2	17.5
United Kingdom	6,795	100	100	269.96	100	196.44	100	11.6

Source: Economic Trends, November 1989; Regional accounts, *Employment Gazette*, February 1990

88.5 per cent of the GB figure, are the lowest of all the regions. Higher rankings are noted for female earnings, but particularly low figures are recorded in the *New Earnings Survey*, 1989, for both males and females in service industry occupations.

Table 2.3 Average gross weekly earnings: full-time employees on adult rates, Wales, GB and regions, April 1989 (£s)

	Manual males	Non-manual males	All males	Manual females	Non-manual females	All females
South-east	233.5	367.0	312.4	149.8	219.5	209.1
East Anglia	219.3	299.2	254.6	129.8	179.4	168.3
South-west	207.9	299.7	253.3	129.3	179.9	169.9
West Midlands	212.7	292.2	246.6	130.4	177.8	165.1
East Midlands	212.8	289.0	242.8	129.1	173.2	158.8
Yorkshire and Humberside	211.7	291.3	244.5	126.2	176.5	164.2
North-west	213.4	295.1	250.9	132.4	182.7	171.0
North	214.1	286.4	243.9	127.3	173.7	161.9
England	219.2	327.4	272.9	135.8	197.1	184.4
Scotland	209.9	300.8	251.2	129.8	181.8	169.6
Wales	209.8	280.9	238.6	131.8	180.5	168.0
Great Britain	217.8	323.6	269.5	134.9	195.0	182.3

Source: New Earnings Survey, 1989

Table 2.4 traces out annual average unemployment rates for each region during the 1980s. The estimated rate of 8 per cent for Wales in 1989 was 1.5 percentage points above that for the UK, the fifth highest amongst the regions and still above the 1980 rate.[4]

Table 2.5 shows that the participation rate in Wales, having picked up slightly, remains low at 70 per cent. The figure is the lowest of all regions and remains below the 1980 level, reflecting the fact that the increase in female participation has been insufficient to offset the decline in the male rate.[5]

4 Table 2.4 is based on the latest complete seasonally adjusted unemployment series as published by the Department of Employment and consistent with current coverage of the monthly count of claimants.
5 The participation rate is calculated as employed, self-employed and unemployed as a percentage of working-age population.

Table 2.4   Annual average unemployment rates, Wales, UK and regions, 1980–9

	1980	1981	1982	1983	1984	1985	1986	1987	1988	1989
South-east	3.1	5.5	6.7	7.5	7.8	8.0	8.2	7.1	5.2	4.0
East Anglia	3.8	6.3	7.4	8.0	7.9	8.0	8.1	6.8	4.8	3.6
South-west	4.5	6.8	7.8	8.7	9.0	9.3	9.5	8.2	6.3	4.6
West Midlands	5.5	10.0	11.9	12.9	12.7	12.7	12.6	11.1	8.5	6.8
East Midlands	4.5	7.4	8.4	9.5	9.8	9.9	9.9	9.0	7.2	5.8
Yorkshire and Humberside	5.3	8.9	10.4	11.4	11.7	12.0	12.4	11.3	9.5	8.0
North-west	6.5	10.2	12.1	13.4	13.6	13.8	13.9	12.7	10.7	8.8
North	8.0	11.8	13.3	14.6	15.3	15.4	15.2	14.0	11.9	10.6
Scotland	7.0	9.9	11.3	12.3	12.6	12.9	13.3	13.0	11.2	9.7
Northern Ireland	9.4	12.7	14.4	15.5	15.9	16.1	17.6	17.6	16.4	15.5
Wales	6.9	10.5	12.1	12.9	13.2	13.8	13.9	12.5	10.5	8.0
United Kingdom	5.1	8.1	9.5	10.5	10.7	10.9	11.1	10.0	8.0	6.5

Source: Department of Employment

Table 2.5   Participation rate, Wales, UK and regions, 1971–89

	1971	1980	1983	1986	1989
South-east	80.1	80.5	80.1	82.1	83.7
East Anglia	70.6	74.5	74.0	74.8	75.9
South-west	68.0	73.6	73.0	75.0	76.7
West Midlands	77.6	77.8	75.7	76.0	74.9
East Midlands	70.1	75.3	73.8	74.7	75.3
Yorkshire and Humberside	73.2	75.2	72.7	74.4	72.7
North-west	77.8	77.7	74.0	75.2	75.2
North	72.9	72.1	69.8	71.6	70.3
Scotland	74.0	76.5	74.2	74.8	74.3
Northern Ireland	67.4	73.3	72.3	72.5	71.3
Wales	69.5	70.6	68.2	70.2	70.0
United Kingdom	75.4	76.9	75.3	76.7	77.0

Source: Regional Economic Prospects, 1990

A divided Wales

The aggregative picture of Wales disguises evidence of considerable disparities in the fortunes of the subregions, as certain areas and people have missed out on any new-found prosperity. Average earnings and unemployment display considerable variations, as do house prices and household incomes. Wales is divided along a number of dimensions, as indicated in a study by Morris and Wilkinson (1989). In general, rural areas are seen to outperform urban areas slightly, but even more striking is the east–west divide. The study ranked each Local Authority District (LAD) in Wales by an 'index of local prosperity' constructed on the basis of a variety of socio-economic indicators. This synthetic index had a top score of 100. With respect to urban LADs, the Vale of Glamorgan registered a value of 73.1, with the Cynon Valley in Mid Glamorgan scoring 8. Amongst the rural LADs, Monmouth in Gwent scored 92.7, while Arfon in Gwynedd came bottom, with 32.6. The urban areas of south-east and north-east Wales together with the rural south-east are seen to perform particularly well. But while south-western districts have recently picked up on a number of indicators, the rural north-west continues to lag behind. At the bottom of the heap come the valley districts of South Wales where, despite new initiatives, circumstances remain chronic in many areas. The latest figures for county income per head place Mid Glamorgan as the poorest county in the UK, with a per capita income of £4,282.

Table 2.6 shows average gross weekly earnings in April 1989 for each county of Wales. The gaps are explained by the sampling restrictions involved in the *New Earnings Survey*, 1989.

Table 2.7 shows unemployment rates by county. A fuller picture, however requires reference to more local statistics. In December 1989 the Aberdare travel-to-work-area (TTWA) recorded an unemployment rate of 11.1 per cent, while Holyhead and Pwllheli recorded rates above 10 per cent. Another three TTWAs had rates above 9 per cent (Bangor and Caernarfon, Merthyr and Rhymney, and South Pembrokeshire).

Table 2.8 shows GDP per county, comparing the latest available figures (for 1987) with those for 1979. It must be emphasized that GDP figures should not be used as indicators of 'wealth' and that care must be taken when making comparisons, but the figures do indicate differences in terms of productive activity. The most noticeable change experienced over the period is that for Clwyd, whose figure relative to Wales increased from 89 per cent to 106 per cent. Mid Glamorgan, already below the figure for Wales in 1979, suffered a further decline to an extremely low 82.5 per cent in 1987.

Table 2.6   Average gross weekly earnings, April 1989. Wales by county (£s)

	Manual males	Non-manual males	All males	Manual females	Non-manual females	All females
Clwyd	217.8	285.4	241.4	-	-	156.2
Clwyd East	(224.8)	-	(247.0)	-	(178.7)	(156.4)
Dyfed (excl.Llanelli)	186.5	-	226.0	-	-	-
Gwent	216.9	266.8	233.4	-	168.1	160.7
Gwynedd	197.8	-	-	-	-	162.6
Mid Glamorgan	209.3	297.4	242.4	-	197.0	176.2
Powys	-	-	-	-	-	-
South Glamorgan	202.4	287.4	248.9	-	182.8	175.8
West Glamorgan (inc.Llanelli)	220.7	259.6	235.8	-	-	162.7
Wales	209.8	280.9	238.6	131.8	180.5	168.0

Source: New Earnings Survey, 1989

Table 2.7   Wales: unemployed by county, December 1989

Workforce base rates	Unemployed			Unemployed Rate		
Counties	Male	Female	Total	Male	Female	Total
				%	%	%
Clwyd	7,477	2,841	10,318	7.1	3.8	5.7
Dyfed	7,262	2,754	10,016	8.1	4.8	6.8
Gwent	10,179	3,296	13,475	8.8	4.1	6.9
Gwynedd	6,423	2,563	8,986	10.6	6.3	8.8
Mid Glamorgan	14,245	4,065	18,310	11.4	4.6	8.6
Powys	1,192	576	1,768	3.6	2.8	3.3
South Glamorgan	10,120	3,012	13,132	8.5	3.2	6.2
West Glamorgan	8,679	2,477	11,156	9.7	3.9	7.3
Wales	65,577	21,584	87,161	8.9	4.2	6.9

Source: Employment Department, Office for Wales

Table 2.8   GDP per head, Wales by county, 1979 and 1987

	1979		1987	
County	£	% Wales	£	% Wales
Clwyd	2237	89.2	5463	106.2
Dyfed and Powys	2584	103.1	5081	98.8
Gwent	2453	97.8	5154	100.2
Gwynedd	2233	89.1	4500	87.5
Mid Glamorgan	2251	89.8	4242	82.5
South Glamorgan	3011	120.1	6248	121.5
West Glamorgan	2774	106.5	5371	104.5
Wales	2507	100	5142	100

Source: Economic Trends, November 1989

These figures for GDP per head, together with those for average earnings by county quoted earlier, reflect the changes which have taken place in industrial and occupational structures within Wales during the 1980s.[6] A significant factor making for these changes has been the unbalanced investment trends. Much of the new investment into Wales has been attracted along a narrow ribbon clinging to the M4 in South Wales and to Alyn and Deeside in north-east Wales; for example, of the £1 billion of inward investment reported for 1988, some three-quarters was accounted for by the Ford Motor Company project announced for Bridgend and Swansea. Table 2.9 is taken from the Welsh Affairs Committee report, *Inward Investment into Wales and its Interaction with Regional and EEC Policies* (December 1988). It shows the distribution of inward investment projects into Wales over the period 1983–7. The report finds that the concentration of inward investment has brought little benefit for rural Wales, with Dyfed, Gwynedd and Powys receiving only twenty-six out of a total of 330 projects in Wales during the period, amounting to £58.6 million or some 6 per cent of the total value.[7]

6   See note 2 above. Estimates of GDP per head by county divide work-place-based estimtes of GDP by the resident population. This procedure is of questionable relevance for counties where commuting is a significant activity. Thus the productivity of urban areas into which workers commute will tend to be overstated by this indicator, while that of surrounding areas in which they live will be understated.

7   Doubts have been expressed concerning the accuracy of inward investment figures, and particular problems arise when making inter-regional comparisons through lack of uniformity. The jobs linked to projects are hypothetical and often relate to some unspecified date in the future.

Table 2.9 Inward investment into Wales by county, 1 April 1983–31 December 1987

County	Number of projects	Total investment (£ millions)
Clwyd	68	284.6
Dyfed	17	56.4
Gwent	79	186.1
Gwynedd	6	1.5
Mid Glamorgan	88	188.6
Powys	3	0.7
South Glamorgan	38	113.8
West Glamorgan	31	66.9
Total	330	898.6

Source: Welsh Affairs Committee. First Report, Session 1988–9

Particular concern has been expressed in many quarters regarding the lopsided appeal to investment which is provided by the Cardiff Bay Development. Despite claims that any investment in the zone would be additional to Wales and capable of generating a spread of economic activity, there are fears that such investment, both private and public, could be at the expense of other areas and intiatives.

The final table in this section shows the variation in house prices between the counties in Wales, with the exclusion of Powys (table 2.10). Some care must be taken when interpreting the figures supplied by the Halifax Building Society, but again they emphasize the relative prosperity of Wales's south-eastern corner. In the late 1980s the region began to feel the ripple effects of the house-price explosion in the south-east of England, which saw a narrowing in the house-price gap between Wales and southern England. Average house prices in Wales rose by 25 per cent over 1989, although the latter part of the year saw a lagged slowing down following the national trend.

Doubts regarding the creation of a stronger economic base

There is some concern that while the economic base of the Welsh economy has been broadened it has not necessarily been strengthened or made more secure. The crucial arguments would seem to rest on the views that

(1) there is a growing dependence on inward investment and multinational company operations, with foreign companies

accounting for approximately one-quarter of manufacturing employment in Wales;

(2) there is a preponderance of low-technology assembly operations in the so-called high-technology industries; and

(3) in general the new jobs created, in factories and services, have been insufficient in terms of quality and quantity to make up for those lost, producing a mismatch in terms of skills and remuneration.

Table 2.10 Average price of semi-detached houses in Wales (4th quarter, 1989)

County	Price (£)
Clwyd	45,593
Dyfed	43,080
Gwent	51,300
Gwynedd	47,477
Mid Glamorgan	44,506
South Glamorgan	56,236
West Glamorgan	46,534
Wales	48,548

Source: Halifax Building Society

The arguments and responses regarding the nature and effects of inward investment have been well rehearsed elsewhere.[8] Criticisms include claims of 'screwdriver' assembly work and low-paid female labour, often non-union, which contribute to a vicious circle involving a labour force which is unsuitable or unavailable to attract the high-value end of high-technology operations. The problems associated with the 'branch-factory' syndrome are identified as: low levels of decision-making; limited integration into the local economy; the location of important entrepreneurial functions such as research and development and marketing elsewhere; and the inherent footlooseness involved in multinational operations. Recent evidence, however, suggests that some of these problems are overstated, or at least being reduced, while the Welsh Affairs Committee Report on Inward Investment (1988) noted that foreign inward investors are not necessarily the main culprits in all these respects.

8 See, for example, Morgan (1987), Morris (1988) and Jones (1988). See also Welsh Affairs Committee (1988).

Once again, care must be taken not to be too cynical about the contribution made by inward investment, but it would seem that, with an increasing dependence on foreign investment, the economy of Wales remains precariously based, but for different reasons than of old. The more diversified economy may be less susceptible to the economic ups and downs associated with traditional industries, but the new order is itself vulnerable to the vagaries introduced by the enterprise calculations associated with the 'branch-factory' syndrome.

Future prospects

1989 saw subdued growth everywhere as the national economy reacted to the Government's tight policies aimed at curbing inflation and reducing the current account deficit. There is clear evidence in Wales of a growing business pessimism after a period of buoyant expectations, as businesses struggle to fund high borrowing charges, and the 'white goods' sector, in particular, has been hit by the side-effects of high interest rates on demand. During 1989 the reported rate of business failures in Wales was worse than the picture across the UK.[9]

There is a view amongst forecasters, however, that the effects of the recession will be marginalized in Wales. Somehow leapfrogging any difficulties in a period of retrenchement, including the uncertain effects of the new Uniform Business Rate and the recent business revaluations, many forecasters produce relatively optimistic projections for the Welsh economy in the 1990s. Several forecasts indicate Wales growing at or around the UK average.[10]

Table 2.11 is based on the recent projections for the 1990s included in the *Regional Economic Prospects* report referred to earlier. The table shows the projected growth rates for each region and for the UK for the period 1989–2000.[11]

9   According to a survey by Dun and Bradstreet UK, Wales recorded 944 business failures in 1989, a rise of 22.1 per cent over the previous year.

10 For example, Business Strategies project an annual average growth rate of GDP for Wales over the period 1990–4 of 2.5 per cent compared with 2.6 per cent for the UK. The rate projected by the National Westminster *UK Regional Review* for the period 1991–5 is 3.1 per cent for both Wales and the UK.

11 The regional model used by *Regional Economic Prospects* basically involves a projection of past trend relationships in regions relative to those of the UK as a whole. The regional projections are consistent with the Cambridge Econometrics Forecast for the UK economy. A number of assumptions are made concerning the management of the UK economy, for example, that interest rates together with intervention in currency markets will continue to be the major instruments of macro-economic policy with the UK joining the Exchange Rate Mechanism in 1992.

Table 2.11   Regional economic forecasts

	Change 1989–2000 (per cent per annum)		
	GDP	Consumers' expenditure	Employment
South-east	2.0	1.6	0.4
Greater London	0.8	1.0	-0.2
Rest of south-east	2.8	2.0	0.8
East Anglia	3.5	2.5	1.4
South-west	3.5	2.3	1.4
West Midlands	2.5	1.5	0.4
East Midlands	3.1	1.8	0.9
Yorkshire and Humberside	2.5	1.5	0.6
North-west	2.1	1.4	0.2
North	2.2	1.3	0.3
Scotland	2.0	1.1	0.3
Northern Ireland	1.5	1.5	0.1
Wales	2.9	1.9	0.8
United Kingdom	2.4	1.6	0.5

Source: Regional Economic Prospects, 1990

The projections for Wales suggest that GDP will grow at 2.9 per cent per annum during the 1990s; above the UK rate and that for seven other regions. Employment will show a lower growth rate, but again above that experienced for the UK. A break-down of the overall figures shows manufacturing output growth slowing down compared with the latter part of the 1980s, but the annual percentage change during the first half of the 1990s will remain above that of the UK at 4.7 per cent. Manufacturing employment is expected to peak around 1992, but will remain stable thereafter, with any decline slower than that for the UK as a whole. Service sector employment will increase more rapidly than for the UK as a whole, but at slightly less than the UK rate with respect to business services.

A key feature in these projections is taken to be business relocation from the south-east of England because of increasing congestion, high property prices and labour shortages.[12] Demographic

12   The jobs gap indicated by the unemployment–vacancy ratio has been estimated as around 1:1 in the south-east of England compared with between 8:1 and 9:1 in Wales.

projections indicate that general shortages in the labour market, particularly of 16–24-year-olds, are not expected to be as great as in Great Britain as a whole, and especially in the south-east. This, together with the persistence of relatively untapped female labour, is assumed to have a potential positive effect on industrial location in Wales in the 1990s.[13]

Several qualifications, however, must be made to the above scenario. The early 1990s will witness the effects of major investment projects coming on stream, but thereafter employment growth in Wales will depend increasingly on the region's locational attractiveness for foreign inward investment, as slower growth within the UK economy would suggest a reduction in the number of domestically generated projects. Longer-term projections are necessarily more conjectural, but forecasts for the second half of the 1990s are particularly uncertain. Clearly the performance of the Welsh economy depends on national and international developments, and European developments after 1992 make predictions particularly problematic.

The implications of full European union and the single market on Wales, with the opportunities and threats posed, are many and varied (see chapter 4). One key consideration which can be elaborated upon at this stage, however, is that involving the ultimate ownership of productive capacity in Wales and the extent to which key decision-making is located elsewhere. It has been suggested that many firms will move their headquarters, while others rationalize and shift their resources to other more favoured areas of Europe, particularly those located in what has come to be referred to as the 'golden triangle' of London–Paris–Hamburg. The footlooseness of the 'branch-factory' syndrome would thus be activated by the open market. An early indication of the new calculations may be seen in the recent announcement by the Ford Motor Company that it is reviewing its manufacturing plans for the 1990s. This review includes the project at Bridgend which was a much lauded inward investment gain in 1988. Ostensibly the reappraisal of the Bridgend project is based on concern regarding industrial disputes, but it is perhaps the first of the black clouds on the horizon. Mention of eastern Europe in the review also suggests that the 1990s may produce a completely new 'ball game' as far as industrial location in Europe is concerned.

The other explicitly European consideration which requires brief treatment is the opening of the Channel Tunnel. Again the effects on

13 Wales has the lowest proportion of economically active females amongst the regions of the UK, at 63 per cent compared with 67 per cent nationally.

Wales are uncertain. Some commentators, including the Henley Centre, have identified several sectors of light industry which could gain because of their lower transport costs. The extent of these gains, however, is heavily dependent on improved infrastructure within Wales and communications with the tunnel. There are also fears that the tunnel will have adverse effects on locational decision-making as far as Wales is concerned by changing Wales's relative accessibility in competition with other parts of Great Britain as well as with Europe.

Many organizations, including the Wales TUC, CBI and the Institute of Welsh Affairs, have emphasized the need for improvements in the transport network to ensure that some gains, let alone maximum benefits, are achieved from the Channel Tunnel and the open market. Recent government responses, however, are not encouraging, based as they are on the view that any improvements are a matter of commerical judgement by the relevant bodies.[14] Such proposals as currently exist are seriously deficient. For example, the British Rail Corporate Plan includes no plans for new and upgraded lines, no further electrification, no major acceleration of services in South Wales and the south-west of England, and no plans for a through train to the continent from South Wales (apart from a possible overnight sleeper service).

Relatively poor infrastructure is viewed as a considerable obstacle to Wales's ability to compete in the European context, and there are major concerns that Wales's grip on inward investment may slip in the 1990s rather than tighten. Thus, whatever the view regarding Wales's current position with respect to the periphery there are clear possibilities of its increasing peripheralization within Europe. To the extent that inward investment continues, the trends should increasingly favour the south-eastern corner and further accentuate differences within Wales.

I shall not attempt a conclusion as such to this chapter. I prefer to end by referring to statements made by Mr Peter Walker, then Secretary of State for Wales, in the St David's Day Welsh affairs debate in Parliament on 1 March 1990.[15] Earlier in the chapter I listed a series of features for the Welsh economy in the 1990s. These can now be compared with the real thing as outlined by Mr Walker in a committed programme for the new decade. Central to this programme is the improvement of facilities for training and

14   See, for example, the Government's response to the Select Committee on Welsh Affairs report on the implications of the Channel Tunnel for Wales (March 1990).
15   Welsh Affairs. Parliamentary Debates, House of Commons Official Report, 168 (62), Thursday 1 March 1990.

education via the new Training and Enterprise Councils. The specific aspects consist of

a substantial programme of developments by the Welsh Development Agency;
completion of the second Severn Bridge, completion of the M4 through to Swansea and plans to improve rail passenger and freight services in South Wales;
the A55 development and its effects on rural North Wales;
the activities of the Development Board for Rural Wales in Mid Wales;
the Cardiff Bay Development;
the Valleys Programme;
the Garden Festival in Ebbw Vale in 1992 with its attendant spin-offs for tourism which will bring to the attention of the world at large the considerable transformation that has taken place in the valleys;
the growth in financial services, particularly in North Wales and in the Swansea Bay area in the south;
and, finally, a 'positive international strategy' involving links with Baden-Württemberg in Germany and such countries as Saudi Arabia and Korea.

These are, according to the Secretary of State, the key points which should turn Wales into 'one of the most prosperous and successful regions of western Europe,'! Of course, Mr Walker has left his post. Was his task complete or are there still unsuspected difficulties ahead?

Bibliography

Cambridge Econometrics/Northern Ireland Economic Research Centre 1990. *Regional Economic Prospects: Analysis and Forecasts to the Year 2000*
George, K. and L. Mainwaring 1987. 'The Welsh Economy in the 1980s', *Contemporary Wales*, 1
George, K. and L. Mainwaring (eds.) 1988. *The Welsh Economy*. University of Wales Press
Henley Centre for Forecasting 1989. 'Regional Futures, a Special Study of the Geography of British Prosperity 1988–1995'. Henley Centre
Jones, A. 1988. Japanese Investment – Welcome to Wales, *Welsh Economic Review*, 1 (2)
Mackay, R. 1988. 'A Review of the Welsh Economy'. Industrial Growth Wales, ICC

Morgan, K. 1987. 'High Technology Industry and Regional Development', *Contemporary Wales*, 1

Morris, J. 1988. 'The Japanese are Here — for Better or Worse?' *Welsh Economic Review*, 1 (1)

Morris, J. and R. Mansfield 1988. 'Economic Regeneration in Industrial South Wales: an Empirical Analysis', *Contemporary Wales*, 2

Morris, J. and B. Wilkinson 1989. 'Divided Wales: Local Prosperity in the 1980s'. Report commissioned by HTV Current Affairs Department for *Wales This Week*. See also 'Wales: the Growing Divides', *Welsh Economic Review*, 2 (1)

Thomas, D. 1988. 'Wales in 1987: an Economic Survey', *Contemporary Wales*, 2

Thomas, D. 1989. 'Wales in 1988: an Economic Survey', *Contemporary Wales*, 3

Welsh Affairs Committee 1988. *Inward Investment into Wales and its Interaction with Regional and EEC Policies*, 2 vols. First report, Session 1988–9, House of Commons

Welsh Economic Review 1988–9, 1 (1,2), 2 (1,2)

Chapter 3

Scotland and European Community Regional Policy in the 1990s

CHARLOTTE LYTHE

In this chapter I shall discuss some of the implications for Scotland of two, in principle separate, major recent influences on EC regional policy.[1] The first is the reform induced by the extensions of the boundaries of the EC by the accession of Greece, Spain and Portugal; and the second is the the Single European Market.

The 1989 reform of EC regional structural policy measures

When Greece, Spain and Portugal joined the EC, this transformed the nature of regional disparities within the Community, and this transformation in turn induced a fundamental rethink of EC regional policy. Regional disparities within the Community are measured in various ways, usually combined into a synthetic index[2] of various indicators. We shall look at the elements of the index in later discussion specifically of Scotland, but the aggregate index serves to make the point here. The index is defined so that the average for the EC as a whole is 100, and index values greater than 100 indicate

1　This chapter draws on unpublished studies prepared for the Commission of the European Community. Neither these studies nor the contents of this chapter can be taken necessarily to represent the views of the Commission.
2　The most recent published version of the synthetic index is described in *The Regions of the Enlarged Community: Third Periodic Report on the Community*, Commission of the European Communities, 1987.

prosperity levels above, and less than 100 below, the EC average. The index values for countries in 1987 are set out in table 3.1; all the regions of Greece, Portugal and Spain have synthetic index values below 100, and in terms of the national average value only Ireland is of a similar order of magnitude.

Table 3.1   Synthetic index values for the level II regions of the EC, 1987 (EC average = 100)

Germany	131	only 2 regions out of 37 below 100, lowest value 92
France	116	5 regions out of 28 below 100, lowest value 84
Denmark	115	all three regions above 100
Belgium/ Luxemburg	101	5 regions out of 10 below 100, lowest value 78
UK	100	26 regions out of 44 below 100, lowest value 64
Italy	96	10 regions out of 25 below 100, lowest value 37
Greece	60	all 12 regions below 100, lowest value 54
Portugal	58	no regional analysis
Spain	53	all 22 regions below 100, lowest value 39
Ireland	48	no regional analysis

Source: The Regions of the Enlarged Community: Third Periodic Report on the Social and Economic Situation and Development of the Regions of the Community, Commission of the European Communities, 1987

Although it is evident from table 3.1 that many of the problems are really national rather than regional, the mechanism within the EC to address the problems is to regard them as regional, which of course is what in Community terms they are. Therefore there was a major recasting of EC regional policy, and in 1989 the Council of the EC adopted new regulations for the conduct of regional policy. The most significant of these redefined the new general framework within which the various structural funds, the European Investment Bank (EIB) and other existing financial instruments would have to operate, by specifying five priority objectives,[3] the fifth of which is subdivided:

3   These are described in Adriaan Dierx, 'The Reform of the European Community Regional Policies in light of the Completion of the Internal Market', unpublished conference paper, July 1989.

(1) promoting the development and structural adjustment of regions where development is lagging
(2) converting areas seriously affected by industrial decline
(3) combating long-term unemployment
(4) facilitating youth employment and training
(5) (a) speeding up the adjustment of agricultural structures
     (b) promoting the development of rural areas.

For objectives 1, 2 and 5(b), EC finance and other aid is channelled to regions which are defined in terms of criteria such as the synthetic index as eligible for assistance, and these have accordingly been dubbed respectively Objective 1, Objective 2 and Objective 5(b) regions in EC nomenclature. Aid under objectives 3, 4 and 5(a) is not tied to specified regions. Objectives 1 and 2 are principally dealt with through the European Regional Development Fund (ERDF), objectives 3 and 4 through the European Social Fund (ESF) and objectives 5 (a) and (b) through the European Agricultural Guidance and Guarantee Fund (EAGGF), but the intention is that the various financial instruments, and the various Commissioners administering them, should operate co-operatively.

The major financial sources available within the EC for regional assistance can best be summarized in table 3.2, also for 1987, in which all figures are in millions of ECUs. We can see in that table that the EIB is the single most important source of finance, but this is of course in the form of loans, not grants. For grant assistance, the ERDF was fractionally more important than the ESF.

The Objective 1 regions designated by the EC contain only one part of the UK, Northern Ireland, which has a synthetic index value of 64. The synthetic index values in table 3.1 give a fairly clear impression of where the Objective 1 regions are to be found – in the southern and western periphery of the EC. Specifically, they are in Greece, the Mezzogiorno in Italy (except Abruzzi), Portugal, Spain and Ireland (including Northern Ireland). They have low per capita income and productivity, and in most cases they have high unemployment, structural underemployment and a rapidly expanding labour force. Their problems are partly associated with their peripherality, and its economic implications of higher transport costs, longer travel times and difficult access to information, because they tend to have small local markets and are remote from the main markets in the centre of the Community. These market disadvantages make it hard for firms to achieve economies of scale. Their production is in general concentrated disproportionately into agriculture and low value-added manufacturing and, in some cases, tourism. The intention of

Table 3.2   EC Regional Assistance, 1987

	(millions of ECUs)
European Regional Development Fund(ERDF)	3662
European Social Fund (ESF)	3524
European Agricultural Guidance and Guarantee Fund (EAGGF)	941
Integrated Mediterranean Programmes	188
Total Grants	8315
European Investment Bank (EIB)	7450
European Coal and Steel Community	969
European Atomic Engergy Community	210
Total Loans	8629

Source: Adriaan Dierx, 'The Reform of the European Community Regional Policies in light of the Completion of the Internal Market' (unpublished conference paper, July 1989)

EC regional policy is to address these problems by promoting growth and industrial restructuring.

In this chapter my concern is with the Objective 2 regions, because this is the heading under which most EC regional assistance finds its way to Scotland. The Objective 2 regions are those in industrial decline: that is, developed and highly industrialized areas which have lost out through structural change. Per capita income is not particularly low, but unemployment rates are high because of job losses and an insufficiently rapid growth of employment in new industries. The problems of these regions stem from overdependence on traditional declining industries, frequently compounded by environmental problems (pollution and industrial dereliction), obsolete infrastructure, poor labour relations and lack of entrepreneurship.

If we look at how Scotland (and its regions) was performing in terms of the synthetic index and its components in 1987, we can see how far, in the relatively measurable elements, it fitted the criteria for Objective 2 regions.

The items in table 3.3 require a word of explanation. 'Population 16–64/total pop.' measures the proportion of the population which is of working age, so indirectly indicating the dependency ratio. 'Participation rate' measures the ratio of the labour force (persons in employment plus the unemployed) to population 16–64. 'Sectoral shares' measures the percentage of all persons in employment whose main occupation is in the sector stated. The unemployment rates are registered regional unemployment (adjusted for different national practices in measuring unemployment) as a percentage of the labour force. 'GDP/pop. PPP index' measures income per head, with the different currencies of the EC related to each other by a purchasing power parity index — that is, it seeks to identify the standard of living. 'GDP/emp. ECU index' measures output per employee, with the different currencies of the EC related to each other in ECUs — that is, it seeks to measure labour productivity. 'Lab. force growth index' considers the additional jobs required because of expected labour force growth between 1987 and 1990. In all the indices, an index value of more than 100 indicates prosperity above the EC average.

Table 3.3 Scottish regions and the EC synthetic index, 1987

	Scotland total	Borders/ Central/ Fife/ Lothian/ Tayside	Dumfries/ Galloway/ Strathclyde	Grampian	Highlands/ Islands	EC
Population 16–64/ total pop.	67.3					65.7
Particip- ation rate	71.2					63.9
Sectoral shares						
agriculture	3.4					8.6
industry	33.4					34.3
services	61.5					57.2
Unemployment rate (1986)	14.4	13.0	16.7	8.2	13.8	10.8
GDP/pop. PPP index	102	103	95	126	108	100
GDP/emp. ECU index	93	92	92	104	97	100
Lab. force growth index	56	56	56	56	56	100
Synthetic index	87	93	76	133	101	100

Source: Third Periodic Report

As is obvious from table 3.3, Grampian and, in some respects, the Highlands and Islands were doing clearly better than the Scottish average. I have presented the data at Level II in the EC's Nomenclature of Territorial Units for Statistics (NUTS), in which Level I is 64 regions of the EC and Level II is 167 regions (there is a more disaggregated Level III, of 824 regions, but there is very little information published at level III). I am confident from the patchy information that *is* available for the Level III regions in Scotland that, if the level of disaggregation were to be increased, we would find that the Borders/Fife/Lothian/Tayside region would display diversity, with the Borders and Lothian doing perceptibly better than Fife and Tayside. At the level of aggregation in the table, only Dumfries and Galloway/Strathclyde is defined as a declining traditional industrial region, but since it embraces half of Scotland in terms of economic activity, that is an important indicator for Scotland as a whole. In addition, some other parts of Scotland, Tayside and Fife in particular, receive ERDF (and ESF) assistance to meet problems of industrial decline. In quantitative terms, the assistance has been, and can be expected to continue to be, significant, especially in the context of the total package of regional assistance made available to Scotland. There is a good deal of year-to-year fluctuation in EC assistance to Scotland, particularly in EIB loans, and the changes in UK regional policy assistance (especially affecting Regional Selective Assistance (RSA) and Grants (RSG)) make fair comparison a little difficult, but table 3.4, which includes UK assistance to Scotland through the Scottish Development Agency (SDA) and the Highlands and Islands Development Board (HIDB), gives some indication of the orders of magnitude.

As is evident from table 3.4, the amount of assistance for industry in Scotland has been fairly consistently constant at about or a little over £300 million in cash terms (though, of course, declining in real terms) since 1981, but the EC share of that total has increased.

With the reform of regional policy, the main focus is on the Objective 1 regions, but the amount of finance for the various instruments of regional policy has been increased to such an extent that the Objective 2 regions can expect to continue to receive broadly the same amount of help as before. However, the framework within which the assistance is available has changed; assistance is now much less to individual piecemeal projects and much more to broad-sweep and long-term programmes, and on a much clearer basis of co-operation in planning between the Commission and EC member governments — the member governments are responsible, at national or local level as they think fit, for the preparation of three- to five-year development plans to achieve objectives 1 to 4 and 5(b), which will then be jointly supported by the EC and the member government. This is at least partly an attempt to address what is for the UK the thorny issue of 'additionality': the envisaged increase in the appropriations for the Funds must have 'a genuine additional economic impact in the regions concerned and [result] in at least an equivalent increase in the total volume of official or similar (Community and national) structural aid in the Member State concerned, taking into account the macro-economic circumstances in which the funding takes place' (article 9 of the co-ordination regulation, 1988, as cited in Dierx).

Table 3.4   Assistance to industry in Scotland (£ million at current prices)

	1981/2	1982/3	1983/4	1984/5	1985/6	1986/7	1987/8	1988/9
UK government								
SDA Acts	58.4	46.4	43.6	23.3	23.8	20.2	20.5	18.2
RSA/RSG	162.3	307.4	167.7	140.9	155.6	205.6	116.3	114.6
HIDB	11.8	15.6	17.3	22.9	17.6	16.6	16.4	18.1
Other	2.0	–	–	–	–	–	–	–
Total	234.5	369.4	228.6	187.2	197.0	242.4	153.2	150.9
EC (note: data apply to calendar years: 1981 etc.)								
ESF	–	9.8	49.2	31.2	29.8	34.3	39.5	52.4
ERDF	70.4	71.6	83.5	103.4	69.4	84.0	92.8	96.4
Other grants	3.5	3.2	3.6	6.9	7.4	9.5	5.9	6.2
Total grants	73.9	84.6	136.3	141.5	106.6	127.8	138.2	155.0
EIB loans	25.0	140.8	40.2	82.0	84.6	107.7	0	0

Source: calculated from *Scottish Economic Bulletin*, December 1989

The consequences for Scotland, therefore, depend more crucially than before on the attitude of the UK government. Financial assistance is in principle available to Scotland in much the same amounts, and for much the same purposes, as before, but the availability in practice depends on the willingness of the government to agree to abide by the additionality ruling and itself to adopt, or permit local authorities to adopt, local planning strategies.

The Single European Market

The second main stimulus to reform of regional policy in the EC is the advent of '1992', which will initiate a new set of policy objectives

agreed by the heads of state of the EC member states in December
1985, when they signed the Single Act to modify the Treaty of Rome.
The new policy objectives are:

(1) the establishment, as far as possible by the end of 1992, of a
     single (or large) market without internal frontiers
(2) economic and social cohesion
(3) a common policy for scientific and technical advancement
(4) strengthening the European Monetary System
(5) the emergence of a European social dimension
(6) co-ordinated action relating to the environment.

What is of concern here is the interaction between the first
two of these objectives. They were agreed together in full realization of the extent to which a policy to achieve cohesion is
required to counterbalance the effects of establishing the single
European market, because it was fully expected that the intensification of competition associated with the single market
would create economic and social tensions, and that countervailing
measures would be required. Specifically, regional policy has a larger
role in enabling regions to adjust to the centripetal forces of the
single market.

The potential gains of the single European market have been
analysed in very concrete, and optimistic, terms in the Cecchini
Report (1988). This report, which was prepared for EC Commission
use but was then widely disseminated, looked at the likely effect of
some 300 specific measures which the Commission regarded as
essential for the creation of a single market. The measures are
designed to remove specific obstacles to the free movement of people,
goods and services within the Community, and fall into four broad
categories:

(1) elimination of delays at intra-Community borders
(2) harmonization of technical regulations in the EC
(3) opening national public procurement markets to EC-wide
     competition
(4) removal of restrictions on trade in services and on the right to
     become established in service activities in other member states.

The Cecchini Report concluded that the completion of the market
would of itself over five to six years result in a 4.5 per cent increase
in Community GDP, a 6.1 per cent reduction in the rate of inflation,
the creation of 1.8 million new jobs and an improvement in
the Community's external balance equivalent to 1 per cent of

Community GDP. These gains would come about through increased competition bringing about increases in efficiency, lowering of prices, economies of scale and quality improvements in products.

The Cecchini Report did not, however, address issues of regional balance, and this is the topic of a series of unpublished studies executed for the Commission to examine the regional effects of '1992'. Increased competition carries obvious threats for less efficient producers and those operating on inefficient scale, and we have already seen that the Objective 1 and Objective 2 regions are likely to have a disproportionately large number of such producers. The research conducted therefore has three stages: first, to identify those sectors of economic activity most likely to be affected by '1992'; second, to look at their regional dispersion; and third, to identify any policy conclusions. Preliminary studies conducted for the Commission indicated that about 20 per cent of the Community's employment was likely to be affected in a direct way by '1992', the biggest threats and opportunities being to firms dependent on public procurement, to a number of agricultural/food industries and to most of the services to industry. Whether in any particular case the single market is a threat or opportunity obviously depends on the individual firm's capacity to accommodate to increased competition, and this in turn depends *inter alia* on its regional location, where relevant considerations include the proximity of suppliers to markets, physical infrastructure, the quantity and quality of the local labour market, and the research and technological development potential.

A series of unpublished studies for the EC Commission has examined specific aspects of the regional impact of '1992'. Two studies looked at sectors likely to be substantially affected – public procurement and financial services – and the others examined more general issues, the most intersting of which were the competitiveness of the problem regions and the problems of traditional industrial regions. The conclusions for Scotland are outlined below.

The report on public procurement (CEGOS–IDET 1990) concentrated on three sectors: telecommunications, electricity generating equipment and railway rolling stock engineering. Of concern to Scotland for telecommunications was Fife (where such employment, mostly in Kirkcaldy, constitutes about 1.6 per cent of total manufacturing employment) and for electricity Dumfries and Galloway (2.2 per cent, mainly in Annan) and Strathclyde (0.5 per cent, mainly in Glasgow). As the figures show, none of these was thus very major in importance to the regional economies. Nor, the report concluded, were the likely effects of '1992' — the pattern of provision within the EC at present ignored economies of scale for the sake of establishing 'national' presence, if only through subsidiaries, and there was no evidence at least in the short term that the opening up of public procurement, which is one of the major elements of '1992', would have much impact on this. Although the report may be a little short-sighted in its conclusion, it seems likely that its findings will be true for more sensitive areas of public procurement, such as defence equipment, which are of particular interest and importance to Scotland.

In the case of financial services, it is important to distinguish 'retail' and 'wholesale' activity. 'Retail' activity occurs where the consumers of financial services are located, and thus the only major regional effect of '1992' on the 'retail' financial services is through the net effect of the growth induced by '1992' on general economic prosperity, and hence on demand for financial services, and on headquarters company location (which is relevant since companies tend to look close to their headquarters for the provision of financial and other business services). Whilst Scotland can be expected to share in the general growth, she may suffer some net loss of headquarters activity, so that the net effect on 'retail' financial services can be expected to be relatively small. For 'wholesale' financial services, '1992' can be expected to cause increased concentration, and this can be expected to be to the advantage of Edinburgh. The work done for the EC Commission (PA Cambridge Economic Consultants 1989) identified potential gainers and losers from greater concentration of 'wholesale' financial services, and put Edinburgh into the former category because of its niche markets. This conclusion was reinforced by a separate analysis (Holmes and Lythe 1990), conducted for the Edinburgh and Lothians 1992 Committee, which found that in UK terms Edinburgh had strengths, particularly in life assurance, in which the Cecchini Report had found the UK generally to be outstandingly price-competitive as compared with the rest of the EC.

The studies undertaken for the EC Commission of problem regions (IFO 1989) and of regions experiencing decline in their traditional industries (IRES/RIDER 1989) are sufficiently complementary, so that their conclusions for Scotland can be discussed together. Both reports included among the areas chosen for special study Strathclyde, in the former study as part of a larger grouping including also Dumfries and Galloway. The problem regions study used a questionnaire, directed at companies operating in the selected regions and asking their views about the present impact, in their experience, of a set of national and regional factors bearing on competitiveness, and enquiring also about what factors were most amenable to improvement; the result for Strathclyde and Dumfries and Galloway was that national rather than regional factors were dominant, and the only regional factors which firms felt reduced their competitiveness were local taxes and local political considerations; in particular, peripherality to markets was *not* regarded as a problem. The study of regions with declining traditional industries relied on the informed judgement of analysts, and its conclusions were rather less optimistic about Strathclyde. As for most of the regions with declining traditional industries, the report found that Strathclyde was inadequate in its approach to labour training and retraining, too complacent and too inflexible. It was felt that in Strathclyde the decline of traditional industries still had some way to go (a view confirmed by subsequent announcements about Ravenscraig steel works), and that, whilst Strathclyde had a fairly substantial representation of modern high-technology industry, this was vulnerable because of external control. The 'branch-factory' syndrome has been quite exensively examined in Scotland (for example, Firn 1975; Hood and Young 1982) because of several unfortunate experiences which have led to the cynical view that if an overseas-owned factory is doing badly it will be closed in order to protect production at the headquarters location, whilst if it is doing well it will be closed in order to shift production to a lower-cost location in southern Europe or in the Third World.

Consumers in Scotland, as elsewhere in the EC, stand unambiguously to gain from the increase in competition engendered by '1992'. Whether producers in Scotland will need special protection, through UK and/or EC regional policy, to help them reduce costs and stand up to these same competitive forces, is unclear. In financial services, Scottish producers should benefit from the absence of protective arrangements. In the areas of declining traditional industries, assistance towards restructuring must be beneficial, provided the will is there for the restructuring to take place.

Bibliography

Cecchini, P. (ed.) 1988. *The European Challenge: 1992 — the Benefits of a Single Market.* Gower

CEGOS–IDET 1990. *Conséquences régionales de l'ouverture des marchés publics: le cas des secteurs des télécommunications, du gros matériel électrique et du matériel ferroviaire* (report for the EC Commission, January 1990)

Firn, J. R. 1975. 'External Control and Regional Development: the Case of Scotland', *Environment and Planning* A, 7, pp. 393–414

Holmes, Mark and Charlotte Lythe 1990. 'The Impact of 1992 on Employment in Lothian Financial Services', Edinburgh and Lothians 1992 Committee Working Paper No. 2 (May)

Hood, N. and S. Young 1982. *Multinationals in Retreat: the Scottish Experience.* Edinburgh University Press

IFO 1989. *An Empirical Assessment of Factors Shaping Regional Competitiveness in Problem Regions* (report for the EC Commission, October 1989)

IRES/RIDER 1989. *Conséquences socio-économiques de l'achèvement du marché intérieur pour les régions de tradition industrielle de la Communauté Européenne* (report for the EC Commission, October 1989)

PA Cambridge Economic Consultants 1989. *The Regional Consequences of Completion of the Internal Market for Financial Services* (report for the EC Commission, October 1989)

Chapter 4

Wales in the 1990s: External Influences on Economic Development

LYNN MAINWARING

Introduction

This chapter is concerned with the major influences on the Welsh economy, in the coming decade, of events originating largely outside the UK. By its nature the discussion will be somewhat speculative. It will also be conducted in rather abstract terms with no attempt at a detailed statistical analysis of current trends.

The major channel of external influence on the Welsh economy is through the UK's economic relationships with the rest of the world, including commodity trade and flows of international investment. How the costs and benefits of these relationships are distributed within the UK is largely a matter of natural regional advantages and of domestic regional policies. Up to 1973 the UK's overseas relationships had no particularly remarkable pattern. Compared to today, a greater share of commodity trade was conducted with less developed countries and there also existed an important system of imperial preferences. But neither of these features was problematic for Wales since, on the whole, these kinds of trade accorded well with Welsh comparative advantages. The postwar period has, however, seen a gradual shift of UK trade (both imports and exports) towards other industrialized countries. This pattern was reinforced in 1973 when the UK acceded to the European Community (EC).

Membership of the EC has led to a steady diversion of both commodity trade and of other economic relationships away from non-EC members and agencies to the Community itself. So persistent and so pronounced has this process been that it is fair to say that the external influences on the Welsh economy are now almost completely dominated by developments within the EC. This applies even to such issues as the nature and extent of direct investments from North

America and Japan, since these are now dictated to a considerable degree by the need to service a European rather than merely British market.

The gradual unification of the West European market since the mid 1970s has already had a significant impact on the way that the Welsh economy has developed. Of particular importance is the way in which the steel industry, once comfortably insulated in a protected British market, has had to contract and restructure in response to Community directives aimed at eliminating overcapacity. The imposition of milk quotas is another specific example of EC policies contributing to changes in Welsh economic welfare. More indirectly, Wales has proved an attractive location for non-European manufacturers looking for European production platforms, and, in the case of the motor industry, for investments forming part of a Continental production strategy.

The speed of current developments suggests that the European dimension will assume even greater significance in the 1990s than it has in the past. There are, as I see it, four major issues that require immediate discussion. These are:

(1) The completion of a single European market in 1992. This is not, of course, something new. It is merely the continuation of a process that began with the formation of the original common market aimed at eliminating tariff barriers between member states. The tariffs have long since gone: 1992 should see the end of non-tariff barriers.

(2) Progress towards monetary integration. Again, this is part of a continuing process but one in which UK governments have, so far, been reluctant to participate. There is, at present, considerable pressure on the UK to join the exchange rate system of the European Monetary System (EMS) and it is likely that this pressure will prove irresistible. It appears to be the intention of most member states to continue the movement in the direction of complete monetary union.[1]

(3) Developments within the Common Agricultural Policy (CAP). The magnitude of agricultural spending has been the major cause of recurrent budgetary crises. Efforts to bring it under control must inevitably affect Welsh agriculture.

(4) Developments in eastern Europe. Any remarks on this issue must be extremely tentative, but an eastward extension of the Community cannot be ruled out. This may be limited to

1 This chapter was, of course, completed before the UK's entry to the exchange rate mechanism.

embracing the former German Democratic Republic within the existing structure, but it may also involve conferring associate membership or some other status on remaining countries. Such an extension would be bound to affect the budgetary claims of regions within the present twelve members.

The list appears to leave out regional policy but, as we shall see, regional policy has a bearing on each of these issues. At an abstract level, assessments of the first three issues lead to rather similar conclusions. The analysis is, perhaps, more clear-cut in the case of monetary integration, and we shall begin with that.

European monetary integration

I should start by stressing that complete monetary integration, such as exists within the UK, for example, is a long way from being fulfilled at the European level. The present arrangement — the EMS — is merely a step in that direction and one which not all member states have fully taken. Nevertheless it will be useful to conduct the argument by looking initially at the implications of full monetary union. In that way we can gain much insight by examining existing integrated monetary areas like the UK to see what lessons they hold for an extended union.

The UK is a complete monetary union because it has a single currency which is used as a means of payment in any part of the realm. The currency is convertible into other currencies at the same rate whether the exchange is made in Aberdare or Aberdeen. Monetary expansion and contraction and, by implication, the setting of interest rates, are undertaken by a single central authority, the Bank of England. The Bank draws on a single pool of foreign exchange reserves to help maintain the value of sterling against other currencies at what is deemed an appropriate rate. Is a single UK currency area a sensible arrangement, or would it be better if Wales and the other regions and nations of the UK had their own currencies, pursuing their own monetary policies, co-ordinated by their own central banks, the currencies being free to rise and fall relative to one another as economic needs dictate? (The question is obviously parallel to the wider one of comparing UK monetary autonomy with complete European integration.)

Up to a point, such an arrangement — monetary disintegration — would have considerable advantages. In so far as the fundamental structural conditions of these individual national and regional economies differ, separate monetary systems would allow each to pursue policies appropriate to its particular needs. Consider the present state of the UK economy. The generally held view is that the economy of late has been 'overheating'. The growth of demand has been too rapid relative to the availability of productive capacity, skills, natural resources and so on. Inflation is uncomfortably high, while the yawning gap between demand and domestic supply is being filled with imports.

Without discussing its merits, consider the government's response to this situation. Basically, it has done two things: one is to keep interest rates high to dampen domestic demand, and the other (a partial consequence of the first) is to maintain a high value of sterling. A high pound means that foreign goods are relatively cheap (in terms of sterling). This avoids a further twist in the inflation index but since cheap imports mean more imports, this has a negative effect on the current account of the balance of payments, and so on British manufacturing generally. Inflation, of course, ranks higher in government priorities than unemployment.

What relevance does this have for the concept of monetary disintegration? Simply that if there is overheating in the UK economy then this is very much a regional problem. In particular, it is a problem for the south-east of England. If high interest rates and a high exchange rate are the appropriate ways of dealing with this problem (itself a debatable proposition) then these are appropriate policies for that part of England. From a Welsh perspective things look rather different. Overheating is not a great problem once you get ten miles out of Cardiff. High interest rates are crippling investment plans of local firms, and the high exchange rate is undermining the profitability of companies which have to compete in international markets.

In principle, the problem of subjecting all the regions of an economy to unified monetary and exchange rate policies that may suit only one of them could be avoided if each region had its own currency. Wales could have its own central bank, setting its own minimum lending rate and determining the value of the Welsh pound not only in relation to the dollar and the yen but to the pound sterling as well. (The Irish, of course, already have such an arrangement.) But if that is wholly advantageous, why stop at Wales? It has already been remarked that Cardiff, in many respects, is different from the rest of Wales, so why not separate currency areas for South Glamorgan, Gwynedd and so on? Once the question is posed in that form the disadvantages of monetary disintegration become immediately apparent. Obviously there are costs in converting one currency into another. If every Welsh county had its own currency, then the journey from Chepstow to Caernarfon would be even more of a challenge than it is at present. But administrative and transaction costs are not the only problem. The biggest disadvantage of small currency areas, where currencies are allowed to float freely in relative value, is uncertainty. A manufacturing firm needs to have a good idea when starting production on an export order what the price of the product will be when it is sold.

The removal of transaction costs and the reduction of uncertainty as a result of monetary integration promote growth in international trade and, hence, according to the conventional gains-from-trade arguments, enhance across-the-board welfare. But if there are also costs, in terms of the loss of regional or national economic sovereignty, what is the correct balance? What, in other words, is the optimum size of a currency area?[2] In a sense the question is misleading. For if monetary union yields sufficient gains to the union, taken as a whole, it ought to be possible to use part of these gains to compensate the regions which suffer most from the loss of economic control. In the UK context, for example, the gains from reduced uncertainty and transaction costs are shared by all regions. But if the government pursues macro-economic policies that are primarily appropriate for the south-east of England then that region has, in effect, a double gain, while the remaining regions will have varying degrees of offsetting losses. Geographical equity then requires appropriate compensating transfers from the south-east to other parts of the UK. From this standpoint, regional programmes should not be considered a symptom of peripheral dependence. In principle, the arrangement is, or should be, a straightforward quid pro quo that is potentially in every region's interest. Unified monetary policy and regional policy go hand in hand.

I have spent some time examining the UK monetary system because it is something with which we are all familiar. The principles involved in an integrated European system are exactly the same. The question then is: what implications does the extension of monetary union have for Wales? In theory, Wales should have no more to fear from being part of a European system than from being part of the UK arrangement. But that, precisely, is why there is reason for concern. When, in the early 1980s, Welsh industry was devastated by the combined effects of excessive interest rates and an overvalued pound, regional aid was itself being cut back. The current picture is similar, if slightly less severe. Recent history of the UK system suggests that Wales is not getting a particularly fair deal from integration.

2   The question was first addressed systematically in Mundell (1961) and McKinnon (1963).

Within Europe, a unified monetary system would probably be run from Frankfurt, along the lines of the Bundesbank, which is far more competent and politically independent than the Bank of England. But with Germany being the dominant and most dynamic European national economy, it is unlikely that policy will be pursued with the weaker peripheral economies in mind. So do the proponents of monetary union see a need for a complementary package of regional policies? The 1970 Werner Report on 'Economic and Monetary Unions' did refer to 'structural and regional action needed to contribute to the balanced development of the Community', but it did not relate this directly to the problems created by monetary union nor clarify how much of a contribution such action was meant to make. It will, of course, be some time (if ever) before union is complete. But each step in that direction entails a loss of UK sovereignty and shifts part of the responsibility for regional support from London to Brussels. The role of Community regional policy is thus crucial in assessing the impact of these developments, and I shall come back to it later.

The single market

The general implications of further goods-market integration are very like those of money-market integration. That is, we can expect the gains at an all-Europe level to be positive, but we should also expect them to be unequally distributed. Indeed, for some regions, most likely those in the periphery, the net benefits may be negative. Thus, again, regional redistributions will be required if all parts of the Community are to gain from the completion of the market.

The gains from the removal of non-tariff barriers can be broken down into their 'static' and 'dynamic' components. The static gains are of the same nature as those arising out of the formation of a customs union (that is, from the removal of tariff barriers). The view of international trade theorists is that protection, in most instances, benefits particular interest groups rather than society in general. The ability of consumers to buy Continental goods more cheaply, as a result of dismantling protective barriers against the rest of the Community, should force British industry to restructure in a way which corresponds more closely to its comparative advantages. It is true that a customs union may also have a trade-diverting (and hence welfare-reducing) effect because common external tariff and non-tariff barriers are maintained against third-party countries. Thus Britons may be importing goods from the Continent that could be produced more efficiently elsewhere simply because the former are no longer subject to barriers while the latter are. Nevertheless, most estimates of the early gains from the European Common Market suggest that trade creation effects were roughly ten times the trade diversion effects.[3]

It is these static effects which are emphasized (and estimated) in the Cecchini Report (1988) on the completion of the single market. The size of the predicted gains has tended to mask issues of how they will be distributed. Precisely what the regional pattern of static gains will be is unclear. There is no doubt that Welsh consumers, along with consumers elsewhere, will benefit from increased competition and lower prices. The real question is what will happen to the supply side, given that industrial restructuring is an important element in trade creation. This is something I shall discuss briefly a little later. For now, let us turn to the dynamic effects of integration.

Again, experience of an existing single market like the UK provides a useful starting-point. Of particular relevance is the, by now commonplace, observation of a north–south divide. Arguably the polarization between metropolis and periphery is a consequence of what Myrdal (1957) calls cumulative causation. That is to say, inequalities become self-reinforcing: success breeds success, failure breeds failure. This is not simply a matter of quoting clichés. There are good theoretical explanations why positive feedbacks arise and they generally run in terms of external economies. Once a concentration of a particular type of production or service activity occurs, the development of supporting infrastructure creates an attraction for other enterprises engaged in that or similar types of activity. The supporting infrastructure may be a transport or communications network, or a pool of skilled labour, or the availability of complementary services.

Such 'agglomeration' externalities are clearly manifest in the south-east of England, with the concentration of central government functions and of financial services in the City of London providing very powerful attracting poles. Thus one finds in the Home Counties an extraordinary concentration of corporate headquarters or 'higher-order' functions like research and development activites, financial and professional services etc. Because the externalities attract the higher functions, the associated incomes are higher, and these provide a further attraction for industry. Even this secondary attraction will have further favourable effects. For higher incomes tend to be more responsive to newer, high-technology goods and services. There is quite clearly in operation a virtuous circle which

3   For a brief survey see Swan (1988), ch. 4.

could be elaborated further, though the principles should now be obvious. No doubt agglomeration externalities also exist in the periphery, but they are more likely to exist in traditional and declining industries (steel, coal, textiles, shipbuilding) or, if they do obtain in modern manufacturing industry, then they are generally in the lower-order functions (routine assembly) associated with lower incomes. Here the process of cumulative causation is likely to confirm the sluggish and relatively backward status of the economy.

The point of returning once again to the UK experience is that the wider European prospect is simply a magnified version. The exploitation of agglomeration externalities is likely to be a major component of the dynamic gains from the single market. But the periphery's share of the larger cake is likely to be smaller.

Integration and regional policy

What emerges from this discussion is that regional policy has a key role in spreading evenly the potential benefits of market unification. But the obligations fall on both London and Brussels. The original decision to enter the EC, current support for the single market and any move towards monetary union presumably reflect the UK government's view that such moves are in the UK interest. The government thus has a responsibility for ensuring that its own regions do not suffer. But there are also Community-wide gains: Brussels too has a responsibility to the regions of Europe. The real question is how far these obligations will be fulfilled.

Recent UK experience is not at all promising. The present government is committed to keeping public expenditure to a minimum, and regional spending has suffered along with much else. It also sees regional intervention as contrary to its free-market philosophy. In the last ten years regional programmes have declined markedly in real terms. Nor is there much cause for optimism when looking towards the European Regional Development Fund. Presently the Fund constitutes a very small proportion (about 7 per cent) of the EC budget (which itself is only 1 per cent of EC GNP). For Wales there is a further problem in being part of the UK because most EC regional spending is channelled through central governments of member states. In principle, regional funds from the EC budget are meant to be additional to each state's own expenditures and not to substitute for them to any degree. In practice, this is almost impossible to verify or enforce. Governments can simply say (as the UK government frequently does) that without money from Europe their regional programmes would have been that much thinner. There is no shortage of circumstantial evidence, much of it from House of Lords Committees (for example, House of Lords 1988) to suggest that the UK government is using European funds to help reduce its own public expenditure burdens. But concrete evidence remains elusive.

Cheating on the principle of regional fund additionality can be totally avoided only if the regional programmes of member states are handed over entirely to Brussels. There are, however, two disadvantages in this strategy. First, it releases the UK from its own regional obligations. Second, it requires funds which are commensurate with the problems that integration entails. It is at this point that we are forced to broaden our outlook. If we consider recent developments in the Community, namely the Mediterranean extension, and if we look to the possibility of some form of eastward extension, then we have to ask: Is Wales still on the periphery?

It is far too soon to say what impact events in eastern Europe will have. But despite the absence of existing formal links, there is already talk of a 'Marshall Plan' for these countries. In the short term I suspect, and regret, that it will be the overseas development programme that will suffer most from the diversion of funds. In the longer term it may be that the status of regions like Wales will be revised to cope with these new financial burdens. Even in the present context of Europe-12, Welsh GDP per capita is roughly equal to the EC average and in line with the great mass of non-metropolitan France, Belgium and northern Italy. The ten poorest regions of the Community are all, with the exception of Northern Ireland, in the Mediterranean (Begg 1989).[4] This does not mean that the south presently has a prior claim on the regional fund, since the Community currently recognizes two categories of deserving region: those that are relatively underdeveloped and those, like Wales, which are suffering from the decline of traditional industries and are undergoing restructuring. It would not be surprising, however, if in Community thinking 'restructuring' is seen as a finite process rather than as an open-ended commitment.

The CAP

The chronic problem of EC agriculture is overproduction. This is an inherent consequence of the nature and magnitude of the agricultural support system embodied in the CAP. This inefficient use of large

4 It should be said that the present assessment of the regional effects of European integration comes to very similar conclusions to those of Begg (1989).

sums of money is a problem not only in itself but, given the limits on the EC budget, for the funding of other programmes also. As with the structural funds, the amounts available for agriculture have come under increasing pressure as a result of recent accessions of countries with large agricultural sectors. Attempts have already been made to control CAP expenditure, most dramatically — in the case of Wales — by the imposition of milk quotas. These are now being followed by quantity restrictions on the support available to sheep and cattle farmers. Moreover guaranteed prices for most products appear to be falling in real terms.

From a Welsh perspective one may feel a certain ambivalence about these developments. A serious attempt to restrain agricultural spending is essential to budgetary reform and the proper funding of structural programmes. On the other hand, there is little doubt that reduced support will create hardship in the rural economy. In particular, farm economies will be attempted through mechanization and increasing farm size, thus continuing trends that have been apparent since the Second World War. These make it increasingly difficult for young farmers to establish themselves and they reduce the number of full-time jobs available. It is, of course, arguable that, because the CAP support system is inherently inefficient,[5] a different system would allow the same level of effective support for a lower expenditure of resources. Such radical reform is, however, unlikely. The prospect is really one of piecemeal restrictions within the same basic framework. With this gradual diminution of support, resources will have to be found to help diversify the rural economy if we are serious about our desire to maintain these communities. Thus we come back to the central theme: a surrender of sovereignty, in this case over agricultural policy, requires compensating redistributions of a magnitude sufficient to deal with the problems of following a common policy.

Specific issues

With the exception of some references to policy changes in the CAP, the discussion so far has been rather abstract, but there are issues of a more concrete nature that need attention.

Steel and coal

Historically these industries have come under the authority of the

5   For an explanation see George and Mainwaring (1988).

European Coal and Steel Community and have been treated differently from other industries, with production being openly subsidized by member governments. A determined effort has already been made under the d'Avignon plans to phase out state support in steel. While this has proved costly in terms of Welsh jobs, the situation is now stable. Provided that British Steel's current level of competitiveness is sustained, there is little to fear on this front. Parallel efforts are now being made to eliminate uneconomic capacity in coal production. The industry, throughout Europe, is still heavily subsidized, and though the removal of these subsidies is likely to be beneficial to the generally more efficient UK industry, the South Wales coalfield (or what remains of it) has rather more in common with the rest of Europe than it does with the rest of the UK. It is probable that subsidies will go with privatization anyway. In either event, there seems little future for large-scale deep-mining operations in Wales.

Inward investment

Wales is an attractive location for foreign investors. The Invest in Britain Bureau estimates that presently some 20 per cent of inward investment, by projects and by employment, comes to Wales.[6] Such investments have contributed to the debate on the merits of attracting branch plants. The argument is that multiplant firms tend to dispense first with peripheral operations when hit by recession. Economic instability is thus magnified in an economy with a large number of such plants. Even if this hypothesis were valid in the past in the case of non-EC investors, is it still valid? Up until the early 1970s, overseas investors set up in the UK mainly to service the UK market. This is no longer the case. The absence of internal tariffs and the dismantling of non-tariff barriers means that non-EC firms can set up in any part of the EC to service the entire Community without the penalty of artificial impediments. Given the size of the EC market such operations can no longer be regarded as peripheral. Many current Japanese investments, for example, are major components of global corporate strategies. Where the 'branch-plant' syndrome may still be valid is in relation to UK firms setting up 'overspill' capacity in the regions. With the removal of barriers, that also now applies to Continental EC firms which have established regional 'outposts'.

If current non-EC investments are a stable source of employment and, therefore, welcome, the question that arises is: Will Wales continue to be an attractive location for such investors? In northern European terms, Wales is still a relatively low-wage area, yet one

6   For further details see House of Commons (1988).

able to offer the kinds of skills that manufacturers seek for assembly operations. Its problem, again, is competition from southern Europe, where wages are even lower and where a vast reserve army of labour in inefficient agricultural production and the female population are waiting to be tapped. The competitive position of the northern periphery thus hinges on superior transport and communication links to the European core. The second Severn bridge and various east–west improvements in the Welsh road networks will help in this respect, but there are two sources of concern. One is the absence of a direct high-speed rail link to the Channel Tunnel; the other is the relatively underdeveloped infrastructure within Wales itself. The latter means that whatever benefits accrue from new investments will tend to be concentrated in the north-east and south-east corners.

1992 and particular industries

The problem of communications applies to all industry and not just to new investments. Existing firms also have to come to terms with the implications of the single market. The extension of competition will almost inevitably mean the contraction of some sectors as comparative advantages and disadvantages become manifest. It has already been noted that, in the absence of counteracting regional measures, Wales could find itself becoming specialized in the less dynamic sectors of manufacturing. Here we shall consider the matter at a more basic level by looking (briefly) at the types of existing industry that may prove vulnerable to freer competition. The types of industry where the risks are highest are those where (1) existing non-tariff barriers are of sufficient magnitude to yield significant protection, and (2) where further economies of scale are possible.[7] Sectors with moderate or high non-tariff barriers include machine tools, car manufacturing, domestic appliances, electronics, pharmaceuticals and some food and drink products. Without an intimate knowledge of production technologies it is not possible to say whether these industries are fully exploiting scale economies, but it is reasonable to suppose that in some cases, at least, there is scope for further gain. A specific, if somewhat speculative example of a high-risk sector is the kitchen appliances industry, represented in Wales by Hoover and

7 See also Wales TUC (1989). This document also identifies the existing degree of import penetration as an indicator of risk. However, in industries where products are highly differentiated, intra-industry trade tends to be high, and the degree of import penetration should not be taken, on its own, as implying low efficiency of domestic production.

Hotpoint. These firms have already been struggling in recent years against increased foreign competition despite the presence of non-tariff barriers, the removal of which may well prove to be the last straw.

It is even less obvious where comparative advantage gains could be made. They are unlikely to be in what are generally thought of as dynamic sectors since Wales has little presence in such sectors at the moment, when the markets are still protected to some degree. Thus, we are again left to contemplate the possibility of expanding routine assembly-type operations — providing, of course, that wage costs can be kept at a competitive level. The alternative is high unemployment.

Conclusion

The basic theme of this chapter is simple. An integrated economy made up of disparate regions cannot pursue unified policies that are optimal for all the regions. Indeed, by surrendering sovereignty some regions may become worse off. This principle has been recognized by most governments in the UK since the Second World War and has provided a rationale for regional policy. It appears, however, to be denied by the present government. With the increasing integration of the UK into the EC, an increasing part of the responsibility for regional support shifts to the Community. But, at a time when UK regional policy is being downgraded, there are few signs of a real commitment to the regions from Brussels. Without a fundamental reversal in Community economic priorities, the 1990s could prove hard times for the periphery.

Bibliography

Begg, I. 1989. 'European Integration and Regional Policy', *Oxford Review of Economic Policy*, 5

Cecchini, P. E. (ed.) 1988. *The European Challenge: 1992 — the Benefits of a Single Market*. Gower

George, K. D. and L. Mainwaring 1988. 'Agriculture' in K. D. George and L. Mainwaring (eds.), *The Welsh Economy*. University of Wales Press

House of Commons 1988. Welsh Affairs Committee Report on 'Inward Investment into Wales and its Interaction with Regional and EEC Policies'. HMSO.

House of Lords 1988. Fourteenth Report of the Select Committee on the European Communities (Reform of Structural Funds). HL Paper 82

McKinnon, R. I. 1963. 'Optimal Currency Areas', *American Economic Review*, 53

Mundell, R. A. 1962. 'A Theory of Optimal Currency Areas', *American Economic Review*, 52

Myrdal, G. 1957. *Economic Theory and Underdeveloped Regions*. Duckworth

Wales TUC 1989. *1992: the Economic Impact on Wales — a first assessment*. Wales TUC.

Swan, D. 1988. *The Economics of the Common Market*, 6th edn. Penguin

Part 2
Politics and Culture at the Periphery

Chapter 5

Politics and Society in Modern Scotland

DAVID McCRONE

Scotland in 1990 is a more politically disaffected place than it was in 1980. Despite the fact that a majority of voters had voted for devolution in the referendum of 1979, the size of that majority seemed to indicate that there was insufficient support for Home Rule north of the border. The subsequent decade, however, has strengthened that cause, and it is probable that the commitment of Scots to the Union is weaker now than at any time this century. At the same time, however, the fortunes of the Scottish National Party (SNP) have not waxed accordingly. Whereas in 1979 17.3 per cent of the electorate voted SNP, in 1987 only 14 per cent did so, a far cry from the 30 per cent who voted for the party in October 1974. This chapter will examine two related issues: the growth of 'small n' nationalism in the 1980s, and the relative failure of 'large N' Nationalism.

In 1987, 24 per cent of Scots voted Conservative, the lowest percentage since 1868, when the franchise was extended to male householders and tenants. What is remarkable about that figure is that it compares very unfavourably with past performances (the Tories were the only party in postwar Scotland to achieve 50 per cent of the popular vote – in 1955), and with its electoral success in England where it took 46.2 per cent in 1987. In the last thirty-five years, there has been a systematic swing away from the Conservatives in Scotland towards the opposition parties, notably Labour, but also the SNP. The long-term consistency of the Tory decline has been the central factor in Scottish politics (Kendrick and McCrone 1989). The major beneficiaries of this swing have been the Labour Party (in 1964 and 1966, and since 1979) and the SNP (in 1970 and 1974). Recent opinion polls do not herald a Tory revival, for support runs at between 15 and 20 per cent.

The divergence between Scotland and England in terms of electoral behaviour is underpinned by growing disenchantment with the governance of Scotland. Eight out of every ten Scots are dissatisfied with how Scotland is governed; a recent MORI Opinion Poll (*The Scotsman*, December 1988) reported that around one-third want outright independence, and over 40 per cent some devolved system of power while remaining within the UK. Even a minority of Conservatives (48 per cent) are unhappy with the status quo. Political disenchantment is underscored by a consistent and substantial assertion of national identity. Polls carried out in the 1980s reveal that seven out of ten Scots either reject or downgrade their identity as 'British' (Moreno 1988, p. 171).

Table 5.1   'National identities' of Scots (percentages)

Scottish not British	39
More Scottish than British	30
Equally Scottish and British	19
More British than Scottish	4
British not Scottish	6

Source: Moreno 1988.

A majority of Scots (54 per cent) claim a dual identity; of the rest, by far the largest number opt for a single Scottish identity.

What these data show is a deep and growing disenchantment with Scotland's place in the UK. It does not simply reflect government unpopularity nor simple dislike of Mrs Thatcher, but a developing sense of cultural and political distinctiveness over the last three or four decades.

Scotland in Britain

Since its Union with England and Wales in 1707, Scotland has sat uneasily within the United Kingdom. The Union, usually portrayed in the South as expanding England to the north, allowed Scotland to retain key institutions like its legal system, its education system and its state religion of Presbyterianism. These institutions provided a base of cultural identity as well as for social interests, but plainly are insufficient to explain why Scottish identity has grown in the twentieth century rather than diminished. If anything, this institutional distinctiveness has been eroded as Westminster has extended its remit to all parts of the kingdom. In the last few years, the clamour against the Anglicization of Scottish institutions has grown significantly, despite the fact that this process has been proceeding for at least 250 years. What is striking about campaigns against the 'Englishing' of Scottish education, for example, is not that they highlight new concerns, but that they mobilize under this essentially 'nationalist' banner. Tom Nairn (1988) has pointed out that complaints about the 'Englishing' of Scottish universities are not new; what is different is that they reflect growing nationalist sentiment throughout the 1980s. The current fashion for Scottish culture, notably in theatre, arts, music and literature — both Scots and Gaelic (two current bestsellers are the *New Testament in Scots* and the *Concise Scots Dictionary*) — testify to a burgeoning nationalist sentiment north of the border. In many respects, then, Scotland has retained a 'civil society' long after its incorporation into the British state, a civil society which has proved resistant to abolition (such as Victorian attempts to recast Scotland as 'North Britain'), and which provides the basis for cultural and political distinctiveness.

What is all the more remarkable, therefore, is that the nationalist party, the SNP, has failed to cash in on these new enthusiasms. The relationship between 'cultural' and 'political' nationalism in Scotland is complex. Since its formation in 1934 (out of two smaller political formations), the SNP has struggled to make political capital out of cultural concerns. The sense of being 'Scottish' is not readily translatable into political nationalism, and the SNP's breakthrough in the late 1960s owed far more to economic concerns over North Sea oil than to defending Scotland's cultural heritage. In any case, nationalism in Scotland is — unusually — not linked to linguistic concerns or religious distinctiveness. There is no cultural defence to be mounted against alien impositions of language, religion or, indeed, as in the case of the Baltic states, or even Wales, people. Scottish Nationalism, therefore, has modelled itself not on cultural movements like those, perhaps, in Wales and Ireland, but imagines an independent Scotland on Scandinavian lines. This 'political' nationalism is reinforced by the belief that much of Scottish culture is deformed or tainted, that Tartanry and Kailyardism have so infiltrated Scottish culture that underscoring a cultural basis for political nationalism is dangerous.[1] As a result, cultural concerns provide some of the raw materials for Nationalism in Scotland, but rarely are its *raison d'être*. As a consequence, the tariff for becoming a Nationalist in Scotland is that much lower; one does not require to

1   For a critique of this view see McCrone 1989a.

speak the language, for example, nor to practise one religion, nor to undertake a searching examination in one's cultural capital.

The electoral fortunes of the SNP, are, as a result, quite unpredictable. Indeed, the 1970s were a much more profitable decade for the party than the 1980s (see table 5.2). In general terms, then, the electoral performance of the SNP is only a modest indicator of 'nationalism' in Scotland. This paper argues that to conflate the two is misleading, for other parties, notably Labour, have been able to translate nationalist sentiment into electoral strength. The capacity of Labour to do so has reflected trends within the Conservative Party in general, and Thatcherism in particular.

Table 5.2 SNP votes (percentages) and seats in general elections

	Votes	Seats
1970	11.4	2
February 1974	21.9	7
October 1974	30.4	11
1979	17.3	2
1983	11.7	2
1987	14.0	3

The 'Englishing' of conservatism

The Conservative Party has the oldest pedigree north of the border, and was known as the Unionist Party from 1912 until 1965, before it was incorporated into its southern counterpart (Fry 1987). Throughout much of the nineteenth century it took second place to the Liberals, but after 1886 and the débâcle over Irish Home Rule, it offered a home to disaffected Liberal Unionists. By the mid 1920s, the Conservatives had overtaken the Liberals, and consolidated their dominance throughout the interwar period, to reach its peak performance in the mid 1950s.

This 'Unionist' Party was thoroughly Scottish. Its leaders were drawn from the ranks of Scottish capital, especially in the west of Scotland, reinforced by an officer core of small businessmen and petty capitalists (Checkland and Checkland 1984). While we have argued that religion has played little part in cultural politics in Scotland, there is evidence that it helped to mobilize the Protestant working class, which found Unionism, with its Protestant patriotism and militarism, a congenial political ideology. In this respect, religion has mattered in Scottish politics. As late as the 1960s, surveys showed a greater propensity of Protestant workers to vote Conservative than their Catholic counterparts. Kirk-going members of the working class were six times more likely to vote Tory than Catholics were (Bochel and Denver 1970). We have suggested elsewhere that the link between Conservatism and Protestantism in Scotland is an expression of a much wider 'ideological bloc' which lay at the heart of the Conservatives' mid-century appeal in Scotland (Kendrick and McCrone 1989). Protestantism, Orangism and Unionism were connected by a strong sense of British national and imperial identity, symbolized by the Union Jack. We have written:

> This was an age in which Conservative rhetoric in terms of British national and imperial identity and interests chimed quite naturally with a powerful strand of Scotland's national identity, which, in the context of the militarism which ran deep through Scottish society, accepted happily and proudly its imperial nature. They fitted harmoniously together, the connection reinforced and cemented by the religious factor. (p. 593)

It is the disintegration of the associated ideological complex and its links with Conservatism which helps to explain the loss of Tory strength in Scotland. The coalition between local capital and Scottish workers remained in place until the 1950s. Thereafter the Scottish capitalist class went into steep decline, losing out to UK and international competition. Politics became progressively secularized, the religious divide less rigid, and the links between Unionist leaders and Protestant workers less meaningful. If Conservatism had benefited from the sense of Scottishness which was nested within the wider British imperial identity, so its diminishing social base eroded its capacity to mobilize its ideological legacy. The election of 1955 was the high point of Unionist support in Scotland; by the late 1980s, its political performance had been halved.

The *coup de grâce* to Conservatism in Scotland, however, has been dealt by Mrs Thatcher. It is difficult to envisage a political ideology more at odds with Scottish sensibilities and identity than that which has emanated from the South during the 1980s.[2] Historically, the Conservative Party has been most adept at mobilizing national sentiment within the British state. In Andrew Gamble's words:

2   This is discussed at length in McCrone (1989b).

The Conservatives have always viewed the British state as their state. There may be a Whig history of England, but there is also a Tory history, the history of a nation-state, its expansion within the British Isles and throughout the world. The success of the British state in avoiding both internal overthrow and external defeat for so many centuries has ensured that most of the national myths are Tory myths, and most of the rituals and institutions are Tory rituals and institutions. (Gamble 1988, p. 170)

Given the reliance of first the Liberals, and latterly the Labour Party, on disproportionate support from the 'periphery' where alternative conceptions of 'the nation' resided, other parties had a distinct disadvantage in associating themselves in an unequivocal way with 'England'.

Within Thatcherism there is an uneasy alliance between neo-liberal and neo-conservative ideas, the former lauding the market and consumer freedom, the latter demanding more authority and social control (Elliott and McCrone 1987). If the notion of the 'citizen' derives from liberal ideas of the state, then conservative thinking about 'the subject' draws upon an allegiance to 'the nation'. Whatever the balance within Thatcherism between liberal and conservative ideas, it is not possible to comprehend its political project without appreciating the importance of conservative motifs.

In the postwar years, Britain shared an assumption with other advanced capitalist economies that politics was about managing the national economy, an assumption which carried within it an implicit economic nationalism. The state would be the key agent of modernization and development, and whichever party managed this function best would form the government. The desperate state of the Scottish economy in the postwar years, the collapse of indigenous industry and the need to diversify the economic base brought the state into play as the agent of modernization quite early on. All parties, including the Conservatives, shared the general common sense of diversifying Scotland and encouraging industry into its most deprived sectors. Collectivism of this sort was approved of by the right and left alike.

The emergence of Mrs Thatcher and her attack on 'state dependency' came as a very rude awakening north of the border. So vital had the role of the state been in economic regeneration that her assault on the state was perceived as an attack on Scotland itself. Of course, in the 1950s and 1960s when the role of the state was not a politically contentious issue, there was little likelihood of any party being perceived as 'anti-Scottish'. Thatcherism shattered the all-party consensus by politicizing all aspects of state activity, in which Scotland had much more to lose than England. The political agenda in Scotland, which had been formed in the postwar period, suffered a major disjuncture, and it was Labour rather than the Nationalists which was in a better position to present itself as the defender of Scotland, if only because of its local government strength.

Mrs Thatcher's skilful turning of the political tables in the south was reflected in growing unpopularity in the north. She was able to highlight traditional English motifs and themes. As Gamble (1988) has put it, 'Thatcherism has reinvigorated it [the old Tory state authority], and restored the confidence of the party in its basic appeal to the English. This is not Unionism. The Scots, Welsh and Irish are increasingly detached; but then so too are the former colonies of greater Britain. There can be no return to the dreams of Empire' (p. 172).

Adventures such as the Falklands War in the early 1980s simply reinforce this triumphalist little Englandism, and battles with Brussels and speeches at Bruges, based as they are on 'national' appeals, have less ideological power outside this territorial base. Scots, for example, have inherited a nation of their own, which has survived the Union, and Mrs Thatcher's vision of re-creating bourgeois England is out of kilter not only with material interests in the north, but with our own sense of national identity. Thatcherism is a religion of little England; her 'one nation' is not ours.

Why was such a revival of nationalism necessary? The Thatcherite revolution is based upon opening up the economy to the cold winds of change, by encouraging overseas investment by British capital, and incoming plants to the UK. Such a strategy is replete with social danger in so far as it disrupts economic practices and drives many companies (and communities) to the wall. It requires dislocation and relocation. It celebrates what Raymond Williams (1974) called 'mobile privatization', whereby people were detached from stable communities and localities which had acquired a patina of age and tradition. The reassertion of nationalism of the centre became necessary because the problem of social stability and order became more obvious. The state had to reassert its right to govern in case the system became destabilized and dangerous. The radical right in Britain produced a potent mix of anti-state rhetoric ('freeing' the market) and pro-state rhetoric (law and order, and national stability).

Faced with this reassertion of nationalism from the centre, and confronted with major economic and social dislocations, the periphery has hit back using similar but competing nationalist symbols. In Raymond Williams's (1983) words:

> It is clear that if people are to defend and promote their real interests on the basis of lived and worked and placeable social identities, a large

part of the now alienated and centralised powers and resources must be actively regained, by new actual societies which in their own terms, and nobody else's, define themselves. (p. 197)

This is the framework within which we can understand the flourishing of new forms of nationalism and the recasting of the old to meet new challenges.

The Challenges of Nationalism

Nationalism provides a sense of historical continuity, in the words of Milan Kundera, a 'struggle of memory against forgetting'. It permits a framework against which present discontents can be laid alongside those of the past, and connected together. The events of 1989–90 in eastern Europe highlight how potent and varied a political ideology nationalism is. And yet, what Gellner called the 'Dark Gods' interpretation of nationalism has surfaced once more. Consider the comment by one interpreter of recent events:

> It [nationalism] remains a powerful concept precisely because it promises all things to all men [*sic*], combining a tribal feeling of kinship with religion, cultural traditions and an attachment to land, and by holding the promise of economic prosperity as well as a rosy if undefined future. (Eyal 1990)

Such a view of nationalism is not unusual. It implies that it happens in cultural and economic backwaters which the world has passed by, where the vestiges of old ways remain. The use of the terms 'tribal', 'kinship', 'religion', 'traditions' and 'land' implies that nationalism belongs to pre-modern formations. Should the forces of modernism get to work, all that will vanish. Some writers have built into their understanding of nationalism 'progressive' and 'reactionary' forms. Plamenatz (1973), for example, distinguished between 'western' nationalism, which was culturally equipped to foster success and excellence, and 'eastern' nationalism, whose culture was not adapted to new conditions. Such an ethnocentric, even racist, account fails to notice that nationalisms of the periphery are often simply mirrors of nationalisms of the centre. At the centre, even the language of nationalism may be implicit. Raymond Williams (1983) again: 'It is as if a really secure nationalism, already in possession of its own nation-state, can fail to see itself as "nationalist" at all' (p. 183).

Given that most nation-states in the postwar world have operated an (at least) implicit economic nationalism, and that since 1979 the British government has operated with a fairly explicit variety of nationalism, there is little justification for arguing that 'peripheral' nationalism is simply the cultural discontent of a few people living in the backwoods.

The second conventional assumption about nationalism which has to be jettisoned is that it is about cultural or ethnic concerns, notably language and religion, which have fallen into disuse in the modern world. In this respect, nationalists are presented (and often present themselves) as backward-looking figures struggling to retain dead or dying cultures in a world wedded to universalistic values of achievement and progress. This view presents the 'nation' as a historic artefact or moment which struggles for survival. But identities are rarely like that. As Tom Nairn (n.d.) has pointed out, 'New identities have to be made. Nationalists like to imagine them as pre-existing — Sleeping Beauty awaiting her Prince's speech — but they are not in fact a ready-made inheritance' (p. 3). The nation is an aspiration, something to be projected on to the future, rather than the simple reconstruction of the historical article.

Finally, nationalism cannot be located simply on the social spectrum, any more than it can be identified simply on the periphery rather than at the centre. Seeking to safeguard the past may be a means for engendering new forms of solidarity and identification. Alberto Melucci (1989) has argued that social movements expose problems related to the structure of complex societies while they are also rooted in history. To grasp their meaning, therefore, we have to avoid conflating these two components. If we treat them as historical by-products, we risk ignoring the issues of structural transformation. If we handle them as merely highlighting structural contradictions, then we risk ignoring their origins in 'national questions'. He comments:

> The ethno-national question must be seen, therefore, as containing a plurality of meanings that cannot be reduced to a single core. It contains ethnic identity, which is a weapon of revenge against centuries of discrimination and new forms of exploitation; it serves as an instrument for applying pressure in the political market; and it is a response to needs for personal and collective identity in highly complex societies. (Melucci 1989, p. 90)

Nationalist movements, therefore, will encapsulate cultural defence and the pursuit of political resources from the centre, and will also serve as the vehicles for social identity in societies undergoing rapid rates of social change. We would find it impossible to separate out these cultural, political and social aspirations within nationalism in any neat and meaningful way. Above all, the relationship between political behaviour and cultural identity is complex.

Nationalism in Scotland

Given the considerable political and economic destabilization of Scotland in the last decade, why has the SNP not taken advantage of such conditions? The rejection of the postwar political agenda by a government led by a leader who speaks the political language of English nationalism would seem to provide a major opportunity for the Scottish National Party in a country in which all other parties are 'unionist'.

The answer lies in the weak association of 'nationalism' with 'Nationalism' north of the border; with the failure of the party to capture the support of the substantial number of Scots who claim to want independence; and finally with the alternative conceptions of self-determination which are on offer. In so far as the SNP envisages the creation of an orthodox nation-state, its project fails to find favour with sufficient Scottish voters.

The complex association between voting behaviour and preferred constitutional options highlights the difficulty for the Nationalists.

Table 5.3 Preferred constitutional option of party supporters (percentages)

Constitutional option	Cons.	Lab.	SNP	SLD/SDP	All
Independence	13	36	60	21	35
Scottish assembly	38	46	36	55	42
Status quo	48	14	3	23	20

Source: MORI Opinion Poll, December 1988.

Table 5.4 Party composition of preferred constitutional options (percentages)

Constitutional option	Cons.	Lab.	SNP	SLD/SDP	All
Independence	8	46	41	6	100
Scottish assembly	19	48	20	12	100
Status quo	54	33	4	10	100

Source: MORI opinion poll, December 1988

These data show that substantial numbers of party supporters in all parties dissent from the party line. Hence, only a minority of Tories

(48 per cent) opt for the status quo; a large number of Labour voters (36 per cent) want independence; and 40 per cent of SNP voters do not want independence. If, on the other hand, we examine the party composition of those opting for each option, we have the figures given in table 5.4.

These data, reflecting as they do the strength of Labour in Scotland, reveal the substantial support for the independence option in Scotland. The often bitter battle between the SNP and Labour reflects the fact that the largest number of supporters for independence is to be found among Labour voters. The problem for the Nationalists is that while a substantial number (40 per cent) of their supporters do not want independence, only 41 per cent of those who want independence are found in the SNP. In other words, there is a marked lack of correspondence between party positions on the Constitution and the views of party supporters. Many nationalists (even Nationalists) do not vote SNP.

Since the election of Mrs Thatcher in 1979, the Labour Party in Scotland has increasingly played, by choice or not, the nationalist card. When, as at the last election, fifty Labour MPs were elected and only ten Conservatives, it was an obvious political charge to claim that Mrs Thatcher had no mandate in Scotland: that while there was a constitutional right, there was no moral one. Since 1979, the increasing concentration of Tory MPs in the south of England, and Labour's reliance on Scottish and Welsh MPs reinforces the 'ethnic' differences between the parties. Labour's problem is amplified by the political difficulty it has in playing the tartan card, because it is, at root, a unionist party, and the Scottish party does not have constitutional independence.

In the late 1980s the battle between Labour and the SNP has grown more bitter, culminating in Nationalist success at Glasgow Govan in November 1988 (where Sillars took the seat with 49 per cent of the vote), and Labour victory at Glasgow Central in June 1989 (with 55 per cent of the vote). Subsequent to that, Labour has found itself playing the nationalist card in the Scottish Constitutional Convention, set up under the auspices of the Campaign for a Scottish Assembly in July 1988. There can be little doubt about the nationalist thrust of this initiative. Its testament, the impressive *Claim of Right for Scotland* (Campaign for a Scottish Assembly 1988), makes it plain that as a nation, Scotland has a right to develop the kind of government it wants. When it met in March 1989, all participants signed a Declaration of Sovereignty which read: 'We, gathered as the Scottish Constitutional Convention, do hereby acknowledge the sovereign right of the Scottish people to determine the form of government best suited to their needs, and do hereby declare and

pledge that in all our actions and deliberations, their interests shall
be paramount.'

The Convention sought to invite both the Nationalists and the
Conservatives to participate. While there was little likelihood
of the Tories joining in under their leader at the time, the SNP
rejected involvement, fearing that they would suffer the same fate
as in the early 1980s, following their association with the
'Yes' campaign in the 1979 devolution referendum. Whereas in the
1970s the SNP was divided between the 'fundamentalists' ('Independence, Nothing Less') and the 'gradualists', in the 1980s the
former (particularly associated now with the powerful left-wing
figure of Sillars) had outflanked the latter, who were tarred with the
1979 failure. Such self-exclusion from the Convention has encouraged the Labour Party to be more enthusiastic and 'nationalist'
than hitherto.

The failure of the SNP to participate in this wider 'home rule'
movement has called down upon its head the wrath of many
nationalists such as Tom Nairn, who has directed this withering
comment in their direction: 'All nationalisms have a purist wing: but I
can think of no other where the wing has flown the bird so constantly,
or with so little *objective* justification' (n.d., p. 5). Nairn argues that
the Scottish middle classes are involved in a 'very sideways and
hesitant motion towards political nationalism rather than the SNP',
much to the latter's annoyance. It seems that, by default, it has been
left to other parties, notably Labour and the Liberal Democrats, to
deliver home rule to Scotland.

Conclusion

Perceptibly, over the past decade, the agenda of Scottish politics has
altered. Neal Ascherson (1989) has commented that by 1989 Scotland
had crossed an important threshold: its politics had become
'Scottish':

> Today, politics north of the border operates inside a web of references
> — past and present manifestos, conference resolutions, factions and
> splits, psephological allusions in a country now used to a four-party
> system, formal and informal institutions — which are simply not
> shared with the rest of the UK . . . the language being used in this
> theatre is no longer 'British'.

In this context, nationalism is less concerned with resurrecting the
ghosts of the past, than with finding new solutions to new conditions.

Central to this endeavour is to find the successor to the nation-state, which rapidly falls into disuse (Held 1988). Economically, there is a diminishing coincidence between political and economic systems; the nation-state is in danger of losing its place in a world of multi-nationals and flexible specialization. Militarily, the *raison d'état* — to monopolize violence and defend the citizenry — has been undermined by the possibility of nuclear war which stops at no frontiers. Culturally it is no longer feasible in multi-cultural societies to indulge in what Max Weber called 'Kulturpolitik', using the power of the state to defend mono-culture (Beetham 1974). The search is on for political structures which recognize the new realities of the twenty-first century, and which acknowledge limited, multi-level sovereignty rather than the absolute form which welded the state to 'the nation'.

Such recognition is manifestly made in the new SNP slogan of 'Independence in Europe', which acknowledges that an *'Europe des patries'* would inevitably limit national sovereignty in return for broader political recognition. To their critics like Nairn and Ascherson, it seems, however, that the Nationalists currently believe in the slogan rather than its substance, for they refuse to recognize that the 'national movement' is broader than the party itself.

Faced with strong central control of the British state, it might seem fanciful to argue that of all the western European states, Britain is the most susceptible to break-up. Nevertheless the paradigm of economic decline and political decay has been on the agenda since the 1950s, and the reassertion of centralism might be seen as the final defence in a breached wall, rather than proof of the soundness of the fortifications. We have only to look to eastern Europe to see how centralist and seemingly impregnable political structures collapsed so easily, eaten away from within. There are, perhaps, distinct parallels in both east and west of this prophetic statement: 'Whenever civil society becomes more confident . . . the state rapidly loses its grip; its structural weaknesses and powerlessness become evident. Civil society tends to swell from below. It feeds upon whatever gains it can wrench from the state, which normally lapses into confusion and paralysis' (Keane 1988, pp. 4–5). Czechoslovakia today; Scotland tomorrow?

Bibliography

Ascherson, Neal 1989. *The Observer (Scotland)*, 12 March
Beetham, D. 1974. *Max Weber and the Theory of Modern Politics*. Allen & Unwin

LIBRARY

Bochel J. and D. Denver 1970. 'Religion and Voting: a Critical Review and a New Analysis', *Political Studies*, 18

Campaign for a Scottish Assembly 1988. *A Claim of Right for Scotland* (report of the Constitutional Steering Committee presented to the Campaign for a Scottish Assembly)

Checkland, S. and O. Checkland 1984. *Industry and Ethos: Scotland, 1832–1914*. Edward Arnold

Elliott, B. and D. McCrone 1987. 'Class, Culture and Morality: a Sociological Analysis of the new Conservatism', *Sociological Review*, 35

Eyal, J. 1990. 'On History's Hopeful Edge', *The Guardian* (18 January)

Fry, M. 1987. *Patronage and Principle: a Political History of Modern Scotland*. Aberdeen University Press

Gamble, A. 1988. *The Free Economy and the Strong State*. Macmillan

Held, D. 1988. 'Farewell to the Nation-State', *Marxism Today* (November/December)

Keane, J. 1988. *Civil Society and the State*. Verso Books

Kendrick, S. and D. McCrone 1989. 'Politics in a Cold Climate: the Conservative Decline in Scotland', *Political Studies*, 37

McCrone, D. 1989a. 'Representing Scotland: Culture and Nationalism' in D. McCrone *et al.* (eds.), *The Making of Scotland*. Edinburgh University Press

McCrone, D. 1989b. 'Thatcherism in a Cold Climate', *Radical Scotland* (June/July)

Melucci, A. 1989. *Nomads of the Present*. Hutchinson Radius

Moreno, L. 1988. 'Scotland and Catalonia: the Path to Home Rule', *Scottish Government Yearbook 1988*. Unit for the Study of Government in Scotland, Edinburgh

MORI Opinion Poll, *The Scotsman* (December 1988)

Nairn, T. 1988. 'The Tartan and the Blue', *Marxism Today* (June)

Nairn, T. n.d. 'Identities' (mimeo)

Plamenatz, J. 1973. 'Two Types of Nationalism' in E. Kamenka (ed.), *Nationalism: the Nature and Evolution of an Idea*. Edward Arnold

Williams, R. 1974. *Television: Technology and Cultural Form*. Fontana

Williams, R. 1983. *Towards 2000*. Penguin

Chapter 6

Lived Experience, Social Consumption and Political Change: Welsh Politics into the 1990s

DAVID ADAMSON

Introduction

> Our world is out of joint: societies are disintegrating, our lifelong
> hopes and values are crumbling. The future ceases to be a continuation
> of past trends. The meaning of present development is confused; the
> meaning of history suspended. (Gorz 1985, p.1)

Gorz's statement is perhaps one of the most lyrical representations of
a growing body of opinion in sociological and political analysis which
expresses the belief that society and the theories which seek to analyse
it are entering a period of considerable change. Gorz and others see
the motor of change as a reconstruction of the capitalist mode of
production in which new patterns of capital accumulation are
redrawing relations of production and the boundaries between the
classes. For Gorz, this process bids 'Farewell to the Working Class'
(1983), as the traditional, highly organized, largely male working
class of heavy industrial production is being replaced by a section-
alized, disorganized, marginalized and increasingly female workforce
associated with the much enlarged tertiary sector.

The processes of economic change recognized by Gorz and other
contributors to this debate have been clearly evident in Wales since
the 1960s, and the sociological analysis of Welsh society has been
dominated throughout the 1980s by a concern, firstly to map the
industrial restructuring that has been taking place (for example,
Edwards 1985) and secondly to assess and classify the corresponding
changes in social and political relations (Cooke 1982; Rees and Rees
1983; Adamson 1988b). It seems self-evident that, as changes in the
economic structure deconstruct and reconstitute traditional divisions
of labour, forms of political organization and representation will be

influenced. This is not to suggest that a crude form of economic determinism should inform political theory, but that economic relations should be one of the principal points of departure in any sociological analysis. However, in recent years, sociological theory has increasingly distanced itself from such an assumption, and any reference to an economic influence on political and ideological formations incurs the risk of being labelled 'essentialist' (Laclau and Mouffe 1985). Of course, this raises the question of whether the previous work in the sociology of Wales has been misinformed and erroneous in its attachment of primacy to the process of economic restructuring. This would certainly be held to be the case by a number of contributors to the 'retreat from class' (Meiskins Wood 1986).

Despite this climate of thought, in this chapter I shall adhere to a perspective which analyses the social and political effects of economic restructuring, assuming that this method of analysis has done much to explain the workings not only of Welsh society but of society in general. I shall assume that a suture exists between the economic, ideological and political levels of the social formation, and that major insights into the social relations of individual actors and classes can be gained by an examination of the complex processes through which economic change is mediated. However, an important part of this chapter will be an attempt to complete the often partial picture which is gained by emphasizing the link between economic change and social change. This will be achieved by suggesting that as well as recognizing the importance of relations of production, it is also necsessary to inform political analysis by an examination of patterns of consumption in society. In the light of the social changes of the 1980s, it is essential to recognize the limits of a conventional class analysis and to attempt to redefine the concept of class in a way which reflects the complexity of class relations in advanced capitalism. I shall suggest that such an exercise leads us to recognize a 'new working class' rather than to bid the working class prematurely farewell.

Among the central failings of class theory have been the inadequacy of analysis of the growing importance of 'non-productive workers' and the discussion of the class location of managers. The failings of orthodox Marxism in these areas are self-evident, but it is also true that Weberian models of social stratification have failed to be predictive of the political and social effects of a large 'middle class' (Abercrombie and Urry 1983). The rise of the 'middle class' is a major characteristic of advanced capitalism, and a consensus exists which grounds explanation of that rise in the tertiarization of capitalism as manufacturing appears almost universally to give way to a service economy.[1] For Winckler (1985) the effects of tertiarization of the Welsh economy have been more pronounced because of the previous predominance of manufacturing industry and the compression of tertiarization in the short time scale since the 1970s. Consequently, to understand Welsh society it is perhaps even more essential to derive a meaningful analysis of the effects of the growth of the service sector.

In a recent article (Adamson 1988b), I suggested that when consideration is given to the lived experience of the relations of production, it is possible to recognize that economic relations are not the sole determinant of class position but that ideological and political relations have considerable effect in the drawing of class boundaries. The article was based on a discussion of the work of Poulantzas (1975) and Cottrell and Roslender (1986) and their respective formulations of a distinction between mental and manual labour, and between managed and managers. I suggested that the authors' claims to identify new classes on the basis of these distinctions could not be supported, but rather that the ideological effects of the mental–manual division of labour produced a 'new working class' as a fraction of the traditional working class. I suggested that, whilst this class fraction shared the objective, economic class position and class interests of the traditional working class, the lived experience of service workers who fell on the mental side of the mental–manual division of labour gave them a greater disposition to respond to managerial ideologies and bourgeois class identities. Furthermore, this change in consciousness is not linked simply to wage levels as in the 'affluent worker thesis', but is determined by a complex process in which the subjectivity of the individual is partially constituted by the place occupied in the social hierarchy of the workplace. The consequence of this ideological positioning is the creation of a complex and contradictory fractional class ideology in which members of the 'new working class' are pulled in different directions by the ideologies of the traditional working-class communities of which they are products and by the ideology of managerialism which shapes their lived experience of the relations of production. The political consequences of the growth of the 'new working class' in Wales has been an increasing fluidity of political praxis; the traditional working-class support for the Labour Party has declined as the 'new working class' has sought forms of political representation which reflect its hybrid ideological formation.

1 In considering whether the growth of the service sector is a universal feature of advanced capitalism Offe (1985) writes: 'In agreement with the entire literature and data on this subject, it is assumed that this question has already been answered in the affirmative' (p. 103).

In this chapter, I wish to support this previous analysis, but also to suggest that it represents an incomplete picture. Whilst the lived experience of work relations is of major significance in the understanding of the dynamics of any social formation, it is also necessary to recognize that many of the meaningful practices of social actors take place outside the working environment and in social relationships that cannot simply be categorized according to class.[2] Part of the reconstruction of social theory in recent years has been the recognition of non-class bases for political and social action. Particular emphasis has been placed on gender and racial differentiation, but the increased sectionalization of the working class has also been recognized (Marshall *et al.* 1988). In the discussion of this sectionalizing of the working class, considerable attention has been paid to changing patterns of consumption and their effects on traditional class political cultures. For Hobsbawm (1981), the traditional solidarity of the working class has been lost to a 'consumer society individualism' which erodes the forms of consciousness associated with the earlier phase of capitalist development in which the primary industries were dominant. Much of this analysis has been linked to the rise of New Right neo-liberalism and the perception that, in Britain, Thatcherism has established a new social consensus which emphasizes market relations instead of productive relations and has created a hegemony which excludes the values of collectivism from popular culture (Hall and Jacques 1983; O'Shea 1984).

The study of culture should represent a fundamental element of any attempt to come to terms with the effects of the postwar reconstruction of capitalist economies. Class consciousness is clearly derived from and reproduced in cultural processes as well as in economic relations. A fully developed concept of the notion of lived experience must recognize the cultural sphere as a primary site of experience and also as a site of struggle over the interpretation of experience. Such a conception of lived experience is most clearly developed in the work of Antonio Gramsci (1971). For Gramsci individuals arrive at a commonsensical understanding of their place in productive relations through the direct sensual experience of everyday life which lives out those relations. In the workplace,

2   The starting point for an analysis of the relationship between class and politics must be rejection of an economistic reading of ideology and politics from 'objective economic' class positions. Class and class consciousness are not determined solely by economic relations but also by political, ideological and cultural relations. In the work of Poulantzas (1975) this is theorized as a complex 'structural' determination of class in the economic, the political and the ideological instances of the social formation.

individuals derive an intuitive understanding of their exploitative relationship to capital. However, that commonsensical awareness is limited in its capacity to theorize and conceptualize that relationship, and the guidance and direction of 'organic intellectuals' are necessary to raise the consciousness of the workers to an understanding of their objective class position.

Gramsci's work stresses the importance of lived experience as a site of struggle. The interpretation of experience is not given, but is the subject for contestation between classes. The very nature of hegemonic struggle is that it is a struggle to define a certain kind of common sense as legitimate and of greater authenticity than other versions of common sense. For Gramsci the ruling class, with the support of its organic intellectuals, attempts to establish its morality and ethics as superior and its ideology as the legitimate, inevitable and necessary basis of social organization. Much of this struggle takes place in the cultural sphere.[3] Culture exists as an arena of struggle in which classes contend for dominance just as they do in the political structures of a social formation. No analysis of hegemony could be undertaken without a full discussion of cultural practices and how they are articulated with the morality and ideology of the class formations which express them. Culture represents a major component of any 'national popular collective will' (Gramsci 1971, p. 131) and plays a significant part in the creation of the social cement which binds classes together in 'historical blocs' (Bocock, 1986).

An analysis which goes a long way to bring together such a view of culture and the economic restructuring discussed earlier can be found in the work of Lash and Urry (1987) and their development of the notion of 'disorganized capitalism'. In describing contemporary capitalism as 'disorganized', they compare it with an early period in which it was highly organized.[4] The economy of Wales at the turn of the century shared many of the fourteen characteristics they identify as typical of an 'organized' capitalism. These include a concentration of capitalism in relatively few sectors of production, particularly

---

3   See McIntyre (1985) for a discussion of the way in which peripheral film cultures provide a site of resistance to Thatcherism as an illustration of the way in which hegemonic struggle takes place in cultural production in society.

4   It is important to stress at this point that their concept of 'disorganized capitalism' differs considerably from what Lash and Urry identify as theories of 'post-industrial' capitalism. They maintain that 'capitalist social relations' continue in existence and in fact suggest that, contrary to Gorz's claims, working-class politics may become more pronounced but more 'sectional'.

'extractive/manufacturing industry'; a regional concentration of specific industries; and a 'growth of collective organizations' representing employee and employer interests. In contrast, 'disorganized' capitalism is characterized, amongst other features, by a decline in the significance of extractive/manufacturing industry, a weakening role for collective bargaining, a 'decline in the absolute and relative size of the core working class' and a 'decline in the salience and class character of politics'. Of particular interest here is their identification of the expansion of white-collar workers and a managerial or 'service class' which, for Lash and Urry, grows out of the bureaucratization of 'organized capital'. They regard the development of an 'educationally based stratification system' as contributing to the fragmentation of society which detracts from the class basis of political action.

Whilst their whole framework has considerable relevance to the analysis of contemporary Wales, for the remainder of this chapter I shall attempt to develop a particular aspect of 'disorganized capitalism'. This feature is what they describe as the appearance and mass distribution of a cultural-ideological configuration of postmodernism. In discussing the role of postmodernism in contemporary culture, Lash and Urry suggest that class identities are in part culturally determined and fixed. Anyone familiar with the social history of Wales will have little difficulty in supporting such a claim given the distinct cultural forms that have grown around the working class created by the Welsh economy. This is perhaps most evident in the mining communities of the South Wales valleys, which demonstrate a distinctive Anglo-Welsh culture grounded in a collectivist ethic. Nor is it difficult to see that cultural practices are not only consequences of class configurations but also reproduce class relations. Consequently, in a disorganized capitalism which features changing class configurations, we shall expect to find emerging cultural formations and to see these innovative cultural practices in turn accelerating the shifts within the class structure. There is therefore a complex process of articulation between class and culture.[5] In discussing this articulation and the appearance of postmodern culture, Lash and Urry draw on the work of Baudrillard (1981) and Bourdieu (1984) to develop a political economy of postmodernism. For the purposes of this chapter, I intend to develop their application of the work of Pierre Bourdieu and the significance he attaches to cultural consumption. I also intend to demonstrate that

5   Lash and Urry are careful to point out that postmodernism cannot be seen as a simple ideological/cultural reflection of 'disorganized capitalism'. Rather they suggest that it links with certain aspects of it 'as cause but mostly as effect of disorganization' (p. 286).

his ideas can be applied to the analysis of consumption in general, with considerable effect for our understanding of contemporary Wales.[6]

Consumption and class relations

Bourdieu's central argument is that the social position of individuals has a direct bearing on their pattern of tastes and their consequent behaviour as consumers. His concern is with the consumption of cultural products and how these reflect the lifestyles of individuals. For Bourdieu taste is not determined by individual preferences, but has its origins in the 'habitus', which is a set of 'predispositions' derived largely through a process of socialization which is internalized in a way which ensures that we 'forget' the social learning of taste. The tastes expressed by individuals reflect a correspondence between a social hierarchy and a cultural hierarchy of art forms. 'To the socially recognized hierarchy of the arts, and within each of them, of genres, schools or periods, corresponds a social hierarchy of the consumers. This predisposes tastes to function as markers of "class" ' (Bourdieu 1984, p. 1).

The expression of tastes serves to mark individuals' class position, their patterns of consumption serve to classify them and additionally, in the act of classifying someone, classifiers are themselves classified. This reflects Bourdieu's assertion that we largely indicate our taste through the negative evaluation of the tastes of others. Thus for him the act of distinction is carried out through the 'visceral intolerance (sick-making) of the taste of others'. The consequence is that 'aversion to different life-styles is perhaps one of the strongest barriers between the classes' (1984, p. 56). Consequently, the lifestyle derived from the class-determined habitus of an individual reflects the class relations in society. This view of the relationship between class and culture goes beyond sociological concepts of class consciousness and social class perspective and suggests a thorough, almost psychologistic, process of internalization of taste and cultural norms, to the extent that the individual's physical representation of the self, for example in the style of walking, is conditioned by the 'habitus'.

One of the most important of Bourdieu's claims is that taste and cultural consumption in society also serve to reproduce class relations:

6 This account of the thinking of Bourdieu is heavily indebted to a paper by Shaun Moores (1989) of the Department of Behavioural and Communication Studies, Polytechnic of Wales.

... the games of artists and aesthetes and their struggles for the monopoly of artistic legitimacy are less innocent than they seem. At stake in every struggle over art there is also the imposition of an art of living, that is the transmutation of an art of living into the legitimate way of life which casts every other way of living into arbitrariness. (1984, p. 57)

Consequently, the class struggle is reflected and reproduced in the competition between forms of culture. For Bourdieu this is a struggle between the 'dominant class' and the 'dominated class'. Cultural consumption provides arenas in which the distinctions between classes are demonstrated, but it also provides a basis for the reproduction of the class structure and corresponding values. We can also assume that in the articulation of taste and class, sites of resistance are carved out as consumption of certain cultural forms provides markers of resistance to the dominant culture and the dominant class.

In the remainder of this chapter, I am going to suggest that many of Bourdieu's insights into the class significance of cultural consumption can be applied to the consumption of the majority of goods and services in society. Moreover an analysis of the patterns of consumption in contemporary Wales can illustrate the rise of the new working class and the process through which its lived experience of the relations of production both gives rise to and is reinforced by different patterns of consumption from those associated with the traditional working class.

Sociological analysis of class relations has traditionally emphasized relations of production and has rarely engaged adequately with the role of consumption in the reproduction of class structures (Warde 1990). However, it is very clear that production and consumption are part of the same process and should not be separated in any analysis which wishes to achieve an overview of class relations and adequately examine the cultural practices which participate in the reproduction of class (Tomlinson 1990). In the capitalist mode of production consumption has a dual role. Firstly, consumption is a fundamental element in the process of capital accumulation. The surplus value of labour expressed in finished commodities is only realized when those goods are exchanged for money, that is, when they are consumed: 'To each capitalist, the total mass of all workers, with the exception of his own workers, appear not as workers, but as consumers, possessors of exchange values (wages), money, which they exchange for his commodity' (Mandel 1972).

Mandel sees each worker as an 'independent centre of circulation' in the process of capital accumulation. However, the additional role of consumption is to tie the worker to the system of capitalism through both coercive and consensual means. The biological need to consume certain fundamental goods and services binds the consumer to the provider of them in a quite fundamental way. Part of the 'dull compulsion' of capitalist relations is the monopoly of the market-place by the bourgeoisie creating a mode of consumption in which individuals are forced to participate by their needs for certain goods and services. Just as workers are forced to labour in capitalist relations to survive, so they are forced to consume to survive.

In earlier periods of capitalism, we can see this relationship particularly clearly through the use of the truck shop system. This directly coercive relationship of consumption created a dependency of worker on employer which was direct and unmediated. In this sense the relations of consumption are a direct reflection of the relationships of production but also help to reproduce them.[7] In contemporary advanced capitalism this same mechanism is mediated through a complex market-place and a huge variety of retail outlets which offer the consumer 'choice'. This pattern of consumption should not disguise the basic principle at work, but must be recognized as a hegemonic method of achieving both the realization of surplus value and the reproduction of class relations. In advanced capitalism the latter objective is achieved less through coercion and to a greater extent through consensus. Current patterns of consumption reflect the consensual ideological basis of the reproduction of class relations in contemporary capitalism. The institution which performs the equivalent role to the truck shop, but through its contribution to consensus, is the 'out-of-town store', which offers a 'lifestyle' rather than a range of products. In the contemporary mode of consumption, the act of shopping itself becomes transformed from a necessity to a leisure activity which involves the whole family. In this way an act of ideological interpellation is hidden behind the shelves of Tesco and Sainsbury. Through adopting postmodern consumption practices, consumers of the lifestyles offered by superstores undergo a process of subjection, they are created as particular subjects by the act of shopping, in that

7   In this context we can see the rise of the co-operative movement as a direct form of class resistance through creating alternative modes of consumption. The sphere of consumption can be recognized clearly in this context as an important site of the class struggle.

their lifestyles are echoes of the images, explicit and coded, in the goods and services they consume.[8]

In areas such as South Wales, where traditional patterns of shopping have been successfully challenged by the leisure shopping of out-of-town superstores, the class consequences have been significant. The act of shopping has become another element of a generally more privatized lifestyle than we might have found in Wales until recently. The virtual demise of the co-operative movement has been an obvious consequence, but the major challenge has been to the corner shops of small communities and to the high streets of the valley towns. Shopping has been transformed from a communal activity to a leisure activity of the nuclear family. Additionally, as well as contributing to the breakdown of the communalism of working-class culture, leisure shopping has an added divisive effect in that the ownership of private transport is a prerequisite. As a consequence key social groups are excluded from the practice, particularly the elderly and the poor. Thus the mobile working class enjoys the savings and greater choice of superstore shopping, whilst those without private transport suffer the high prices of local stores. In this way consumption patterns reflect and reinforce divisions within the working class and enhance the poverty of its lowest levels.

In relation to the existence of a 'new working class' in Wales, it is clear that this class fraction will have a perception of itself which predisposes its members to take up contemporary patterns of consumption as a means of positioning themselves in Welsh society. They will choose consumption practices which reflect the self-perception and ideological values determined by their lived experience of capitalist work relations. I have already suggested that this is a lived experience which opens them to more 'bourgeois' interpellation than experienced by the traditional working class. Their consumption will also reflect this. In turn, the lived experience of consumption will distance them further from the practices of the traditional working class and supplement and enhance their lived experience of work relations which already serve to fracture them from the traditional working class.

8   We might even identify a hierarchy of lifestyles on offer in such stores in much the same way that Bourdieu identifies a hierarchy of art forms. From the relative sophistication of Habitat, we could move down through Sainsbury, Tesco to Kwik Save. Nor is it a coincidence that the high streets of the valleys gave birth to the cheap discount stores such as Poundstretcher and Hypervalue at the height of the unemployment crisis of the early eighties.

To summarize: a lifestyle emerges which reflects the subjectivity of the new working class, initially derived from its lived experience of production relations. This leads to tastes and patterns of consumption that are used as social markers to distance its members from the traditional working class. Changes in diet, dress, place of residence, car ownership, holiday-making and leisure activity will be some examples of an infinity of means through which the 'new working class' will exert its distinction from the traditional working class. Additionally, the more developed such a lifestyle becomes the more its participants link with a social network and forms of behaviour which serve to reproduce it. The consequence is a hegemonizing influence on the wider society as people judge themselves and are judged by others according to the criteria of the lifestyle of this class fraction.

A key determinant of the response to the hegemonizing influence of the new working-class lifestyle is the individual's financial capacity to engage with emerging patterns of consumption. Many of the members of the new working class are in occupations which may create an ideological distinction from the traditional working class, but not always a financial one. Many members of the class fraction are routinized clerical workers or peripheralized female workers, and are not unionized. Wages in the service sector usually reflect such structural weaknesses. Consequently the rise of new patterns of consumption has been dependent on the relaxed credit environment of the 1980s. Personal credit has provided the foundation of the growth of the new working-class lifestyle. Whilst not always in well-rewarded jobs, they are often jobs of permanence and comparatively high status and consequently credit is relatively easy to come by in comparison to members of the traditional working class. The credit boom has affected all sections of society, but I would suggest it is particularly those in the new working class who have been well placed to take advantage of it.

Members of the new working class in contemporary Wales thus are developing a 'habitus' which is a product of a complex dialectic between their lived experience of work relations and their lifestyle patterns of consumption. Just as we can recognize sectors of production where we can identify the creation of the new working class, then so are there aspects of consumption which point to the activities of this class fraction. In what follows, I sketch some impressions of an emerging new working-class lifestyle. I believe anyone resident in Wales in the last ten years will recognize some of these features as considerable departures from past patterns of consumption. However, considerable further research is clearly required to establish a comprehensive empirical basis for this analysis.

Housing and home-based activities.

Housing, in the postwar period, has become one of the primary spheres of consumption which offers the individual an opportunity to create social distinction. The superior social status accorded to owner-occupation in comparison to tenancy has created one of the key social divisions in contemporary Britain and provided the basis of a fundamental 'consumption cleavage' (Dunleavy and Husbands 1985). State sponsorship of private ownership has created a social ideal of home ownership which has obscured the many advantages of state and collective provision.

Housing in Wales represents one area in which there has been considerable change, with a general increase in the levels of owner-occupation. Of particular significance has been the number of local authority tenants purchasing their properties, which has been higher in Wales than in any other part of Britain. Between 1980 and 1987, 10.2 per cent of the housing stock has been sold compared to 9.3 per cent in England, 5.5 per cent in Scotland and 8.9 per cent in Northern Ireland (Department of the Environment 1989). Additionally, the pattern of house prices has reflected a particular buoyancy in the housing market. Of particular interest in South Wales has been the expansion of large British house-building companies, saturating the middle sector of the housing market. The lifestyle image of this housing has been particularly significant in its targeting of the consumer. The use of materials and designs associated primarily with the south-east of England has invited consumers to link themselves with an imagery of affluence and upward mobility which has become a reality through the relaxation of building society mortgaging practices throughout the 1980s. This trend is indicative of a lifestyle imagery which creates in the consumer a personal distance from the traditional terraced accommodation and its connection with working-class culture.

The distinction between owner-occupancy and tenancy is also apparent in council housing in Wales, where those who have purchased their housing immediately attempt to make a visible statement of their social distinction through external decoration and renovation. For many tenants the sharp rent rises of the early 1980s provided a strong economic incentive to purchase, but the element of social distinction has also been a factor. For Tomlinson (1990) the purchase of council housing represents a route from the public to the private sphere and symbolizes the privatized and individualistic lifestyle which has become ascendant in the Thatcher era.

Linked to the housing market has been the increasing trend toward house improvement and DIY, representing another indication of lifestyle trends which link particularly with new modes of consumption and shopping. DIY activites are some of the most significant leisure practices, after 'eating and drinking out' and appear to cross class and gender divisions (Tomlinson 1990). The role of DIY activity is to offer an opportunity to make a statement about individual taste. It allows the privatized home-owner to customize a dwelling in an almost unique expression of individuality. Additionally it is the DIY superstore which has led the shopping revolution in South Wales, ensuring the privatized activity of DIY is mirrored by the consumption process which leads to the purchasing of DIY goods. Furthermore, the out-of-town location of DIY superstores renders the act of shopping for such goods a leisure activity in its own right. DIY is also clearly linked to the ideology of home-ownership and consequently is a practice which reinforces a commitment to private provision of housing and to the individual's responsiblity for the quality of that housing.

The search for lifestyle enhancement is also evident in the trend of increased levels of ownership of key household goods; over the period from 1980 until 1985, the proportions of households owning tumble dryers increased by 8 per cent, deep freezers by 14 per cent and telephones by 8 per cent (Central Statistical Office 1989). These trends are despite quite acute levels of unemployment during this period. This perhaps reflects the pattern of that unemployment, which fell more heavily on certain sectors of the Welsh economy, especially the traditional industries associated with the period of 'organized capitalism'. Tomlinson (1990) cites the rise of ownership of video cassette recorders (VCRs) as a specific example of a move away from a collective provision of leisure to a privatized mode of leisure consumption: 'If the cinema could be seen as a symbolic site of commercialized but collectively experienced leisure, the growth of the VCR has been an index of the increasing grip of the privatized context in which leisure is now consumed' (p. 61). It is important to add that cinema has not been the only casualty of the rise of home video, but other collective arenas of leisure activity such as the pub and club are now in competition with the video shop, which often provides off-licence facilities as well.

In housing provision and in home-based activities changes have occurred which emphasize an individualistic and privatized lifestyle and remove many of the collective elements of working-class culture from contemporary lifestyles. Such activities articulate with the individualistic perspective derived from the workplace experiences of the new working class, and a basis for new cultural and political practices emerges.

Out-of-home activities

An increased sophistication of leisure activities has developed in the last decade, especially the growth of sporting facilities, which reflects an increasing demand for healthier lifestyles. The provision of extensive leisure and sport facilities by local authorities has represented a growth area during a period when other services, particularly housing, have been suffering decline. Activities such as road running and cycling have also gained in popularity, suggesting a concern with health which has not normally been reflected in working-class culture. Participation in such activities would also suggest that more traditional male activities, such as rugby, darts and other pub and club activities are being given up as collective activities, in favour of more individualistic leisure activities. The concern with healthy lifestyles has also been reflected in dietary concerns, and health and wholefood shops have become a high street norm rather than a back street exception. Food outlets also now offer more varied and exotic provisions, and the restaurant trade has become increasingly sophisticated and expensive, relying on marketing images of exclusivity.[9]

Personal transport has also reflected lifestyle change as car ownership has become easier in a decade which has seen the car market flooded with the used stock of the commercial and leasing sectors of the car trade. Outlets for the sale of used cars, particularly at the lower and middle sectors of the market, can be found in most South Wales communities, and relaxation of credit regulations on car purchase has made car ownership a reality for the majority. Additionally there has been a growth in the number of dealers catering for the luxury end of the market, with dealerships for BMW, Porsche, Rolls Royce, Saab and Volvo either opening or expanding in the area. Of all consumer goods the car has the most clear role in the classifying processes identified by Bourdieu. Distinction between social classes is almost instantly recognizable in car ownership, a characteristic easily and expertly exploited by marketing strategies. Car commercials make clear reference to the lifestyle implications of their product, linking with images of sophistication, affluence and personal success. Additionally, the car market is hierarchical, offering clear distinction not only between marques but also in the internal differentiation within marques and even between different versions of the same models. Furthermore, car ownership has considerable consequences for sustaining the privatized activities of leisure shopping and the new leisure practices identified earlier. In this way, transport plays a fundamental role in the restructuring processes under discussion.

9   For Bourdieu (1984), food is the most basic indicator of 'taste'.

Finally, we can see changes in the drinking and entertainment facilities provided by public houses and private clubs in Wales. The political and working men's clubs which have traditionally dominated the region have suffered the effects of the economic depression in the 1980s, and many have faced declining membership and closure. This has partly been caused by their entrenchment in patriarchal practices and their failure to link with the 'family' market in the style of their North of England counterparts. Additionally, the smaller and independent public houses have fared badly, whilst larger premises have improved services, especially in the provision of food, and have developed a theme approach to capture a declining market. As a consequence, key social institutions which originated as a cultural form in the 'organized' period of capitalism are in decline, adding to the cultural restructuring processes evident in Welsh society.

These preliminary observations are intended to stimulate responses and hopefully provide the basis for further research, rather than to make any definitive claims for accuracy and relevance. However, they are indicative of the considerable change which has already taken place and of greater change to come. In the final section of this chapter I propose to examine briefly the political consequences of these economic and cultural patterns of change.

Welsh politics into the 1990s

The most obvious casualty of this pattern of economic and cultural change will be the political practices which have characterized Welsh society since the turn of the century. The major feature of the Welsh political structure in this period has been its domination by the Labour Party and the labour movement more widely. As generally recognized (Hobsbawm 1981; Goldthorpe 1980), decline in the forms of economic activity which gave birth to this political formation threaten its demise.[10] In Wales, the programmes of steel plant and pit closures have done much to destabilize the organizational structure and socializing mechanisms of the labour movement. This process is accelerated by the tertiarization of the economy and the consequent growth of the new working class. The initial consequence of the complex ideological position of the new working class is the

10   For Lash and Urry (1987), however, the numerical decline of the working class, together with the 'decline in the significance of a distinctively proletarian pattern of life' (p. 211) does not necessarily mean that the 'forward march of Labour' (Hobsbawn 1981) has been permanently halted.

distancing it experiences from traditional working-class political ideology. This creates a more open ideological terrain and a more unpredictable pattern of political practice on the part of the new working class.

Inevitably, in this process of change it is the Labour Party which is most likely to lose support, especially given its municipal conservatism in Wales, which has grown from its position as the party of the 'establishment' at the level of local government. In retaining a traditional form of political address and of organization, it has remained largely patriarchal and has done little to encourage participation of those outside the labour movement. It seems unlikely to be able to respond positively to the politics of the 1990s, which appear to be already dominated by consumer issues rather than producer issues.

I have already suggested (Adamson 1988b) that the Conservative Party is unlikely to benefit from the rise of the new working class, in that it represents too long an ideological journey for those whose social origins are so recently connected to traditional working-class communities and who maintain links with strong family and communal socializing influences. In many ways the rise of the centre parties in the early 1980s represented a likely avenue of expression for the interests of this class fraction. However, the organizational disarray of these parties precludes this, at least in the short term.

It must also be questioned whether the programmes offered by parties fixed in the postwar consensus can retain any relevance in the post-Thatcherite era, which has demonstrated most convincingly the failures of Keynesianism. The debate as to the degree of success of the Thatcherite project (O'Shea 1984) in undermining collectivism in British culture is particularly difficult to resolve in the peripheries. However, it does seem likely that few voters would wish to return to the same mechanisms of a mixed economy which demonstrated their failure in the 1970s. This does not however suggest a rejection of welfarism, but of the mode of provision of welfare services within a bureaucratic, impersonal state sector.

If, as I have suggested above, it is consumer issues which now structure political demands, then the emergence of the ecological perspective in politics will be of considerable significance in the 1990s. It is quite clear that 'green' issues are, first and foremost, consumption issues. Their point of entry into popular culture has been through issues such as food quality, and the popularity of the Greens in the European Community election of 1989 came hot on the heels of several major food scares. Additionally, green political issues link fundamentally with lifestyle and are addressable by the individual in terms of personal conduct. Political issues can be resolved at the individual level by altering one's personal lifestyle. Animal cruelty can be redressed through vegetarianism, ozone damage by boycotting implicated products; each individual can take political actions by altering his or her patterns of consumption. Nava (1990) sees such consumption practices as enabling a new popular radicalism, in which individuals make consumption choices on the basis of ethical considerations and exercise power through participation in boycotts of certain products. She regards the organization of such political actions as being achieved through the activities of publications such as *The Ethical Consumer* and *The New Consumer*. Futhermore, consumer power 'enfranchises' marginal groups such as women and the young, who have little opportunity for influence in conventional party political processes.

However, the close link to the mode of consumption, evident in green, consumer-based politics, constitutes the weakest characteristic of the way the green perspective has entered popular culture and politics. Firstly, if issues can be addressed at the personal, lifestyle level, individuals may not feel disposed to active participation in formal organizational structures. Political organization will be correspondingly weak, and the difficulty facing the Green Party is to persuade the electorate that such a political movement is necessary. Secondly, Nava (1990) has ignored the extent to which a political praxis founded on consumption strategies can be incorporated into marketing techniques. In fact there is a growing sense in which the green perspective has been appropriated by manufacturing capital as a highly successful marketing strategy. The consequence is that the implicit radicalism of a perspective which offers a critique of capitalism and state capitalism is rendered ineffective. Individuals are no longer asked to question the ecological sustainability of their lifestyle, but merely to consume certain ecogically sound products. The green perspective is in the process of being commoditized.

Finally I would suggest that a popular, mass political movement must have some basis in the mode of production. I have suggested here that the consciousness of the new working class is in part determined by the lived experience of the relations of production, and in part by the lived experience derived from consumption patterns and lifestyle. I regard the sphere of production as a crucial component in the creation of a political movement, and social movements must inevitably reflect in some way work and production relations. Until now the Green movement has not linked with this sphere of individuals' activity and consequently has failed to develop a popular basis of support. In South Wales the 'jobs at all costs' pressures created by high levels of unemployment have often led to environmentally disastrous investment decisions being made by the local and central state. No one has yet addressed this issue in a way which also engages with the need to secure livelihoods in a capitalist society. Green perspectives have yet to link with the 'quality' of people's working lives in the same way they have linked with patterns of consumption. There has been little debate about the exploitative nature of work in capitalist society, and instead the critique has been of industrialism rather than capitalism. Green politics may offer alternative modes of consumption, but it has yet to formulate a coherent ideology of work and production in society.

Given the current failure of all political perspectives to link with the lived experience of the new working class, we must draw the conclusion that politics in Wales is entering a period of unpredictability and uncertainty, in common with much of the rest of the world. It seems clear that the social basis of the Labour Party is in decline, but no alternative movement has appeared which demonstrates the potential of being a mass, popular political organization. Given this absence of an alternative, it appears likely that the Labour Party in Wales will continue to draw a grudging support from much of the electorate. Nationalism appears to have lost an opportunity to tap Anglo-Welsh nationalist sentiment and has failed in its attempts throughout the 1980s to make inroads into the Labour heartlands of South Wales. In the latter half of the 1980s, Plaid Cymru has once again experienced conflict between the ideological strands of culturalism and leftism (Adamson 1988a) and until this issue is resolved it appears unlikely that any broad basis of electoral appeal will emerge from the party.

The only certainty in this open juncture is that it is the new working class which is likely to form the basis for the social movements which will carry Wales into the next century. A cultural and political hegemony grounded in the era of 'organized capitalism' will inevitably give way to the social movements of the era of 'disorganized capitalism'. In common with Lash and Urry (1987), I believe that such movements will not reflect the demise of working-class politics, and that disorganized capitalism remains characterized by the conflicting interests of capital and labour in much the same way as the period of organized capitalism. It is the division of labour which has changed, not the relations of production. This new division of labour now reflects new interests, perhaps best illustrated by recognizing the feminization of the workforce which has accompanied its tertiarization (Winckler 1985). The political interests of the new working class cannot be represented through the patriarchal and sectionalist structures of the labour movement as it is currently constituted.

Finally, I think it is crucial that we avoid the conclusion that working-class radicalism will disappear with the traditional organizations of the working class. The new working class and the social movements to which it will give rise are potentially as radical as the traditional working class and its organizational forms. Whilst it is clear that much of the historical basis for collectivism has eroded in the lived experience of this class fraction, it would be premature to write off collectivism completely. Nor is it impossible to visualize radical forms of individualism which appear, at least in embryonic form, in the Green movement. Perhaps, like Gorz (1985), I must conclude that as Wales enters the 1990s, the only certainty is uncertainty.

Bibliography

Abercrombie, N. and J. Urry 1983. *Capital, Labour and the Middle Classes*. Allen & Unwin

Adamson, D. L. 1988a. 'Community, Ideology and Political Discourse: the Concept of Community in Welsh Nationalist Politics' (paper presented to the International Conference on Utopian Thought and Communal Experience, New Lanark, July 1988)

Adamson, D. L. 1988b. 'The New Working Class and Political Change in Wales', *Contemporary Wales*, 2. Board of Celtic Studies, University of Wales Press

Baudrillard, J. 1981. *For a Critique of the Political Economy of the Sign*. Telos Press

Bocock, R. 1986. *Hegemony*. Tavistock

Bourdieu, P. 1984. *Distinction. A Social Critique of the Judgement of Taste*. Routledge & Kegan Paul

Central Statistical Office 1989. *Social Trends 19*. HMSO

Cooke, P. N. 1982. 'Class Interests, Regional Restructuring and State Formation in Wales', *International Journal of Urban and Regional Research*, 6, pp. 187–204

Cottrell, A. and R. Roslender 1986. 'Economic Class, Social Class and Political Forces', *International Journal of Sociology and Social Policy*, 6, pp. 13–27

Dunleavy, P. and C. Husbands 1985. *British Democracy at the Crossroads. Voting and Party Competition in the 1980s*. Allen & Unwin

Edwards. A. J. 1985. 'Manufacturing in Wales: a Spatial and Sectoral Analysis of Recent Changes in Structure, 1975–85, *Cambria*, 12, pp. 89–115

Goldthorpe, J. H. 1980. *Social Mobility and Class Structure in Britain*. Clarendon Press

Gorz, A. 1983. *Farewell to the Working Class*. Pluto Press

Gorz, A. 1985. *Paths to Paradise. On the Liberation from Work*. Pluto Press.

Gramsci, A. 1971. *Selections from the Prison Notebooks*, edited and translated by Q. Hoare and G. Nowell. Lawrence & Wishart

Hall, S. and M. Jacques (eds.) 1983. *The Politics of Thatcherism*. Lawrence & Wishart

Hebdige, D. 1979. *Subculture: the Meaning of Style*. Methuen

Hindess, B. 1987. *Politics and Class Analysis*. Blackwell

Hobsbawm, E. 1981. *The Forward March of Labour Halted?* Verso

Laclau, E. and C. Mouffe 1985. *Hegemony and Socialist Strategy: towards a Radical Democratic Politics*. Verso

Lash, S. and J. Urry 1987. *The End of Organized Capitalism*. Polity Press

Mandel, E. 1972. *Late Capitalism*. Verso

Marshall, G., H. Newby, D. Rose and C. Vogler 1988. *Social Class in Modern Britain*. Hutchinson

McIntyre, S. 1985. 'National Film Cultures: Politics and Peripheries', *Screen* 26, pp. 66–76

Meiskins Wood, E. 1986. *The Retreat from Class: a New 'True' Socialism*. Verso

Moores, S. 1989. Untitled/unpublished paper, Department of Behavioural and Communication Studies, Polytechnic of Wales

Nava, M. 1990. 'Consumerism Reconsidered: Buying and Power' (paper presented to the British Sociological Association, Annual Conference, University of Surrey, April)

Offe, C. 1985. *Disorganized Capitalism. Contemporary Transformations of Work and Politics*. Polity Press

O'Shea, A. 1984. 'Trusting the People: How does Thatcherism Work?' in T. Bennet *et al.*, *Formations of Nation and People*. Routledge & Kegan Paul

Poulantzas, N. 1975. *Classes in Contemporary Capitalism*. New Left Books

Rees, G. and T. Rees 1983. 'Migration, Industrial Restructuring and Class Relations: an Analysis of South Wales' in G. Williams (ed.), *Crisis of Economy and Ideology: Essays on Welsh Society, 1840–1980*. SSRC/BSA Sociology of Wales Study Group

Saunders, P. 1990. *A Nation of Home Owners*. Unwin

Tomlinson, A. (ed.) 1990. *Consumption, Identity and Style: Marketing, Meanings, and the Packaging of Pleasure*. Routledge & Kegan Paul

Warde, A. 1990. 'On the Relationship between Production and

Consumption' (paper presented to the British Sociological Association, Annual Conference, University of Surrey, April)

Winckler, V. 1985. 'Tertiarization and Feminization at the Periphery' in *Restructuring Capital. Recession and Reorganization in Industrial Society*. Macmillan

Chapter 7

Intellectuals and the National Question in Ireland

LIAM O'DOWD

Intellectuals and national identity

Many studies of nationalism have noted the key role of intellectuals in constructing national identity and in 'inventing' or 'imagining' the nation (Anderson 1983; Gellner 1964; Smith 1971). In 'newer' post-colonial states, the role of political intellectuals is clear. Before independence they mobilize popular support behind the demand for a new nation-state while seeking to legitimize it thereafter against internal and external threats to its existence. In longer-established states, the role of intellectuals as definers of national identity is less prominent. In the absence of war, mobilization or major internal strife, appeals to national identity may take a different form. As Raymond Williams (1983) observes, 'It is as if a really secure nationalism, already in possession of the nation-state, can fail to see itself as nationalist at all' (pp. 182–3). The 'national question' is always someone else's problem.

This chapter examines the responses of intellectuals in both parts of Ireland to twenty years of ethnic-national conflict in Northern Ireland. It suggests that these responses are conditioned in part by the growth and changing composition of an intelligentsia increasingly in the service of both capitalist states in Ireland. Secondly, the responses are structured by the different historic roles of intellectuals within Irish nationalist and Ulster unionist blocs.

Both Northern and Southern experience indicates the continued importance of national identity as a source of political legitimacy. In the North, intellectuals' inability to contruct, or appeal to, a common national identity has continued to undermine the legitimacy of the state. They have been unable to construct a shared political language which might facilitate structures based on the active consent of both communal blocs. In the Irish Republic, however, the Northern conflict has been used as a means of redefining the 'Irish nation' in order to make it coterminous with the Irish state. Intellectuals in the South have been rather more successful in using national identity as a flexible source of political legitimation.

Changing size and composition of the 'intelligentsia'

One of the secular trends in all advanced industrial societies is the growth in size of the 'intelligentsia' and in their degree of specialization. The limiting factor is a society's capacity to divert substantial material resources from the daily process of production and reproduction to support extended intellectual labour.

The *intelligentsia* is defined for present purposes as 'mental' or non-manual workers with relatively high levels of education whose work is based on specialized knowledge. Their hallmarks are formal educational credentials and professional bodies organized on a national or international basis. *Intellectuals*, on the other hand, although they may claim specialist expertise, are willing to go beyond it to address non-specialist audiences and wider questions of social organization and political direction. In seeking to influence the moral or political leadership of a society, they may seek either to sustain or to challenge the status quo. Their status is politically contested in a way in which that of the intelligentsia is not.[1] Nevertheless, intellectuals are drawn increasingly from the ranks of the intelligentsia, who are frequently dependent on material support from the state or the corporate sector.

If the census category 'professional' is taken as a crude proxy for the intelligentsia, it is clear that the latter have greatly expanded as a percentage of the 'gainfully occupied', particularly since 1951. In that year they accounted for 6 per cent of the workforce in the Irish

1 The term 'intelligentsia' is used here in a sense close to the corresponding census category as used in some state socialist systems to incorporate those in professional, administrative, managerial, academic and technological occupations. 'Intellectuals' and 'intelligentsia' do not carry for present purposes the necessary connotations of radical dissent associated with their eastern European origins (see Williams 1976, pp. 40–2). Instead, the distinction used follows Konrad and Szelenyi (1979) and Etzioni-Halevy (1979) among others.

Republic and 5 per cent in Northern Ireland, increasing to 12.2 per cent and 14.3 per cent respectively in the 1981 census.

Table 7.1 indicates significant differences in the composition of the intelligentsia in both parts of Ireland, although by 1981 there are clear signs of convergence.

Table 7.1   Changing composition of professional category

% of total professions	1926		1951		1971		1981	
	IR	NI	IR	NI	IR	NI	IR	NI
Clergy	26	10	39	8	19	4	10	2
Teachers	31	46	21	31	24	31	27	28
Judges, barristers, doctors	6	8	7	7	6	4	6	5
Engineers, scientists	3	3	4	6	6	11	6	6
Other professionals*	34	33	29	48	45	50	51	59

* Nurses are the largest group within this category accounting for 20 per cent of professional occupations in each part of Ireland in 1981. In each case the rest of this category consists of a wide and diverse range of specialist professional occupations. *Source*: Census of Northern Ireland and Irish Republic.

The most striking point of contrast is the much greater proportion of clerical intellectuals in the South. This difference understates the differences between nationalist and unionist Ireland as the Northern Ireland figures include large numbers of Catholic clergy.

The influence of the Catholic Church on Irish nationalism has been well rehearsed (see e.g. Inglis 1987). The point here however is that the Church provided a powerful institutional basis and model for Irish intellectuals and professionals, establishing lasting channels of communication between an intellectual elite and a mass following. After partition until the mid-1950s, clerical intellectuals sought to construct a social order based on Catholic corporatist principles in the South (Whyte 1971) This social order was to be built on a small property-owning class concentrated in rural areas, with a decisive role for the Church in education, health and welfare and a very circumscribed role for the state.

Underpinning this ideology was a dramatic rise in the number of clergy. Whereas the Irish population decreased by 2.6 per cent between 1901 and 1951, the number of priests, brothers and nuns increased by 40, 40 and 66 per cent respectively. This followed an increase of 137 per cent in all religious in the last forty years of the nineteenth century at a time when the population decreased by 27 per cent (Titley 1983, p. 146). In numbers and influence the Catholic clergy were to reach their zenith in the 1950s in the Irish Republic. By then, however, the material basis of the existing social order in the Republic was crumbling. The clerical intellectuals had no answers to the mass emigration of the 1946–61 period or to the stagnation of the Irish economy. The Catholic social movement lacked a convincing economic ideology in a Europe moving to free trade, the creation of the EEC and the internationalization of capitalist production.

Alongside the clergy, professionals such as teachers, journalists and lawyers had always played an important role in the nationalist leadership both before and after partition (Garvin 1987; Chubb 1982, p. 93; Hutchinson 1987). In this, there are similarities between the Irish case and some eastern European nationalist movements where entrepreneurial capitalism was poorly developed (Hroch 1985). By the 1950s, however, both clerical and non-clerical nationalists were facing the failure of their social projects. Nationalist goals like the ending of partition, the revival of Irish as a spoken language, the stemming of emigration and successful indigenous industrialization seemed further from realization than ever. The ideal of a rural-based society under clerical guidance and built around an Irish-controlled economy was revealed now to be utopian.

It was precisely at this point that one element within the secular intelligentsia, led by civil service and academic economists, and with the support of the new Irish prime minister, Lemass, came forward with an alternative programme based on free trade, state-sponsored multinational investment, and membership of the EEC.[2] Initially presented as an alternative means of achieving traditional nationalist goals, the implication was the radical revision of the social content of Irish nationalism. Significantly, too, as one political scientist put it, 'The Church had lost, almost without realising it, the role of intellectual and cultural arbiter it once had' (Garvin 1982, pp. 31–2).

The belated adaptation of the Irish state to the postwar capitalist economy involved replacing the Church as the major institutional focus for the Southern intelligentsia. A new, larger and more specialized intelligentsia now found employment within a state apparatus geared to economic modernization. As the national

2 Terence Brown (1981, p. 241) represents a virtual consensus about Southern Irish intellectuals when he points to the period 1958–63 as the 'major turning point in post-independence nationalist politics'. For a critical account see e.g. Crotty 1986.

education system expanded at second and third levels, its intellectual beneficiaries used educational credentials to consolidate their status within the new order (Breen *et al.* 1990).

A range of new state agencies were established to effect and monitor the new socio-economic policies. The creation of a state-owned television service in 1962 and a series of new professional publications provided the vehicles for communicating the new ideas to a wider audience. Professional economists, planners and media experts began to replace clergy and traditional nationalist ideologues in reshaping the language and agenda of Southern politics.

By the 1960s, Northern Ireland was having to come to terms with the same global capitalist economy as the Republic. Under the aegis of a more active regional strategy in Britain, the Stormont government embarked on a programme of economic modernization aimed at diversifying industrial structure through the sponsorship of multinational investment. Although Stormont adopted a similar strategy to that of the Republic in response to the same set of global economic conditions, it was doing so from a very different base. Unlike the Republic, the class structure was rooted in the nineteenth-century industrial revolution, with a substantial skilled working class centred on Belfast and a more complex bourgeoisie. The 'intelligentsia' carried were relatively less significant than in the South – they constituted just one element in a Protestant coalition of interests which also included old landed gentry, large farmers and industrial and commercial entrepreneurs. Furthermore Northern Ireland's class structure was divided sharply on religio-national grounds.

Again, unlike the Republic, there were no nationalist intellectuals on hand in Northern Ireland to legitimize the transition to state-sponsored modernization programmes. Deep ethnic-national divisions ensured that appeals to national identity were more likely to challenge rather than bolster the legitimacy of the new state policies. The Catholic intelligentsia, lawyers, journalists, doctors, teachers and clergy, serviced their own community. Excluded from positions of political influence in a Protestant state, they were reluctant to see it as a 'neutral' agent of socio-economic development.

For their part, Ulster Protestants had not produced nationalist intellectuals. This is part of what Nairn (1977, p. 241) terms the 'pathological asymmetry of the Irish Question', i.e. the failure of Protestants to develop a fully-fledged Ulster nationalism to counter Irish nationalism. It would have been a contradiction in terms for unionists to have sought actively a separate sovereign state in order to accomplish specific economic, political or cultural goals. From the outset, the Stormont statelet was perceived not as a positive initiating agent but rather as a bulwark of Britishness and Protestantism against Irish Catholicism and nationalism (Bell 1985; O'Dowd 1990a).

Historically, a politically-minded intellectual elite had drifted away from Ulster unionism either to the cause of Irish nationalism or to that of British imperialism. What was left was a powerful popular culture of Loyalism, often exclusivist, reactionary and anti-Catholic which required little in the way of intellectual elaboration (see Brown 1985; Bell 1985) As the literary critic and Ulster Protestant, J. W. Foster (1988) puts it, 'Ulster did not need thinkers or apologists. It was set on automatic pilot, set by grey and visionless men. Unionism as an intellectually defensible or culturally defensible belief withered away' (p. 412).

Given Northern Ireland's large Catholic minority, the slippage between 'Ulster' and 'Protestant' is perhaps important in Foster's observation. Nevertheless, his general point about Protestant and unionist intellectuals holds. Their role in mobilizing popular support behind the Northern Ireland state was very limited, as was their part in sustaining the Protestant class coalition. Aside from the absence of nationalism, its unionist substitutes, evangelicalism and Protestant contractarianism, accorded relatively low status to an 'intellectual clerisy'. This distinguished Ulster Protestantism from its Irish Catholic counterpart and linked it to elements in wider British political culture (see Ignatieff 1990 on the anti-intellectualism of British culture).

The scarcity of politicized intellectuals in Northern Ireland should not be confused with the lack of an intelligentsia. As table 7.1 shows, this was rapidly expanding in the 1960s and 1970s as state institutions expanded to manage both economic modernization and the emerging political conflict. This intelligentsia was very fragmented, however, in terms of its educational and institutional orientations. Alongside the Protestant and Catholic intelligentsia was a resident British intelligentsia prominent in academic life and in some professions. The diversity of communal and national reference points was a major barrier to the emergence of intellectuals with coherent political and ideological programmes.

There was one major similarity with the South however. Both the Northern and Southern intelligentsia were now more directly affiliated with their respective state institutions. Adaptation to the changing capitalist order was being accomplished alongside, and through, both states. In the North however, the central British state had supplanted the Northern Ireland statelet as the focus of the intelligentsia. Both states and their respective intelligentsias were facing increasingly similar socio-economic problems: mass unemployment, loss of manufacturing employment, increasing dependence on public expenditure, competition for similar types of multinational investment and joint membership of the EEC.

Intellectuals and the Northern crisis

The eruption of the Northern conflict in 1968 not only threatened new policies of economic modernization in both parts of Ireland, it raised apparently intractable questions associated with national identity and partition. Throughout the 1970s and 1980s, two sets of problems have intersected: (1) those engendered by state management of economic modernization and the impact of global capitalist restructuring; (2) those engendered by the Northern conflict with its implications for the relationships between communal and national identity and for British–Irish relationships more generally. The combination of these issues had important implications for intellectuals and the intelligentsia on either side of the Border.

For the historical and structural reasons outlined above, the responses of intellectuals and the intelligentsia in both parts of Ireland differed. In the North, the outbreak of the conflict exposed the political weakness of intellectuals and intelligentsia alike. In the South, the initial impact was to fuel a process already under way in the early 1960s – a redefinition of Irish national identity and a marginalization of more traditional forms of nationalism.

One of the novel features of the Northern Ireland Civil Rights Movement in the 1960s was the way in which Northern nationalist intellectuals initially sought to develop their politics within the context of the Stormont statelet. Programmatic demands for reform were no substitute for the power to realize them, however. While support came from a minority of Protestant liberals and socialists, the latter lacked substantial influence within their own bloc. Instead, the civil rights agitation provoked intense *popular* unionist opposition. This opened the way for a popular nationalist response under the aegis of the IRA. While many professionals and intellectuals distanced themselves from the IRA, subsequently the revitalized republican movement was able to draw on an ideology informed by a long history of interaction between intellectual and popular culture. Even if modern nationalist intellectuals wished to distance themselves from new manifestations of republicanism, the latter was a more accessible intellectual currency than that of Ulster loyalism.

The outbreak of the Northern Ireland conflict quickly became a focus for intellectual attention internationally. The burgeoning media and social science interest in the 'Northern Ireland Problem' was reflected in an apparently endless stream of sponsored seminars in Ireland, Britain and the US where, it was hoped, the contending parties might resolve their differences in rational discussion. The major impetus for outside interest was, of course, the apparent anomaly of violent political conflict over issues of religion and nationality – issues which had been allegedly settled long ago within the broader American–western European context.

From an early preoccupation with the Catholic and nationalist case, attention began to be diverted to the 'real kernel of the problem'. This was the virulent popular opposition of Loyalists to the more readily understandable demands of nationalists for equitable participation in state institutions. A gap in the comprehensibility of both sides began to appear. While students of Irish nationalism could fall back on a host of conventional literary sources, political histories, pamphlets and creative literature, information on Loyalism was not so easily accessible. This in turn opened the way for closer examination of the Ulster unionist community. Not surprisingly, the new research focused more on popular culture – on sources such as ethnographic accounts, Orange songs, Free Presbyterian sermons, banners, graffiti and popular newspapers. One of the unintended effects of this research was to illuminate the limits of intellectual influence on unionist political culture.

While Richard Rose had already delineated the political attitudes of the 'Protestant ultras' in his survey in the late 1960s, popular Loyalism now came in for more sustained empirical scrutiny.[3] The object was to make sense of what Geoff Bell (1976) termed 'the most misunderstood and criticised community in western Europe'. Sarah Nelson (1984, p. 9) aptly summarizes the problem of comprehensibility:

3   Examples include Geoff Bell, *The Protestants of Ulster* (Pluto, 1976); David Miller, *Queen's Rebels: Ulster Loyalism in Historical Perspective* (Gill and Macmillan, 1978); Ron Wiener, *The Rape and Plunder of the Shankill* (Forset Press, 1980); Richard Jenkins, *Lads, Citizens and Ordinary Kids* (Routledge & Kegan Paul, 1983); Sarah Nelson, *Ulster's Uncertain Defenders* (Appletree, 1984); Roy Wallis, Steve Bruce and David Taylor, *'No Surrender': Paisleyism and the Politics of Ethnic Identity in Northern Ireland* (Queen's University Press, 1986); Steve Bruce, *God Save Ulster! The Religion and Politics of Paisleyism* (Clarendon, 1987); Desmond Bell, *Acts of Union: Youth Culture and Sectarianism in Northern Ireland* (Macmillan, 1990). Besides Bruce's work there are now no less than four biographies of Paisley: Patrick Marrinan, *Paisley: Man of Wrath* (Anvil Books, 1973); Ed Moloney and Andy Pollak, *Paisley* (Brandon Press, 1986); Clifford Smyth, *Ian Paisley: the Voice of Protestant Ulster* (Scottish Academic Press, 1987); and Rhonda Paisley, *Ian Paisley: My Father* (Marshall Pickering, 1988).

They [the Loyalists] are loyal to Britain, yet ready to disobey her; they reject clerical tyranny, yet oppose secularism; they proclaim an ideology of freedom and equality, except for Catholics; they revere law and authority, then break the law. And they refuse to do the rational obvious thing.

What these accounts show *inter alia* is the way in which these ideas, in opposition at the abstract level, are reconciled at the level of direct and popular political *activity*. They show the centrality of Orange marches, of the mobilizing power of Paisley's revivalist style, of confrontations with Catholics, of the flags, arches and graffiti in delineating Loyalist territory. To working-class Catholics this is merely supremacism, to Loyalists it is an important part of their social and political identity.

The research on Ulster Protestants reveals the various interlocking strands of popular Loyalism as an ideology – its evangelical Protestantism, anti-Catholicism, racist views of Catholics as 'filthy Fenian scum', the feeling of being 'outbred', a pro-letarian suspicion of the 'fur-coat brigade' yet a deep suspicion of socialism, its sense of being an 'elect' and embattled people with a mission of recalling the British state to its old political and religious values.

Overall adherence to communal exclusivism is linked to an understanding of 'the privileges of British citizenship as *exclusive entitlements* bequeathed to Protestants *qua* Protestants rather than as *inclusive rights* afforded to every member of a country' (Bell 1985, p. 93). Clearly the gulf between this popular exclusivism and the inclusive ideology of many liberal democratic, socialist and nationalist intellectuals is considerable. It may be argued that all *popular* political ideologies contain contradictory and exclusivistic elements. In the case of unionism, however, intellectuals have failed to forge an enduring link between a popular political culture and any major political ideology such as liberal democracy, socialism or nationalism.[4] One of the reasons is the popular and visual, rather than literary or intellectual, nature of Loyalist culture; another is the structural weakness of intellectuals. As Bell (1985) observes, 'It is the sound of the Lambeg drum, rather than the resonance of political ideology, which brings tears to the eyes of a Loyalist' (p. 95).

4 The United Irishmen, the fate of nineteenth-century Liberal Unionism, the Labour and socialist movements in Ulster, and more recently, O'Neillism, are examples of failed attempts to make lasting links between Loyalism and nationalism, liberal democracy and socialism.

More importantly, perhaps, popular Loyalism is not easily translatable into a mere collection of abstract ideas because it has proved so successful as a vehicle of popular *power*. There are parallels here with British conservatism – which itself had long and intimate links with Ulster Loyalism.

Direct Rule and the restructuring of Northern Ireland's economy have altered the parameters within which popular Loyalism operates. With the major exception of the security forces, it is no longer married to the formal exercise of power as it was under Stormont. At most it retains *in extremis* the power of popular veto over internal political arrangements. Its decline does create limited political space for intellectuals under the aegis of the British central state.

Southern intellectuals and the Northern crisis

As indicated above, the retreat from traditional nationalism among Southern intellectuals had begun before the upheavals in Northern Ireland. By the early 1960s the economic determinants of Irish history were being stressed in opposition to the traditionalist nationalist emphasis on political factors . The new intelligentsia was formulating a new political vocabulary in the South centred on economic development. Despite initial sympathy with the plight of Northern nationalists, the re-emergence of the IRA encouraged a distancing of the Northern conflict. After 1973, the Northern crisis featured only as a marginal issue in Southern party politics.[5]

A rather one-sided debate proceeded between revisionist historians and adherents of traditional nationalism. The thrust of revisionism was to challenge some of the claims of physical force nationalism and anti-colonial interpretations of Irish history (for a classic synthesis see R. Foster 1988). British administrators, landlords, collaborationist and reformist national movements were rescued from the opprobrium heaped on them by traditional nationalists. The empirical basis of this new scholarship was impressive and its interpretative framework placed Ireland firmly within a British Isles context, rather than within the wider context of colonialism and decolonization.

One of the striking features of the output of this intelligentsia, notably in the area of economics and social science, is reluctance to engage in any empirical analysis of contemporary Northern Ireland. This reluctance contrasts sharply with the widespread interest of British, American and other 'external' intellectuals in analysing Northern Irish society.

5 Sinn Fein polled less than 2 per cent of the vote in the 1989 general election in the Irish Republic.

Nevertheless, a number of Irish intellectuals did develop an analysis which, if it seldom addressed the realities of contemporary Northern Ireland, at least took it into account. This group casts the Irish problem in culturalist terms portraying the conflict as a clash of identities or cultures. The relationship between tradition, modernity and post-modernity, the cultural basis of political violence and, above all, the relationship of the Irish literature to politics is central to this approach.[6] Although self-consciously revisionist with respect to the Catholic nationalist tradition, it shares many of its characteristics. Intellectuals continue to be seen, implicitly or explicitly, in a vanguard role as arbiters of national identity, as purveyors of ideas rather than as signposts of particular material or class interests. The failure to recognize the material base of culture and intellectuals' wider structural role has at least two consequences. It obscures the widening class divisions in Southern society and how intellectuals relate to them, and it illuminates the limits of a comparable intellectual or culturalist analysis among Ulster Protestants (O'Dowd 1985, 1988).

By the 1980s, however, it was possible to discern the outlines of a new if somewhat contradictory 'national consensus' which is the product of both the new intelligentsia and the reformulated intellectual perspectives on cultural identity. The key elements include: the indefinite postponement of Irish reunification, the recognition of the 'Britishness' of unionists, and the containment of violence and the 'national question' within the boundaries of Northern Ireland (*New Ireland Forum Report* 1984; Anglo-Irish Agreement, 1985). To this is added a Europeanism which allows Irish national, i.e. state, interests to be pursued within the EEC. This has the practical benefit of widening the scope of occupational opportunities for the highly educated intelligentsia. Against this background, the old form of the 'national question' may be portrayed as increasingly irrelevant in a 'Europe of regions' which is allegedly superseding the old nation-states (Kearney 1988).

Underpinning this political and cultural programme is an Irish version of neo-conservative economics aimed at controlling public expenditure, and the massive public debt while integrating the Irish Republic further into the international capitalist economy. Here the legitimacy of the state can be bolstered by pointing to its lack of real

6 Examples of this approach may be found in Garrett Fitzgerald, *Irish Identities* (BBC Publications, 1982); F. S. L. Lyons, *Culture and Anarchy in Ireland* (Clarendon, 1982); *The New Ireland Forum Report* (Stationery Office, 1984); Roy Foster and the Northern Ireland Cultural Traditions Group in Maurna Crozier (ed.), *Cultural Traditions in Northern Ireland* (Institute of Irish Studies, Queen's University, 1989); and in the prolific writings of Conor Cruise O'Brien.

policy options as a member of the EEC. The revival of mass emigration in the 1980s also removes many sources of political discontent. Threats to the new 'consensus' exist, however, including the debt crisis, increasing social inequality and the indirect effects of the Northern Ireland conflict. Dissenting intellectuals abound, of course, although the basis of their opposition is diffuse and lacks coherent political support (e.g. Crotty 1986; O'Connor 1989). The new 'regime' has been shrewdly summed up by one 'dissenting' journalist:

> In the 1970s the Southern middle class conceded traditional nationalism to the Northern (Catholic) working class. Since then their intellectuals have been trying to fashion an ideology which can integrate their material interests with a sense of national purpose. Many have found an obsession with the budget deficit, but that hardly constitutes an ideology. (Kerrigan 1989)

The redefinition of the national question and the declining ideological role of the Church has led another intellectual critic to term Irish (i.e. Southern) society of the 1980s 'ideologically vacuous' (Lee 1982, p. 16). Importantly, however, the dissenters share with their opponents a sense of the 'mission of intellectuals' which is missing from Ulster unionism.

A solution in the North?

In the North, of course, appeals to national identity, Irish, British or Ulster, are divisive almost by definition. From within the expanded intelligentsia, now containing a growing number of Catholics at junior levels,[7] attempts are being made to forge a new vocabulary for cross-communal understanding. This is being supported by the British government through programmes such as Education for Mutual Understanding and the new Community Relations Commission.

The gulf between such intellectualist programmes and popular Loyalism seems as wide as ever. In addition, Northern republicanism has become an increasingly populist ideology. Under intense pressure from the British state, the Catholic Church and Loyalists, it can no

---

7   Fair Employment Agency reports have shown that there has been a substantial rise in the proportion of Catholics in the Northern Ireland civil service, especially at junior levels. Catholics are much less well represented in universities, however.

longer rely on support from middle-class intellectuals. Like Loyalism it too is becoming impervious to cultural engineering.

A whole range of minority and sometimes exotic ideologies exist, often propagated by small intellectual coteries. These range from militant republicanism to the British national movement and attempts to 'invent' a past for an Ulster nation. None of these movements can mobilize a majority of the population behind a positive political programme.

The 'national question' in its most virulent and confrontational forms is now more of a class marker in Northern Ireland than ever before. It finds its most intense expression — the rhetoric and practice of the colonizer and colonized, 'settler' and 'native' — in working-class communities throughout the province. It is precisely this spectre — i.e., that Northern conflict is the latest episode of British decolonization — that haunts both national states and the middle class on either side of the communal divide. Both states and their respective intelligentsia wish to forget the colonial past. Northern Ireland is a reminder of its legacy, and a reminder that the process of decolonization in the old imperial heartland may not be complete (for discussion of this issue, see O'Dowd 1990b).

The Anglo-Irish Agreement is a remarkable acknowledgement by both governments of the necessity for 'containing' the political conflict within Northern Ireland. It seems to institutionalize official scepticism about the possibility of mobilizing active cross-communal consent behind agreed structures within Northern Ireland. Opinion polls continually reveal lack of popular support for the Agreement. The main point is, however, that it has proved impossible to mount sustained popular resistance to it either, which perhaps indicates widespread scepticism among the population that any alternative is feasible.

Conclusions

This chapter has attempted to show that the obstacles to political accommodation between unionists and nationalists in Ireland are at least partially rooted in the contrasting historical roles and ideologies of intellectuals. Intellectuals have not played equivalent roles on each side for deep-rooted political and structural reasons. This has inhibited the construction of a common political discourse which might inform political accommodation. It may be that this conclusion also embraces British nationalism. However much Ulster unionism might be seen as a dispensable element in the UK, it may be that it shares much with British nationalism. It may share, for example, a popular identification with the Crown, the army and the remnants of empire, as well as a lack of reliance on politicized intellectuals to elaborate notions of British identity. The question may be posed therefore whether the British nation-state depends less on intellectuals' use of national identity as a source of identity than on a mixture of popular beliefs, acquiescence, apathy and coercion.

The Irish case suggests that nationalism needs to be analysed, not as an abstract doctrine, but as a specific ideology. It is necessary to locate its chief promulgators and to examine their relationships to the class and institutional framework of the capitalist state.Where the state necessarily plays a large role in mediating the impact of the wider capitalist system, national identity remains a critical source of political legitimacy prompting agreement with Benedict Anderson's (1983, p. 12) observation, 'The end of the era of "nationalism", so long prophesied, is not remotely in sight.'

Bibliography

Anderson, B. 1983. *Imagined Communities: Reflections on the Origin and Spread of Nationalism.* Verso.
Bell, D. 1985. 'Contemporary Cultural Studies in Ireland and the Problem of Protestant Ideology', *Crane Bag*, 9 (2)
Bell, G. 1976. *The Protestants of Ulster.* Pluto.
Breen, R. *et al.* 1990. *Understanding Contemporary Ireland.* Gill and Macmillan
Brown, T. 1981. *Ireland: a Social and Cultural History.* Fontana
Brown, T. 1985. *The Whole Protestant Community: the Making of a Myth.* Field Day Pamphlet, Derry
Chubb, B. 1982. *The Government and Politics of Ireland.* Longman
Crotty, R. 1986. *Ireland in Crisis.* Brandon
Etzioni-Halevy, E. 1979. *The Knowledge Elite and the Failure of Prophecy.* Allen & Unwin
Foster, J. W. 1988. 'Who are the Irish?' *Studies*, 77 (308)
Foster, R. 1988. *Modern Ireland, 1600–1972.* Allen Lane
Garvin, T. 1982. 'Change in the Political System' in F. Litton (ed.), *Unequal Achievement: the Irish Experience, 1957–1982.* Institute of Public Administration
Garvin, T. 1987. *Nationalist Revolutionaries in Ireland, 1858–1928.* Clarendon Press.
Gellner, E. 1964. *Thought and Change.* Weidenfeld & Nicolson
Hroch, M. 1985. *Social Preconditions for Nationalist Revival in Europe.* Cambridge University Press

Hutchinson, J. 1987. *The Dynamics of Cultural Nationalism: the Gaelic Revival and the Creation of the Irish Nation State.* Allen & Unwin

Ignatieff, M. 1990. 'A Country Fit to Think in', *The Observer* (25 February)

Inglis, T. 1987. *The Moral Monopoly: the Catholic Church in Ireland.* Gill and Macmillan.

Kearney, R. (ed.) 1988. *Across the Frontiers: Ireland in the 1990s.* Wolfhound Press

Kerrigan, G. 1989 in *Sunday Tribune* (12 March)

Konrad, G. and I. Szelenyi 1979. *Intellectuals on the Road to Class Power.* Harvester

Lee, A. 1982. 'Society and Culture' in F. Litton (ed.), *Unequal Achievement: the Irish Experience, 1957–1982.* Institute of Public Administration

Nairn, T. 1977. *The Break-up of Britain.* New Left Books

New Ireland Forum Report 1984. Government Publications Office, Dublin

Nelson, S. 1984. *Ulster's Uncertain Defenders.* Appletree

O'Connor, U. 1989. *Crisis and Commitment: the Writer and Northern Ireland.* Elo Publications

O'Dowd, L. 1985. 'Intellectuals in Twentieth Century Ireland and the Case of George Russell (AE)', *Crane Bag*, 9 (1)

O'Dowd, L. 1988. 'Neglecting the Material Dimension: Irish Intellectuals and the Problem of Identity', *Irish Review*, 3

O'Dowd, L. 1990a. 'Intellectuals and Political Culture: a Unionist–Nationalist Comparison' in E. Hughes (ed.), *Culture and Politics in Ireland.* Open University Press

O'Dowd, L. 1990b. New Introduction to reissue of A. Memmi, *The Colonizer and the Colonized.* Earthscan Publications

Smith, A. 1971. *Theories of Nationalism.* Harper

Titley, E. B. 1983. *Church, State and the Control of Schooling, 1900–44.* Gill and Macmillan.

Whyte, J. 1971. *Church and State in Modern Ireland.* Gill and Macmillan

Williams, R. 1976. *Keywords: a Vocabulary of Culture and Society.* Fontana

Williams, R. 1983. *Towards 2000.* Penguin Books

Chapter 8

Popping the Cork: History, Heritage and the Stately Home in the Scottish Borders

ANGELA MORRIS

Introduction

In recent years commentators such as Patrick Wright and Robert Hewison have expressed concern over a growing public obsession with the past. The most explicit statement of this concern is Hewison's *The Heritage Industry* (1987). This study was inspired by the fact that 'every week or so, somewhere in Britain, a new museum opens' (1987, p. 9) and Hewison's fear that the UK will soon become 'one vast museum' (ibid.). *The Heritage Industry* is not confined to museums but traces 'the growth of a new cultural force of which museums are only a part' (ibid.). Hewison calls this force

> the 'heritage industry' not only because it absorbs considerable public and private resources, but also because it is expected more and more to replace the real industry upon which this country's economy depends. Instead of manufacturing goods, we are manufacturing heritage, a commodity which nobody seems able to define, but which everybody is eager to sell. (1987, p. 9)

In an English context Hewison's arguments are interesting, but not fully convincing. In a Scottish context they are, ultimately, unsatisfactory. In this chapter, I intend, by focusing on the stately homes of the Scottish Borders, to show three things: firstly, why Hewison's arguments do not work north of the border; secondly, how Patrick Wright (1985) gets one step closer, but falls into some of the same pitfalls; and thirdly, how Wright's arguments can be fruitfully extended to cover Scotland.

The ambiguities of the 'national heritage'

Writing about the television dramatization of Evelyn Waugh's *Brideshead Revisited*, Hewison argues that country houses such as Brideshead demonstrate the 'peculiarly strong hold' such places have on 'the British — though for once it seems more appropriate to say English — imagination' (1987, pp. 51–2). Scotland, and in particular the Scottish Borders, has her fair share of country houses. Why then should Hewison say that these buildings and what they represent are an essentially *English* phenomenon? After all, he quite happily equates England with Britain throughout the rest of his analysis. Hewison, it seems, is treading warily. His caution is entirely justified. Fools rush in where angels fear to tread. Hewison is no fool, but he is no angel either. Having put one foot tentatively out, he soon forgets that he is not on firm ground. The result is that while some of his arguments can be applied to Scotland, many of his ideas simply do not work north of the border.

There are two main strands to Hewison's argument. The first, and less contentious, is that the birth of the heritage industry in Britain during the 1970s is essentially a response to the insecurities, economic and otherwise, of the postwar world. It is the second strand, however, that gets Hewison into deep water. Here, he links the growth of the heritage industry with postmodernism, on the grounds that 'they both conspire to create a shallow screen that intervenes between our present lives and our history' (1987, p. 135). I shall come back to this issue later.

Meanwhile, there are no problems in applying the first strand of Hewison's argument about the birth of the heritage industry in the mid 1970s to Scotland. In 1975, while *Brideshead Revisited* was under production for television, Bowhill, Borders home of the Duke and Duchess of Buccleuch, was opened to the fee-paying public during the summer months. It was followed by Drumlanrig Castle, their Dumfriesshire stately home in 1976. Floors Castle, ancestral home of the Duke and Duchess of Roxburghe, opened its doors two years later, in 1978. Until this time it had opened only once a year for charity. And although the Assistant Factor of the Roxburghe Estates is quick to stress that there was 'a willingness to allow the public access to enjoy the many treasures the castle contains', he also points out that the 'high maintenance costs of the Castle were a primary reason for opening Floors to the public in order that the revenue from the Castle opening could help to defray these costs'.[1] Other stately homes in the Borders soon followed suit, including Mellerstain and

1   Floors costs £100,000 a year simply to maintain.

Manderston. Mellerstain is the stately home of Lord and Lady Binning; Manderston was bought by a William Miller in 1864, out of the fortune he made trading with Russia in hemp and herring; it now belongs to Mr Adrian Palmer, William Miller's great-great-grandson. Manderston is particularly interesting because it is a nice illustration of how, in Britain, the bourgeoisie's greatest desire has been to become assimilated into the aristocracy, a process which, as Wiener (1985) has pointed out, is symbolized by the acquisition of a stately home.

It is appropriate here to make the often overlooked point that while the commercialization of heritage – that is, the 'heritage industry' – is a relatively recent phenomenon, 'heritage' *per se* is not. For example, Abbotsford, the home of Sir Walter Scott, just outside Galashiels on the banks of the Tweed, was opened to the public way back in 1833. One hundred and twenty-three years later, but still a good twenty years before the birth of the heritage industry, Traquair House, the oldest inhabited house in Scotland, was opened to the public.

The angle of Hewison's vision is in some ways impressively wide. He argues that heritage has become an industry; there is a product, a set of entrepreneurs, a manufacturing process with its accompanying social arrangements, a market and consumers. At the same time, however, he is aware that 'whatever the true figures for production and employment, this country is gripped by the *perception* that it is in decline' (1987, p. 9; my emphasis). Hence, the heritage industry is, for Hewison, esentially 'an attempt to dispel this climate of decline by exploiting the economic potential of our culture' (ibid.). Its success is grounded on the fact that 'it finds a ready market because the perception of decline includes all sorts of insecurities and doubts (which are more than simply economic) that makes its products especially attractive and reassuring' (pp. 9–10).

These 'insecurities and doubts' are in many ways the key to understanding the stately home/heritage industry in the Scottish Borders. While not intending to imply any direct, overly simplistic causal relationship between the two, it is interesting to note that the involvement of Border landowners, such as the Duke of Buccleuch and the Duke of Roxburghe, in the heritage industry took place shortly after a piece of legislation was passed which placed large question marks over their future role in the everyday life of the Borders. This was the Local Government (Scotland) Act of 1973, which reorganized Scottish local government into a two-tier system of Regions/Islands and Districts, in line with the proposals outlined by the Wheatley Commission.

In Scotland as a whole one of the most important effects of the 1973 Act was that it increased party activity at the local level. However, this was not so in the Borders. With the exception of the District of

Berwickshire, which, because of the strong agricultural interests in
the county, has consistently been held by the Conservatives, the
Borders, along with the Highlands, Dumfries and Galloway (other
rural areas with strong local traditions) has at both regional and
district levels been characterized by a tradition of non-partisan local
politics. A more significant consequence of this Act for the Borders
was that it in fact brought to an end the formal involvement of the
great landowning families in local government. Stripped of their
political function, it seems as if the Border lairds saw the heritage
industry as a way of securing not only their own economic future, but
as a useful way of legitimizing their privileged position within it.

In addition to highlighting many of the 'insecurities and doubts' of
the postwar world, the involvement of Scottish Border landowners in
the heritage industry also raises a whole set of questions about their
relationship to the reading and writing, constructing and creating of
Scottish history. These questions, one is tempted to suggest, are easy
enough to answer. After all, James Fergusson (1949) assures us that
instead of seeing Scottish history in terms of the biographies of
monarchs and nobles, economics or nationalism, 'It would be no
more misleading, and might even be a useful counterbalance, to write
the story of our country as that of the landed families of Lowland
Scotland' (p. 13). Fergusson's reasoning here is that 'their influence
on Scotland's growth and development has been steadier and more
enduring than that of kings and regents and far more direct than that
of popular movements' (ibid.). As a lowland laird himself (Fergusson
is one of the Fergussons of Kilkerran), it is perhaps hardly surprising
that he should want us to think this!

Fergusson was writing in 1949, well before the birth of the heritage
industry, but his example is one which latter-day lairdly entrepreneurs still follow. One has only to open a stately home guidebook
to find a succinct history of the family in question, invariably written
by the family itself. After paying our £1.70, we are expected to take
the guidebook home to read in detail and keep for future reference.
These historical accounts of the great families have a twofold
function. With their family trees, crests and mottoes, they are
intended to be factual and informative. At a deeper and more
significant level, however, their function is legitimatory. To this end,
the guidebook for Bowhill, for example, recites the stirring story of
'Bold Buccleuch', alias Walter, first Lord Scott of Buccleuch. 'Bold
Buccleuch' is supposed to have earned his name as a result of his
exploits in the Border raids. The high point in his colourful career,
however, was his rescue of Kinmount Willie in 1596 from the English
stronghold of Carlisle Castle with only eighty horsemen. This rescue
roused the wrath and indignation of Queen Elizabeth I of England

and was the cause of much bitterness in her relationship with King James Vl of Scotland. Two years later the English Queen came face to face with 'Bold Buccleuch' and asked him why he had embarked upon such a desperate mission. He answered her with the immortal line: 'What is it that a man dare not do?' (Bowhill Guidebook 1981, p. 22). The Queen was apparently so impressed by the bravery and audacity of the man before her that she turned to the bystanders and said, 'With ten thousand such men our brothers in Scotland might shake the firmest throne in Europe' (ibid.). In 1606 'Bold Buccleuch' was created Lord Scott of Buccleuch. Thus an act of heroic bravery, sealed with royal approval, is used to justify and legitimate the acquisition of power, position, influence, privilege and property.

The first major strand of Hewison's (1987) argument can thus be supported to a considerable extent by evidence from the Scottish Borders. It cannot, however, be swallowed whole. The stumbling block is that while he is aware that the country house, and what it represents, is essentially an English, rather than a British phenomenon, he does not develop this point further. His argument remains predicated upon a simplistic and chauvinistic Anglo-British premise, in which the British nation is equated with England and the 'national heritage' thereby reduced to an *Anglo-British* national heritage.

This is a venial sin of which Patrick Wright (1985) is also guilty. Wright, however, can get away with a lighter penance, for he is acutely aware of both the importance and the ambivalence of the symbol of the nation in contemporary British everyday life. Indeed, for Wright, the symbol of the nation is the key to understanding the political situation of contemporary Britain. The nation is 'the modern integration par excellence' (1985, p. 142) and 'a key figure in British politics, one that must be understood and carefully negotiated if we are to move beyond the passive experience of deadlock to an active public engagement with the issues determining our situation' (p. 141). It is therefore necessary to look at Wright's arguments in more detail.

Wright argues that in Britain since 1979 a political conscription of the past has taken place. This has been facilitated by the convergence around the symbol of 'the nation' of the three interrelated themes: the golden age or rural idyll; the search for the unique; and the fascination of remembered war. He suggests that this preoccupation with the 'nation' is indicative of the present crisis within Britain, in which traditions and customs are being destroyed by the process of social development. At the same time that traditions and customs are being destroyed in the name of 'progress', an ever deepening source of cultural meaning is sought through which this changing society can legitimate itself. In this situation 'tradition appears as an artifice, articulated not in particular or essential connection to people's experience, but at the generalised and diffused level of an overriding "national" identity' (1985, pp. 141–2). Thus, the nation is not so much a historical, geographical or political entity, in which the 'nation' to which he refers therefore would have an easy relation to the nation-state. Rather, it is 'a structuring of consciousness, a publicly instituted sense of identity which finds its support in a variety of experiences, and which is capable of colouring and making sense of others' (p. 142).

One of the most fundamental elements of this structuring of consciousness, Wright argues, is a historically shaped sense of the past, which provides the basis for a variety of other definitions of what is normal or appropriate. Thus while everyday life is characterized by 'a shared romantic orientation', which takes the form of an enthusiasm to embrace the past, closer historical attention 'will also reveal that very different versions and appropriations of the past will continue to emerge from different classes and groups' (1985, p. 25).

Wright discusses the possibility of alternative definitions of the past and alternative/oppositional senses of ˙history, in relation to the British labour movement as a whole. He takes, as an illustration of such alternative and oppositional versions of the past, the outrage Michael Foot, as leader of the Labour Party, provoked at the Cenotaph on Remembrance Day 1981, when he wore a green, untailored garment which was either a dufflecoat, with its early CND connotations, or a donkey jacket, resonant of sullen proletarianism. Many people, members of his own party included, felt this to be 'distinctly out of place on the back of the Leader of the Labour Party during the solemnities at the Cenotaph' (1985, p. 135). Foot was attacked by the media for representing 'a recalcitrant and perhaps even oppositional sense of history' (p. 142). Hence, Wright argues, we have to ask the question: 'What is this national past, and how does it bear on the critical expressions of history which come from within the labour movement?' (ibid.).

Wright also refers to the continuing tensions between the different 'nations' of Britain, but does not develop this point. Had he done so, he might well have found that hope need not always be 'the mother of fools' (1985, p. 27); for in Scotland, where the past has not been captured by either the authoritarian right or by the nostalgic left, there is the greatest hope of breaking out of the bell-jar which is Mrs Thatcher's Britain. Because the Scottish past has not been captured and transformed into 'history-that-is-over', it retains a potency that the English past does not have. In this way, then, it fulfils Wright's plea that 'while the earlier Marxist philosophy of history with its assumptions about the inevitable progress of the universal working class should certainly be discarded, there is continuing need for a theory of *possible* history which can be fought for in accordance with the political principles of socialism' (pp. 255–6).

Because competing national definitions of 'the nation' and the 'national heritage' are overlooked in both Hewison's and Wright's accounts, national differences, not just of history but also of historiography, do not feature in either. This is where their arguments are limiting. There is, however, a much more fundamental weakness in Hewison's argument which stems from his failure to see history itself as problematic. A historian by training, he nevertheless sees history as ultimately beyond refute. It is, for him, the final arbitrator, the sword that separates truth from deceit, fact from fiction, appearance from reality. History represents 'our true past' (1987, p. 10), from which we are becoming increasingly separated by the smoke-screen of the heritage industry. While he is worried about the political and ideological (as well as the economic) implications of heritage, history remains essentially unproblematic. It is history, he argues, which will be the Saviour who comes to redeem and release Britain from the menace of heritage: 'we need history, not heritage' (p. 146).

Wright, on the other hand, drawing his inspiration from his reading of the Hungarian philosopher Agnes Heller, is much more cautious about seeing history and heritage in such black and white terms. History for Wright is, as we have seen, extremely problematic, because capturing history is one of the ways in which an elite tries to achieve hegemony. This is precisely what Mrs Thatcher and her government have done. But while they have been successful in projecting the 'unitary image of a privileged national identity which has been raised to the level of exclusive and normative essence' (1985, p. 255), there exists, Wright argues, at the level of everyday life, an expression and recognition of heterogeneity which has the potential to challenge the dominant hegemony. The limitation of Wright's argument, however, is that he ignores Scotland, the very place where this challenge is most likely to come from.

Both Wright and Hewison, then, are united in their concern with the ways in which the heritage industry is stifling the past, keeping its critical power safely within a vacuum. They beg to differ, however, in their suggested ways of escaping from the bell-jar. For Hewison it is history, 'the fierce spirit of renewal' (1987, p. 146), which will shatter the jar. For Wright it is 'a theory of possible history which can be fought for in accordance with the political principles of socialism' (1985, pp. 255–6) If they had removed their Anglo-British spectacles and looked northwards, both might have come up with rather different answers.

Historiography and Scottish heritage

Had Wright and Hewison read the writing on the wall, three things might have made them decide to modify their answers. To understand the first we have to go back to the Scottish Enlightenment. It is a legacy of the Scottish Enlightenment that there is no such thing as Scottish History, but that rather there is a *variety* of Scottish histories, with many focal points and many different perspectives. The parallel here is not with England, but with France where, Neal Ascherson (1988) reminds us, it is taken for granted that French history will be different, depending on whether it is told by a Communist, a Catholic monarchist, or by a middle-of-the-road Republican. This is emphatically not 'Druidic' (that is, English) thinking, because south of the Border 'there is still an assumption that "our" history can only have one focal point, one perspective' (p. 153).

Secondly, not only is Scottish history characterized by a multiplicity of perspectives, but these perspectives are not ordered or enforced by time. As Ascherson (1988) again argues,

> 'It isn't an insult to the enormous pioneering work of historians here in the last forty years to suggest that the public perception of time remains chaotic. Time is not generally used to enforce perspective, and instead there is a scrapbook of highly coloured, often bloody scenes or tableaux whose relation to one another is obscure. (p. 154)

The result is that there is no single venerated and idealized 'Scottish Past' which stands firmly behind the present as something which is essentially over. There is instead a plethora of living histories which are in competition.

It is, however, the third point which questions one of the fundamental themes of both Hewison's and Wright's analyses. This is the suggestion that, in Scotland, history may not have deteriorated into 'heritage', with all its commercial, ideological and, indeed, political implications. Because there is no single Scottish historiography, because there is no sense of a historical continuum transforming a living present into a dead past, there is a sense in which this Scottish past remains relatively open and unfinished.

This need not have been the case, however. Indeed, if Walter Scott had had his way, the Scottish past would long since have been neatly sewn up. As Nairn (1975) argues, Scott 'said nothing about "modern" Scotland. But he did show us what to do with our past. And in the context of nineteenth and early twentieth century social development in Europe, this was a most important thing to do' (p. 14). What did Scott tell the Scots to do with their past, and why was it so important? Marinell Ash (1980) suggests some answers. The key to Ash's critique and to the importance of Scott himself is contained in the following paragraph:

> The Romantic revolution in historical writing was born of Sir Walter Scott and Scotland. The man and the place combined a blend of past and present, uncertainties and assumptions, physical realities and philosophical ideals . . . Scott's historical legacy was both personally unique and yet representative of the changing experience of his country, compounded as it was of the tensions and contradictions of a traditional Scotland merging into a great world empire. (p. 13)

Ash argues that Scott created a picture of the past in his novels and poems which was highly romantic and fictitious, inspired largely by his childhood spent on his grandfather's country farm at Sandyknowe near Smailholm in Roxburghshire, and his early exposure to the oral historical tradition of the Borders. Nineteenth-century historians took Scott's highly romanticized vision of the past and attempted to re-create similar pictures of the past through the recovery and study of historical documents and records. Scott did not just condone this activity; he actively encouraged it. By 1870 most of Scott's historical crusaders, the would-be founding fathers of Scottish historiography, were dead. They left a legacy but no heirs to inherit it.

The point about the Scottish past having an open and unfinished quality is the most important, and Ash's critique is again perceptive. She points to a connection between the death of Scottish history as an academic discipline and a corresponding change in the middle of the nineteenth century from a distinctively Scottish society to one with a British or even imperial outlook. Scottish history had no place in this imperial/British future and was simply tossed aside.

> The Scots were a practical and utilitarian people – or at least thought they were, despite their propensity for tearing one another apart over matters of principle. The spirit of Scott's historical revolution was deeply utilitarian and initially his revolution fulfilled a national need. But when his conception of history was no longer useful to the Scots they abandoned it, speaking as usual in terms of liberation and freedom. The Reformation was freedom, the Union was freedom, the Disruption was freedom and the death of Scottish history was freedom. Perhaps. What was more certain is that by the 1870s Scottish history was no longer a national preoccupation except when it touched national pride. (1980, p. 150)

Scott's revolution, Ash argues, was thus destroyed by the elements of the living historical tradition of Scotland from which it sprang and of which he was the embodiment. Ultimately, then, her conclusion is pessimistic. Whilst Scott had aspired to create a historical consciousness with which all elements in Scottish society could identify, 'What the Scots grew and planted for themselves from Scott's plantation was a succession of historical kailyards' (p. 152). Such pessimism, I would argue, is uncalled for. The very fact of Scott's failure has turned out to be a blessing. It has meant that while the Border lairds have been able to commercialize the Scottish past, they have not been able to capture and conscript it. They have not been able to do to the Scottish past what the 'Druids' have done to the English past (Ascherson 1988, p. 146). The Scottish past remains alive, open and unfinished, not captured, tamed and neutered. It is colourful, chaotic, confused and dislocated, but this itself constitutes a source of energy, and it is this energy of an unfinished past which is its life force. At the very least it could provide a way out of the impasse which Britain has been in since 1979. For as Ascherson again reminds us, 'live Scottish history was to be feared. People might act upon it, imperilling the stable order of the present' (1988, p. 64).

Because the Druids have failed to capture and conscript the Scottish past into servility and senility, standing in the grounds of a Scottish stately home is in some ways a fundamentally different experience from doing the same thing south of the Border. In England, where there has been, as Hewison (1987) points out, no foreign invasion, civil war or revolution since the seventeenth century, stately homes, both great and small, represent 'a physical continuity' (p. 52) with the past. This clearly does not apply to Scotland. Instead of being a window through which one can look back at an unbroken and continuous past, the stately homes of Scotland form a prism through which we can look at 'the modern Scotland that has so strangely, almost miraculously, survived a thousand years of attacks from without and distress and decay within' (McLaren 1951, p. 22).

The key word here is 'modern'. The Scotland of 1990 remains firmly located within the *modern* age, not as Hewison would have us believe, somewhere in the postmodern. For as John Orr (1988) argues: 'The basic condition for the end of modernism cannot merely be a "post-industrial" age whatever that may entail. It must also be a post-nuclear age, a condition which always remains within the realm of hope but so far outside the realm of possibility' (p. 19).

In Hewison's memorable words, 'It never rains in a heritage magazine' (1987, p. 137). But as we stand on the terrace of an English country house, with its 'carefully-landscaped perspectives of barbered lawns and positioned trees', from which 'The eye is masterfully led down a vista of elements (this battle, that cabinet) chosen to combine with one another into a single artistic experience' (p. 153), the outlook is far from sunny, as the prospects of change seem uncertain. Despite recent political problems, the gas jar of Thatcherite/Tory hegemony still has its cork firmly intact.

However, from the terrace of the Scottish stately home, be it Drumlanrig, Bowhill or Traquair, we are aware that the cork is more likely to pop. For not only are the Scottish stately homes monuments to a nation which, however doggedly, has survived a thousand years of attacks from both within and without; they also remind us that this is a nation 'which has not only survived, but which looks forward to a new and still vigorous life' (McLaren 1951, p. 22).

Bibliography

Ascherson, N. 1988. *Games with Shadows*. Radius

Ash, M. 1980. *The Strange Death of Scottish History*. Ramsay Head Press.

Bowhill Guidebook 1981. Pilgrim Press Ltd

Fergusson, J. 1949. *Lowland Lairds*. Faber & Faber

Hewison, R. 1987. *The Heritage Industry: Britain in a Climate of Decline*. Methuen

McLaren, M. 1951. *The Scots*. Penguin

Nairn, T. 1975. 'Old Nationalism and New Nationalism' in G. Brown (ed.), *The Red Paper on Scotland*. EUSPB

Orr, J. 1988. 'Modernisms and Modernity: a Divided History' (unpublished paper, BSA Conference, Edinburgh)

Wiener, M. 1985. *English Culture and the Decline of the Industrial Spirit, 1850–1980*. Penguin

Wright, P. 1985. *On Living in an Old Country: the National Past in Contemporary Britain*. Verso

Part 3
State Restructuring and Peripheral Development

Chapter 9

Industrial Restructuring, Innovation Systems and the Regional State: South Wales in the 1990s

GARETH REES AND KEVIN MORGAN

Introduction

Even for the most optimistic of commentators, the 1990s promise an uncertain economic future for Britain. The decade of the 1980s ended much as it began, with sharp debate over the real condition of the British economy and, more particularly, over what constitutes the appropriate role of government in managing economic development. Ironically enough, then, over ten years of a neo-liberal regime, pledged to disengage the state from key areas of economic intervention, have served merely to generate new controversies over economic policy. Moreover, as the European Community moves — albeit erratically — towards increasing economic integration, and the competitive pressures on the British economy grow, it seems probable that these controversies will intensify.

A key element in these debates through the 1980s has been the vast amount of evidence which has accumulated to indicate that a central weakness of the British economy has been its poor capacity for innovation. In comparison with its competitor economies, it has lagged behind in the development of new products and production processes, especially in manufacturing; and it has thus failed to capitalize adequately on its managerial and other human resources. Freeman (1987) has argued that this, in turn, is attributable to Britain's characteristic 'national system of innovation', embodying both levels of investment in basic inputs such as research and development and vocational education and training, as well as the institutional mechanisms through which these inputs are exploited.

Accordingly, it is argued, for example, that British research and development has been dominated by military activity to the detriment of civilian applications, whilst the vocational education and training system is poorly adapted to the development of a technologically sophisticated labour force. The social and institutional forms of capital have developed in such a way that the relationships between industry and finance are essentially determined by considerations of short-term profitability, making strategic development difficult. Moreover, far from compensating for these shortcomings, state initiatives have focused upon a relatively small number of high-prestige projects and have failed to secure the diffusion of technological innovation throughout the economy as a whole.

Whatever the other achievements of the Thatcher decade, there is no indication that this system has been effectively overhauled. And the consequences of this failure have been especially acutely felt in the peripheral regions of 'outer Britain', where the down-swings of industrial decline have been, at best, only partially compensated by the roundabouts of economic regeneration. Certainly, there has been a dramatic resurgence of regional inequalities during the 1980s. And it is widely recognized that the south (and, in particular, the south-east) of England has been the principal beneficiary of the economic trajectory of Thatcherism, with the north, correspondingly, faring very much worse (for example, Massey 1988). Not without reason, then, has the 'north–south divide' once more become a commonplace of media discussion and political debate.

Moreover, it may be argued that the relative poverty of development in these 'northern' regions results from their characteristic insertion into the 'national system of innovation'. They are areas whose economies have traditionally been dominated by older industries — such as coalmining, metal manufacture and ship-building — whose record of innovation has been especially poor historically, and whose typical labour markets have constrained the local provision of vocational education and training. Moreover the decline of these traditional industries has been compensated only very partially by new forms of economic activity. Much of the latter, of course, has been concentrated into decidedly 'low-tech' sectors — such as certain of the consumer services — and has made only minimal demands on the provision of vocational education and training (for example, Hudson 1989).

However, one possible exception to this pattern of 'north–south' differentiation is provided by the Welsh experience of economic development during the 1980s. Although Wales has clearly been a 'problem region' of 'outer Britain' for much of the past half-century, the 1980s appear to have witnessed something of a turnround in its fortunes. Unemployment rates have fallen dramatically relative to other parts of Britain; inward investment has reached record levels, with a number of large-scale, high-prestige projects; and there has been substantial sectoral diversification, especially during the second part of the decade, as key manufacturing industries and financial and business services have grown strongly, particularly in south-east and north-east Wales. Indeed, as the trauma of the run-down of the coal and steel industries has faded, attention has shifted to what many commentators have come to see as a 'Welsh economic miracle', proclaiming the thorough-going modernization of the industrial structure.[1]

It is also striking that this 'economic miracle' has become popularly associated with the purportedly distinctive form of state intervention which has been practised in Wales during the decade, a distinctiveness which perhaps reached its height during Mr Peter Walker's tenure of the Welsh Office between 1987 and 1990. Indeed, it has even been suggested (not least by Mr Walker himself) that, whatever the failures of Thatcherism elsewhere, the more explicit state intervention embodied in 'Walkerism' has achieved remarkable improvements in the Welsh economic performance.

Irrespective of the influence of individual Secretaries of State, it is certainly the case that Wales has retained throughout the 1980s a significant institutional infrastructure of state economic management, through the Welsh Office, the Welsh Development Agency (WDA), the Development Board for Rural Wales (DBRW), the Land Authority for Wales (LAW) and so forth. This 'regional state' is clearly much more highly developed than in the English regions and, in the context of mainland Britain, bears comparison only with Scotland.[2] Moreover, in apparent contrast with the Scottish situation, after the intense conflicts of the earlier years of the decade, the relationships between central and local government, as well as with the organizations representing both employers and labour, have been relatively consensual and co-operative. They have been characterized by a residue of 1970s corporatism to a far greater extent than in other parts of Britain.[3] And this, of course, has served to reinforce the peculiarities of Welsh governance during the 1980s.

1　Those with a sceptical disposition may note that the terms of this analysis are remarkably similar to those used to describe the transformation of the Welsh economy which was held to have taken place by the 1960s (Rees and Lambert 1981).

2　The very special circumstances of Northern Ireland make comparisons extremely difficult.

3　It is difficult to produce systematic evidence in support of this argument. However, it has been put to us by a number of respondents, many of whom are from the trade unions and wider labour movement. These, of course, are groups generally held to have been excluded from the determination of economic policy under Thatcherism.

What this implies is that an analysis of this Welsh experience opens up important opportunities to explore some of the wider theoretical issues associated with any conceptualization of economic performance in terms of a 'national system of innovation'. In particular, it poses the question of the limits and potentialities of a *'regional* innovation system' and its capacity to generate characteristic forms of economic transformation within sub-national economies. In short, then, there is a sense in which Wales currently constitutes a 'critical example', in that it provides the most fertile conditions in Britain for the expression of such a 'regional innovation system'.

These concerns, in turn, are likely to have a significance which extends beyond the determination of Wales's economic performance during the 1990s. At one level, the notion of a 'regional system of innovation' provides — at least in principle — a much more convincing link between the promotion of economic regeneration and the decentralization of political control than was ever developed in the 1970s debate over devolution. Potentially, it allows the specification of the mechanisms by which devolved forms of government may bring about enhanced economic growth. Indeed, it is perhaps in this context that the full significance of the Labour Party's current proposals to decentralize industrial strategy lies. Moreover, of course, increasing integration within the European Community implies not only changes in the external relations between the member states, but also in their internal organization. Whilst a 'Europe of the regions' remains somewhat elusive, it is clear that fulfilling obligations to the citizens of all of the Community's regions constitutes a major dimension of the European project. And this may well entail a significant redistribution of power from the central state to sub-national levels.[4]

In what follows, we develop an initial exploration of these issues by reference to an empirical analysis of the patterns of economic change which have characterized, in particular, South Wales during the 1980s. Accordingly, in the next section we present an account of four key sectors of economic activity: coalmining; steel manufacturing; electronics; and financial and business services. This then provides the basis for a discussion of the role of the state in these developments and, more specifically, the functioning of a 'regional system of innovation'. In conclusion, we look forward to the 1990s and return to some of the more theoretical arguments raised here.

4   Williams *et al.* (1989) provide a general discussion of likely future patterns of development within the European Community.

The 'modernization' of the South Wales economy

The broad pattern of economic change through the 1980s in South Wales is rather well known. In brief, the region was especially hard hit during the economic crisis of the late 1970s and earlier 1980s, with massive job losses not only in the (then) public-sector steel industry, but also in private manufacturing (for example, George and Mainwaring 1988). Since then, however, despite the precipitous decline of the coal industry, unemployment has fallen to levels much closer to the British average. Inward investment has been running at record levels, with Wales 'capturing' some 20 per cent of the British annual total, whilst having only 5 per cent of the population. Moreover, this has included some very large 'prestige' projects such as the new Ford engine plant at Bridgend, the Bosch components factory at Miskin and the proposed development of a major British Airways servicing facility at Cardiff Airport. In addition, there has been considerable sectoral recomposition, as employment in financial and business services, other services and some manufacturing sectors — such as motor components — has expanded. All of this, then, is widely held to add up to a fundamental 'modernization' of the South Wales economy.

Further insight into the nature of these economic changes may be gained by a closer examination of some of the key industrial sectors involved. This emphasis upon sectoral analysis is especially significant, as the character of the economic transformation in South Wales is more often than not presented in terms of a shift from 'sunset' to 'sunrise' industries, from an economy dependent upon archaic, outmoded industries to one dominated by new, forward-looking forms of economic activity. The imagery which informs the public construction of this type of account is neatly captured in a recent WDA advertisement. Under the headline 'Brave New Wales', it contrasts a photograph of a splendid new, glass-and-concrete factory, with a line drawing of Scott's Pit Engine House (built around 1817), which — we are informed — has recently been restored as a museum. Thus, coalmining is consigned irredeemably to the past; whilst the future is identified with the 'high-tech' electronics or biotechnology (or whatever) which is housed inside the glass and concrete.

However, it is important to stress here that this conventional distinction between 'sunset' and 'sunrise' industries is *not* a helpful one in understanding the trajectories of regional change. In order to illustrate this, in what follows we examine in some detail two industries which are conventionally viewed as 'sunset' — coal and steel — and two which are perceived as 'sunrise' — electronics and financial services. As will become clear, this categorization obscures as much as it illuminates.

The demise of the South Wales coal industry

The 1980s have been a decade of continuous decline for the South Wales coalfield, especially in the years since the disastrous strike of 1984–5. Hence, in 1979–80, the coalfield produced 7.7 million tonnes of coal from thirty-six collieries, employing 26,400 people. A decade later (1988–9), output was some 4.5 million tonnes from eight collieries, employing some 5,500 (Wass and Mainwaring 1989). Currently (April 1990), there are only six working collieries (of which at least two are under threat) and employment has been reduced to less than 4,000.

However, these gloomy trends have been paralleled by astonishing rates of increase in labour productivity: in 1979–80, output per man shift was 1.4 tonnes; by the end of the decade this had risen to over 2 tonnes per man shift. Wass and Mainwaring (1989) report a 42.4 per cent increase in productivity between 1983–4 and 1987–8 alone. More importantly, they estimate that of this, 23.2 per cent is attributable to the closure of low-productivity pits; 2.5 per cent to the transfer of miners from low- to high-productivity pits; and 16.7 per cent to improvements in the collieries remaining in operation.

It is perhaps the latter which is most interesting. In the immediate aftermath of the 1984–5 strike, there was considerable investment in heavy-duty face equipment for the remaining faces in South Wales, although not in the computerized control systems — MINOS — necessary to deliver the full productivity potential of such investment in the longer term. Nevertheless, this yielded substantial productivity increases, doubtless reinforced by the effects of defeat in the strike on the remaining workforce. In particular, various amendments to the incentive payments scheme, the expanded use of subcontractors and some changes in job demarcations, all contributed to the productivity increase in the coalfield (Winterton 1989). However, as yet, British Coal has been unsuccessful in implementing thorough-going changes in patterns of shifts, the length of the working week and so forth, although it is attempting to use the Union of Democratic Mineworkers to do this in new mines, such as that proposed for Margam.

In many respects, therefore, the coal industry in South Wales (as more widely) has been undergoing a restructuring during the 1980s which parallels that of many manufacturing industries: investment in new technologies; the reorganization of production; new working practices, and so on. Moreover, it is clear that the central impetus to these changes derives from the imposition of a managerial regime which seeks directly to transmit market pressures into the internal organization of the industry. Indeed, the 1984–5 strike was a struggle over precisely this. Certainly, South Wales miners are now left in no doubt that they are in competition not only with alternative forms of fuel, but also with coal which can be imported from other parts of the world, and, of course, the privatization of British Coal's two principal customers, the electricity generation and steel industries, has greatly facilitated this development. Indeed, in addition to the coal already being landed at the Port Talbot steel plant, Milford Haven has been widely reported as a prospective deep-water harbour through which the electricity generation industry may be supplied.[5]

The end-result of all this, therefore, is that, despite the dramatic reorganization of the South Wales industry, the effects on profitability have been insufficient to secure the future of the coalfield. The British coal industry, in effect, is being rationalized into the central areas of the Midlands and Yorkshire. Moreover, the proposed privatization of the coal industry itself implies — at best — the survival of only marginal deep-mining activities in South Wales, although the profitable opencast operations are likely to continue to expand.

What should be clear, however, is that there is nothing inherent in the nature of coalmining which has made this decline inevitable; it is not a natural phenomenon like a sunset. Rather, it reflects the impacts of a particular set of contingencies and, most of all, the effects of British Coal's development strategy, which itself has been formulated within the parameters set by Thatcherite economic policy.

The steel industry: a phoenix from the ashes?

By the mid 1970s, steel-making in Wales appeared to be in a state of almost terminal crisis. It had come to symbolize the more general malaise of manufacturing industry, expressed in persistently low productivity, competitive failure and lack of profitability (Morgan 1983). Clearly, drastic remedial action was required. During the decade after 1974, the Welsh steel industry shed some 50,000 jobs. In addition to closures at Ebbw Vale and East Moors in Cardiff, the two major integrated plants in South Wales contributed substantially to this total; employment in Port Talbot fell from 13,000 to just over 4,500 and in Llanwern from 9,000 to some 4,000. However, by the end of the 1980s the future of the newly privatized BSC seemed assured,

5   General developments in the British coal industry in the aftermath of the 1984–5 strike are usefully reviewed in Gibbon and Bromley (1990).

with lower costs per tonne than its European and North American rivals and buoyant levels of profit. Moreover, the South Wales plants were making major contributions to this success. Indeed, up until now, it is the Ravenscraig plant's future which has appeared in jeopardy, with closure apparently avoided only by the mobilization of a formidable Scottish 'regional coalition'.

This remarkable recovery story in South Wales (as more generally) has been based upon more than simply shedding labour. In particular, there has been massive investment in new steel-making technology, especially the expansion of 'con-cast'; for example, £650 million has been invested in Port Talbot over the past decade and a further £75 million is planned up until the end of 1991. In addition, more 'flexible' working practices have been introduced. An emphasis upon 'total quality performance' has necessitated substantial work reorganization, with new quality control methods, the break-down of job demarcations, the expanded use of subcontracting and much greater attention to training and retraining. Bargaining has been decentralized, and productivity payments have become a key mechanism in implementing these 'flexible' work arrangements (Blyton 1989).

The industry has also made major investments in telecommunications technology, creating the kinds of networking systems — soon to be extended to western Europe — which enable the South Wales plants to respond effectively to the demands of its major customers, such as the motor-car companies. In short, it creates the potential for British Steel to act in the fashion of the so-called 'networked firm'. This is a form of industrial organization which is intermediate between traditional forms of market-based exchange between buyers and suppliers, on the one hand, and the hierarchies of full vertical integration, on the other. Rather, suppliers and users commit themselves to long-term, high-trust relationships or networks (Antonelli 1988). Clearly, these developments are scarcely consistent with the popular image of a 'smoke-stack' industry!

What is striking here is that the pattern of restructuring followed in the steel industry exhibits remarkable similarities with what has been done in coal: labour-shedding; substantial investment in new technology; the introduction of new working practices. However, in consequence of the radically different environments in which the two industries are operating, the *outcomes* in South Wales have been dramatically distinct.

Electronics and the 'high-tech' economy

No other sector has been so heavily targeted by politicians and the economic development professionals as the electronics industry. It has become the most potent emblem of Wales's 'high-tech' future: the veritable epitome of South Wales's economic 'sunrise' (Morgan 1987). It is, of course, true that, by British standards, the electronics industry has experienced substantial growth in Wales during the 1980s. Employment increased from 13,400 to 23,300 between 1978 and 1989, an increase of some 70 per cent in eleven years. By way of contrast, Greater London went through a staggering decline of 46 per cent in its electronics employment base over the same period.

However, for critics at least, it is the character of the jobs which have been created in electronics which is as significant as their absolute number. Certainly, developments during the later 1960s and 1970s gave rise to a persistent stereotype of the Welsh industry as one consisting of branch-plant operations and 'screwdriver' jobs. In fact, perhaps the most substantial empirical study of electronics plants in South Wales concluded that, whilst research and development activities were by no means wholly absent, the large majority of the workers in South Wales firms *were* semi-skilled and unskilled. Indeed, there were reports of major difficulties in recruiting professional and managerial employees (Morgan and Sayer 1988).

However, trends during the 1980s begin to suggest a more complex picture. All occupational categories have been growing at a much faster rate in Wales than in Britain as a whole. But if we take the professional engineer, scientist and technologist (PEST) category, one of the best indicators of higher value-added production, then the result would seem to suggest that Wales may be moving beyond the branch-plant stereotype. Hence, the PEST category grew by 393 per cent in Wales between 1978 and 1983 and by a further 127 per cent between 1983 and 1989. This compares with 45 per cent and 41 per cent respectively for Britain as a whole. A similar picture of differential growth emerges in the case of the manager category: between 1983 and 1989 managers increased by 99 per cent in Wales compared with 21 per cent in Britain as a whole (Morgan and Lawson 1990).

However, these emergent trends have to be set in context. Certainly they should not — as yet — be taken as indicating any radical break with the past employment situation in Welsh electronics. The impressive percentage growth of professional and managerial groups that we have noted has built upon an extremely low numerical base. And PESTs still account for a very small proportion of total electronics employment in Wales: in 1989, for example, they comprised only 5 per cent of the Welsh total, compared with 11.4 per cent in Scotland, 14.4 per cent in the south-east of England and 12.9 per cent in Britain as a whole. Moreover, whilst we know relatively little about the processes underpinning these shifts, it would appear that the geographical distribution of new professional and managerial jobs is highly uneven, with marked concentrations in those parts of South Wales away from the coalfield (cf. Morgan and Sayer 1988).

Even so, these recent trends in Wales do suggest that branch plants are no longer associated with routine assembly and production functions and operator occupations to the extent that they were in the past (Morgan and Lawson 1990). Nevertheless, even the Welsh electronics industry remains a somewhat flawed embodiment of the 'sunrise' economy.

Sectoral recomposition: the financial and business services

According to WDA estimates, the banking, insurance and finance sector employed over 65,000 in Wales in 1989, having risen from 50,000 in 1983. Moreover it is a target for future growth. In 1988, the WDA launched a Financial Services Initiative in south-east Wales, focused on Cardiff, aimed at stimulating further development. Indeed, it is clear that the financial services are held to generate the types of occupations suitable to the 'modernized' South Wales economy of the 1990s.

Whilst considerable growth had occurred earlier, the initiative is nevertheless timely. Financial services in general have been undergoing substantial restructuring, much of which has involved the growth of employment in so-called 'provincial centres' such as Cardiff. Some of this growth has been attributable to the straightforward expansion of existing local firms. Equally, however, many larger companies have been creating networks of branch offices in order to capitalize upon regional markets, whilst others have decentralized at least part of their operations away from the City of London, thus avoiding crippling office costs, high salary pressure and debilitating labour turnover (Leyshon, Thrift and Tommey 1989).

It is upon the latter two processes that the growth of Cardiff's financial services sector has been based; as Leyshon, Thrift and Tommey (1989) conclude:

> Despite the rapid growth in financial producer service employment in Cardiff especially between 1981 and 1984, the city still lacks any substantial base of local financial institutions. More than any other large sub-regional centre, financial and producer service employment growth in Cardiff has been dependent upon the expansion of multi-locational organisations. The paucity of local control over financial institutions is illustrated by the fact that even the Commercial Bank of Wales is owned by the Bank of Scotland. (p. 224)

In this context, then, it is instructive that the WDA has begun to emphasize the role which advanced telecommunications can play in allowing London-based firms to split their support functions from their core trading operations. Although the WDA refuses to concede the point, one of the things that has been happening in recent years is that large London institutions have been utilizing digital communications technology to create closely integrated, but spatially remote 'back offices' in the periphery, where the principal functions are based on routinized processing skills and corresponding occupational categories. Whilst this may be a relatively new feature of the South Wales economy, it is a well-established phenomenon in the Caribbean and the Irish Republic, both of which act as low-skill processing zones for US-based multinationals. In short, then, the much heralded 'distance-shrinking' potential of digital telecommunications can be used to reproduce spatial inequalities in new forms (Morgan 1990).

Clearly, considerations such as these cast some doubt upon the transformative effects of financial services growth on the employment structure of south-east Wales. Whilst professional and managerial occupations have certainly increased, as with services growth more generally, the types of jobs which *predominate* in the new financial institutions seem rather far removed from those predicted by proponents of 'post-industrial' or some other form of 'modernized' economy (Fielder, Rees and Rees 1990).

New labour market structures

The sectoral upheavals of the 1980s have also brought about the transformation of characteristic labour market structures and the consequent access of social groups to employment opportunities. Lovering (1990) provides a general model of this transformation, which he describes as an emergent 'labour market sandwich'. In these terms, then, the 'middle' is constituted by structured internal labour markets (ILMs). In part, these comprise traditional forms of ILM, which have been especially well developed, for example, in the public-sector and certain manufacturing industries, where career progression has been dependent primarily upon the acquisition of 'seniority'. Currently, however, these are both shrinking through de-industrialization and being transformed in the ways in which they operate, as individually based assessment comes to ration promotion. In addition, new forms of 'truncated' ILMs are developing in sectors which have not previously had them, as, for instance, in expanding services such as retailing and catering. The top layer of the 'sandwich' is made up of elite external labour markets (ELMs), especially for professional, managerial and scientific workers who are in relatively short supply. Such labour markets are national (or even international) in extent, and workers may be highly mobile within them, given easily transferable qualifications and previous work experience. Finally, the bottom layer is provided by secondary ELMs, in which routine, frequently low-wage jobs are filled from essentially highly localized labour pools. Clearly, these offer the most precarious and least rewarding forms of employment and may be taken up by highly disadvantaged social groups.

It is clear that South Wales, historically dominated by nationalized industries, has witnessed the sharp decline of traditional ILMs as a result of the sectoral shifts we have described. The coal and steel industries offered relatively good wages and, more significantly, a 'job for life' for those who wanted it (cf. Harris 1987). Equally, however, there is some evidence of the growth of new ILMs in industries such as retailing and catering, although given the overwhelming recruitment of women here, they are by no means a direct substitute (Fielder, Rees and Rees 1990). Moreover, of course, there are substantial numbers of workers who have been expelled from the labour force altogether (for example, Harris 1987; Wass and Mainwaring 1989).

Much less well understood are the ways in which the elite ELMs have been operating. As we have seen, there is some evidence in both electronics and financial services that professional and managerial occupations are expanding in South Wales. However, the impacts of these developments are clearly mediated by the relationships between recruitment into such occupations and patterns of geographical mobility (Savage 1988). Anecdotally at least, it would appear that for many individuals a professional or managerial post in South Wales is something to be endured as a part of a 'spiralist' career pattern. Whether the rising social costs of living in the south-east of England will change this remains to be seen. Nevertheless, this does suggest that the 'service class' in the region may be becoming less dependent on the public sector and possibly less Welsh in character too (cf. Rees and Lambert 1981).

However, it is clearly the secondary ELMs which now comprise the more substantial section of the South Wales labour market. Indeed, there is a sense in which what has been happening during the 1980s may be summarized as a switch from a regional economy dominated by traditional ILMs to one in which secondary ELMs provide the characteristic form of employment. This, in turn, is intimately interrelated with the changing significance of part-time and female employment. As we have seen, even in the so-called 'sunrise' industries, much of the employment is confined to routinized and relatively badly rewarded forms of activity, whilst the decline of the coal and steel industries has been shown to generate the growth of self-employment and subcontracting, but in highly precarious forms which are far removed from the rhetoric of the 'enterprise economy' (Fevre 1989; Rees and Thomas, forthcoming).

In short, then, different social groups in the region are experiencing the impacts of industrial change in contrasting ways. Indeed, there is some evidence of emergent patterns of both social and spatial polarization (Morris and Wilkinson 1989). Equally, the manifest changes in the economy of South Wales are the product of a variety of processes. Certainly, it is not clear that it is especially helpful to reduce this complexity to some neat conceptualization in terms of *either* an emergent 'post-Fordism' *or* a 'sunset' economy eking out an existence on the scraps of de-skilled production. Moreover, this complexity also suggests that simple accounts of the state's role are probably inappropriate too.

The central state, the regional state and innovation systems

The major thrust of central state policy under the New Right administrations of the 1980s has been to disengage, albeit with certain important exceptions, from the economy. This has been so despite the fact that the main elements of our national system of innovation (research and development, vocational education and training and so forth) are either woefully inadequate compared with the leading capitalist economies, or else they are misallocated. For example, over 50 per cent of all state expenditure in Britain on research and development (R and D) goes to the military; the civilian economy is thus very much the Cinderella. Moreover, private sector R and D is also extremely weak: for example, between 1967 and 1982, UK private expenditure on R and D increased by a meagre 0.9 per cent per annum, compared with nearly 10 per cent per annum in Japan and 6 per cent per annum in France and the Federal Republic of Germany. In fact, during the first half of the 1980s, Britain was the *only* country in the OECD where the proportion of national income devoted to R and D actually declined (OECD 1989).

Likewise, Britain's provision of vocational education and training has persistently been adversely compared with that in other countries. For example, recent studies have estimated that whilst some 30 per cent of West Germans leaving school at about sixteen years of age attain an intermediate certificate — with compulsory assessment in German, mathematics and a foreign language — only 12 per cent of British youngsters attain a comparable standard. Ninety-five per cent of Japanese eighteen-year-olds currently remain in full-time education, compared with only 32 per cent in Britain, whilst between 1979 and 1983 the number of apprentices recruited in Britain fell by a staggering 60 per cent (Rees *et al.* 1988).

Regional policy in a neo-liberal regime

Most significantly for present purposes, as we have suggested, the adverse impacts of this poorly developed national innovation system have been experienced especially sharply in the regions of the 'north'. It is here that competitive failures and the deindustrialization which they induce have been concentrated through the 1980s. Moreover, direct state intervention to compensate these imbalances in regional development has declined substantially overall through the decade. Regional policy expenditure has fallen from £1,558 million in 1978–9 to only £738 million in 1988–9, equivalent to a cut of 52 per cent in real terms over the decade. On the other hand, some of this may be offset by the fact that spending on urban policy has increased from £388 million in 1979–80 to £750 million in 1989–90, largely as a result of the expansion of the urban development corporations, arguably the least democratic form of urban renewal.

Regional policy, once a centre-piece of the political repertoire of 'One Nation' conservatism, has been the most dramatic cut so far in traditional forms of territorial management. That it has not been jettisoned completely represents something of a defeat for the New Right, because, initially at least, the Thatcher government, prodded by the West Midlands lobby, wished to dispense with it completely. However, two particular factors persuaded the goverment to change track. First, regional assistance from the British state was a *sine qua non* for access to European Community regional funds. Secondly, regional incentives were thought to be an important means by which to attract internationally mobile capital into Britain; and inward investment is perceived as one of the main methods for reindustrializing Britain.

What lies behind the government's more radical initiatives is an attempt to substitute a neo-liberal for a social-democratic developmental model. In particular, it has tried to stress the contribution which factors other than regional policy can play in regional development. For example, the 1983 White Paper on Regional Industrial Development stresses first and foremost that spatial imbalances must be corrected by 'the natural adjustment of labour markets', that is, through the payment of lower wages in loose labour markets than comparable work commands in tight ones. This conceptual framework, within which centralized wage bargaining is viewed as an impediment to 'natural adjustment', helps to explain why privatization and anti-trade union legislation both figure in a White Paper on regional policy, a development quite without precedent in the history of British regional policy (Morgan 1985).

Equally, the retreat from traditional methods of fostering more balanced regional development has not been compensated by the effects of the new forms of state intervention which *are* deemed consistent with the emergent neo-liberal regime. In particular, it is clear that those policies aimed at stimulating an 'enterprise economy' have had a markedly uneven impact. Certainly, there is by now considerable evidence to suggest that in terms of not only the number, but also the types of small business and self-employment, the 'north' has been significantly disadvantaged (Rees and Rees 1989; Rees and Thomas, forthcoming). In addition, it seems likely that the impact of the development of the Training and Enterprise Councils (TECs), embodying both the privatization and radical decentralization of the delivery of vocational training, will actually intensify pre-existing disparities between local areas in their capacity to foster training opportunities (Rees, 1990a).

The Welsh regional state

The question remains, however, of whether things have been significantly different in Wales. To what extent has Welsh institutional differentiation created a context within which a distinctive 'regional innovation system' has been able to flourish? Certainly, the *appearance* has been different. The Welsh Office and the WDA have been engaged in a sophisticated and remarkably successful process of 'image management', involving the careful manipulation of the media and the selective promotion of 'research' through private consultants.

This perhaps achieved its clearest expression in the 'cult of personality' which grew up around Mr Peter Walker, as the glowing tributes from a wide cross-section of Welsh society on the announcement of his retirement testified. In turn, Mr Walker's apotheosis depended to a considerable extent on a number of special policy initiatives — notably in the valleys of South Wales and in the north of Wales — which owe far more to careful packaging and presentation than to genuine innovation or increased public investment (Rees 1989; 1990b).

More substantively, however, it is also true that the 1980s have seen the development of an effective 'regional consensus' in Wales (cf. Rees and Lambert, 1981), embracing not only the Welsh Office and the WDA, but also the Wales CBI and — especially since 1987 — the Wales TUC. To some extent, then, this pro-growth coalition has been able to operate in a relatively autonomous 'regional space'. For example, it is instructive that the Welsh Office never 'sells' Wales abroad as a location where inward investing firms can set up in a *union-free* environment, which is precisely what London-based central government does. Rather, the Welsh Office stresses the *flexible* nature of unions in Wales (for example, single-union deals, no-strike clauses etc.) and the key role of the Wales TUC in securing *orderly* industrial relations. It is also clear that the Welsh regional state has been engaged in a more concerted and energetic courting of potential inward investors, embodying a more creative use of public investment than has been the case in Downing Street and Whitehall or in the English regions. What is interesting, however, is that currently even this limited autonomy of the regional state is under pressure. In particular, in line with central government priorities, the WDA has changed its mode of operation substantially, with nearly 50 per cent of its budget now deriving from internal sources (it is the foremost industrial landlord in Wales) and the 'privatization' of many of its functions.

Ultimately, therefore, it is difficult to see that the Welsh regional state has had other than rather marginal impacts upon the economic changes which have characterized South Wales during the 1980s. As we saw earlier, the much vaunted 'modernization' process has, in reality, been ambivalent in its effects. Moreover, whatever the peculiarites of the region's economic trajectory, they owe as much to the 'normal' processes of uneven development as to any state intervention. And in respect of the latter, the effects of centrally inspired and controlled policies have far outweighed those of specifically Welsh initiatives. Certainly, one looks in vain for evidence of major initiatives in areas such as R and D or vocational education and training, which would provide a basis for Welsh distinctiveness in terms of the innovation system. In short, then, South Wales's development during the 1980s was dependent — for good or ill — on Britain's *national* innovation system.

However, there are some indications that new priorities are emerging; and these have been stimulated by two rather separate factors. First, the WDA has been *forced* to set a higher premium on stimulating indigenous development, given the drastically reduced levels of central government support for regional development which we noted earlier. Certainly, the almost exclusive focus on inward investment has shifted considerably (although the Welsh Office continues to need the kind of political kudos conferred by major foreign investment 'catches'). Paradoxically, however, the second important influence on the WDA's strategy has come from inward investing companies themselves. It is now widely believed that major multinational companies are demanding far more of the regional infrastructure than was the case in the 1960s and 1970s. Among other things, they require higher technical skills, a supply base that can meet exacting specifications and a more advanced (that is, digital) telecommunications network.

It may be argued, then, that these new orientations are reflected in growing concerns within the regional state institutions in Wales to develop a more vigorous regional innovation system. And here, Europe's more robust industrial regions — for example, Baden-Württemberg in Germany, Rhône-Alpes in France and Emilia-Romagna in Italy — are now held to offer important exemplars. Clearly Wales has nowhere near the development potential of these regions; and this, of course, raises the vexed question of what can be transferred from an advanced region to a less favoured one. Nevertheless, it is instructive that an alliance was formed between Wales and Baden-Württemberg in March 1990, which included a commitment to promote economic co-operation, technology transfer, and to research, education and training links between the two regions (Cooke and Morgan 1990a). Whilst the outcome of this initiative remains to be seen, it is an indication of new strategic thinking within the Welsh regional state system.

In the development of a more vigorous regional innovation system, three dimensions are likely to be of critical importance: vocational education and training; technology transfer; and networking. Indeed, these are widely viewed as three of the core elements of the more advanced regional innovation systems in Europe, and there is some evidence of increasing regional state activity in Wales with respect to all of them.

Vocational education and training

In addition to expanding its own direct role in training, the WDA is showing an increasing interest in identifying and diffusing what it considers to be the best training practices in the region. In this context, the experience of establishing the Bosch plant at Miskin has been of particular significance. Certainly, the company has a high-profile corporate commitment to training and has been extremely active in developing new forms of linkages with local further education colleges, with the latter responding enthusiastically to Bosch's initiatives.

Clearly, however, the wider implications have yet to be fully worked through. It remains to be seen, for example, how far supplier firms and, indeed, other employers in the region are persuaded to adopt new training practices (Cooke and Morgan, 1990b). Moreover, the relationships between the WDA and the TECs have yet to be stabilized. And there may be tensions between the former's emphasis upon the implementation of particular forms of best practice and the latter's dependence — not least for their funding — on the responses of employers, who historically have been loath to make long-term investment in training provision.[6] Nevertheless it is clear that vocational education and training has achieved a more prominent place in the policy agenda of the Welsh regional state than ever before.

Technology transfer

There are two dimensions to technology transfer activity: transfers from the public to the private sector; and transfers from firm to firm within the private sector. The WDA, in particular, is involved with the promotion of both, through the activities of its recently created Technology Marketing Division. More generally too, the significance of technology transfer mechanisms has been underlined through the alliance with Baden-Württemberg, where these mechanisms have played a significant role (Cooke and Morgan 1990a).

Clearly, it is too early to assess the efficacy of these initiatives as yet. However, past evidence suggests that Wales's performance in this area has been particularly poor, even relatively to British standards, which are themselves extremely low in international terms (George and Mainwaring 1988). Accordingly, it is extremely important that the institutions of the Welsh regional state should be addressing these issues at all.

Networking

This rather broad term covers a number of separate activities, two of which deserve to be mentioned here. Firstly, there is the promotion of closer buyer–supplier relations, in an attempt to exploit the trend towards more integrated supply chains, which has been argued to be of increasing importance in such industries as autos and electronics (Womack, Jones and Roos, 1990; Morgan, forthcoming). In this context, one of the key aims of the WDA's strategy is to promote sector-specific networks, in which buyers and suppliers

6　It is instructive that these tensions have been avoided in Scotland by combining the activities of what were the Scottish Development Agency and the Training Agency. It is not clear why this organizational solution was not adopted in Wales.

can forge longer-term partnerships. So far activity has been concentrated on the critical auto components sector and a new institutional forum has been created through which the major UK-based manufacturers can exchange information with firms in the Welsh components sector.

Secondly, there is the attempt to orchestrate the regional system as a whole, such that the stake-holders in the regional development process, public and private, co-ordinate their activities to a much greater degree than in the past. A regional networking strategy of this kind is similar to what is currently practised in some of Europe's more advanced industrial regions (Cooke and Morgan, 1990b). Perhaps significantly, it is also one of the key policy prescriptions in the Labour Party's emergent strategy for industrial development in Britain as a whole. However, the development of an appropriate institutional infrastructure is already being addressed by the WDA.

Once again, it is clearly too early to assess the significance of regional state initiatives in this area. Certainly, Welsh firms seeking to establish long-term supplier relationships with major inward investors will have to be prepared to make large-scale investments — direct and indirect — in order to meet quality, price and delivery criteria. Whilst in the development of wider regional networks, it will be no easy matter to import practices which have emerged in widely different institutional and political contexts. Nevertheless, once more it is instructive that such innovative strategies are on the agenda of the regional state at all.

Concluding remarks

Clearly, the emergent priorities which we have sketched betoken a regional state strategy which is highly ambitious. Equally, however, it is simply not possible to predict at this stage whether the strategy will be developed and implemented in a way which will substantially affect the trajectory of economic change in South Wales (and Wales more generally) during the coming decade. At the least, major obstacles remain to be overcome.

Amongst the principal of these is the very structure of the British state system itself. Comparative evidence suggests that the historical dominance of the national innovation system in Britain may be a *contingent* feature of the highly centralized state apparatus, a centralization which Thatcherism has intensified. Certainly, it appears that some of the most successful European regions (for example, Baden-Württemberg, Emilia-Romagna etc.) enjoy far greater elements of autonomy in their innovation systems than exist anywhere in Britain.

This suggests that a new *political* strategy is every bit as important as an economic programme, if the vision of a more robust regional innovation system is to materialize in Wales and Britain's peripheral regions more generally during the 1990s. Of course, there are *some* grounds for suggesting that the preconditions for the development of such a strategy are emerging. Certainly, for example, the limited opinion poll evidence which is available in Wales suggests that some of the unpopularity of Thatcherism is attributable precisely to its 'authoritarian centralism', with some polls revealing a majority in favour of a Welsh Assembly with substantial powers over public expenditure. It would also appear that part of the Labour Party's transformation has involved a rejection of the worst excesses of its 'social democratic centralism'. In this context, therefore, even a conceptual framework in terms of 'regional innovation systems' may assist in defining the desirable pattern for more decentralized forms of governance.

Ultimately, however, it is in a European context that judgements should be formed as to Wales's performance during the 1990s. What is clear is that with developments after 1992, the need to develop an effective regional innovation system will become even more pressing. As with the other parts of Britain, Wales's future through the 1990s will depend upon its capacity to respond to this challenge.

Bibliography

Antonelli, C. 1988. *New Information Technology and Industrial Change*. Kluwer (Amsterdam)

Blyton, P. 1989. 'Welsh Steel in a Changing UK and World Context', *Welsh Economic Review*, 2 (1)

Cooke, P. and K. Morgan 1990a. *Industry, Training and Technology Transfer: the Baden-Württemberg System in Perspective* (report to the Welsh Office)

Cooke, P. and K. Morgan 1990b. 'Learning through Networking: Regional Innovation and the Lessons of Baden-Württemberg' (Regional Industrial Report No. 5, UWCC)

Fevre, R. (1989). *Wales Is Closed.* Spokesman

Fielder, S., G. Rees, and T. Rees, 1990. 'Regional Restructuring, Services and Women's Employment: Labour Market Change in South Wales' (Project Paper 3, ESRC Research Initiative on the Determinants of Adult Training)

Freeman, C. 1987. *Technology Policy and Economic Performance*. Frances Pinter

George, K. and L. Mainwaring (eds.) 1988. *The Welsh Economy.* University of Wales Press

Gibbon, P. and S. Bromley 1990.' "From an Institution to a Business"? Changes in the British Coal Industry 1985-9', *Economy and Society*, 19 (1)

Harris, C. 1987. *Redundancy and Recession in South Wales.* Blackwell

Hudson, R. 1989. 'Labour-market Change and New Forms of Work in Older Industrial Regions: Maybe Flexibility for Some, but not Flexible Accumulation', *Society and Space*, 7 (1)

Leyshon, A., N. Thrift and C. Tommey 1989. 'The Rise of the Provincial Financial Centre', *Progress in Planning*, 13 (3)

Lovering, J. 1990. 'A Perfunctory Sort of Post-Fordism: Economic Restructuring and Labour Market Segmentation in Britain in the 1980s', *Work, Employment and Society* (Special Issue)

Massey, D. 1988. 'Uneven Development: Social Change and Spatial Divisions of Labour' in D. Massey and J. Allen (eds.), *Uneven Redevelopment: Cities and Regions in Transition.* Hodder and Stoughton

Morgan, K. 1983. 'Restructuring Steel: the Crisis of Labour and Locality in Britain', *International Journal of Urban and Regional Research*, 7 (2)

Morgan, K. 1985. 'Regional Regeneration in Britain: the Territorial Imperative and the Conservative State', *Political Studies*, 33 (4)

Morgan, K. 1987. 'High Technology Industry and Regional Development: for Wales, see Greater Boston?' in G. Day and G. Rees (eds.), *Contemporary Wales 1.* University of Wales Press

Morgan, K. 1990. 'Banking on a New Digital Infrastructure' (Regional Industrial Report, Note). UWCC

Morgan, K. (forthcoming): 'Competition and Collaboration in Electronics: What are the Prospects for Britain?' *Environment and Planning A*

Morgan, K. and G. Lawson 1990. 'Electronics Industry Sparks Skills Growth', *Western Mail*, 14 March

Morgan, K. and A. Sayer 1988. *Microcircuits of Capital: 'Sunrise' Industry and Uneven Development.* Polity Press

Morris, J. and B. Wilkinson 1989. *Divided Wales: Local Prosperity in the 1980s* (report prepared for HTV Wales, Cardiff Business School)

OECD 1989. *R and D, Production and Diffusion of Technology.* OECD

Rees, G. 1989. 'The State and the Transformation of a Region: Thatcherism in South Wales' in P. Ahleit and H. Francis (eds.), *Adult Education in Changing Industrial Regions.* Verlag Arbeiterbewegung und Gesellschaftswissenschaft (Marburg)

Rees, G. 1990a. 'The New Vocationalism and Local Economic

Development' (paper presented at symposium on 'Local Economic Restructuring', Queen's University, Belfast)

Rees, G. 1990b. 'A55 – Whose Opportunity? A Review of Government Strategy in North Wales' (report prepared for HTV Cymru/ Wales)

Rees, G. and J. Lambert 1981. 'Nationalism as Legitimation?' in M. Harloe (ed.), *New Perspectives in Urban Change and Conflict*. Heinemann

Rees, G. and T. Rees 1989. 'The Enterprise Culture and Local Economic Development' (report to the Scottish Development Agency)

Rees, G. and M. Thomas (forthcoming). 'From Coalminers to Entrepreneurs?' in M. Cross and G. Payne (eds.), *Social Inequality and the Enterprise Culture*. Falmer

Rees, G., I. Tweedale, T. Rees and M. Read 1988. 'Adult Training Policy and Local Labour Markets', *British Journal of Education and Work*, 2 (1)

Savage, M. 1988. 'The Missing Link? The Relationship between Spatial Mobility and Social Mobility', *British Journal of Sociology*, 39 (4)

Wass, V. and L. Mainwaring 1989. 'Economic and Social Consequences of Rationalization in the South Wales Coal Industry' in G. Day and G. Rees (eds.), *Contemporary Wales 3*. University of Wales Press

Williams, K., J. Williams and C. Haslam 1989. *1992 — the Struggle for Europe*. Berg

Winterton, J. 1989. 'Technological Change and Flexibility in British Coal Mining' (paper presented at conference on 'A Flexible Future? Prospects for Employment in the 1990s', UWCC)

Womack, J., D. Jones and J. Roos 1990. *The Machine that Changed the World*. Macmillan

Chapter 10

The Political Economy of Regional Industrial Regeneration: The Welsh and Basque 'Models'*

JONATHAN MORRIS, PHILIP COOKE, GOIO ETXEBARRIA
AND ARANTXA RODRIGUES

Introduction

It is arguable that the role of institutions and institutional frameworks in regional and national industrial development has largely been ignored or at least badly underestimated in regional analysis over the past two decades. This is possibly a product of the 'global scenario' of analysis which started with the work of Hymer (1975), Massey (1984) and Frobel et al. (1980). The argument went crudely something like this: multinational capital dominates industrial organization at a global level, it is extremely footloose and it uses space to its competitive advantage by developing international divisions of labour. True, Massey amongst others argued that it would impact in differing ways upon different regions and would interact with existing social formations. Little attempt, however, has been made to understand the role of regional institutions. If multinational capital — and decision-making in Tokyo, Frankfurt or Detroit — set the agenda, then what was the purpose of studying such institutions? Surely such institutions were at best marginal in the global economic order and, as such, took on the part of 'bit players', largely unworthy of study?

The only groups in the UK which took the institutional framework seriously were metropolitan authorities such as Sheffield and the Greater London Council, and the experience of such bodies has largely reinforced the notion that the sub-national, or even national level, is fairly unimportant in framing local policies, given the power

* The original study of the Welsh and Basque economies was carried out with financial assistance from the British Council and Spanish Ministry of Education under the Acciones Integradas Programme.

of multinational capital. More recent research evidence (notably that in Best 1990 and Cooke and Morgan 1990), would suggest that there is more to the institutional framework than previous research might have suggested. Neglect of institutions may be understood in terms of the origin of much restructuring research in the UK or the USA, where national policies have essentially been strongly neo-liberal in an economic sense, certainly for the past decade but generally for longer. Thus foreign multinational capital has been welcomed on a *laissez-faire* basis, and monopolies and mergers policy has been framed mainly according to 'market' rather than 'national interest' criteria. The position has been different in countries such as West Germany, France or Spain.

Most advanced economies have territorially based institutions responsible for economic development at a sub-state level. Development agencies, such as the Welsh Development Agency or SPRI in the Basque Country, are cases in point. However, development institutions also include industry associations, important in the Basque setting, or Chambers of Commerce, important in the West German case. These essentially act as power brokers at various levels.

The aim of this chapter is to highlight the very different models of industrial regeneration used by two development agencies in different countries, Wales and the Basque Country. Both operate within a context of declining older industry, but the different institutional frameworks and outcomes make the cases instructive.

Industrial restructuring in Wales and the Basque Country

Wales and the Basque Country display comparable profiles of industrial change (see Cooke *et al.* 1989; Etxebarria and Rodrigues 1989; Morris 1990). The Basque Country became the industrial powerhouse of Spain, with its three main industries being steel, shipbuilding and metal processing (for the automotive and other industries). In the 1970s, however, the Basque Country was hit much harder than the rest of Spain by economic recession, as the focus of industrial growth shifted to a Mediterranean triangle bounded by Barcelona, Madrid and Valencia. These three cities have been the recipients of considerable investment, often foreign, in the newer industries such as automotives, electronics and services. Barcelona, for example, has major investments from Seat (Volkswagen) and Nissan, while Ford have a major plant at Valencia (Etxebarria and Rodrigues 1989; Morris 1987a). Industrial decline and change in Wales has been well documented in a variety of articles, with the decline of steel and coal and the rise of new industries such as electronics, motor vehicle components and service industries. Foreign capital has become increasingly important in the first two of these sectors (Cooke 1987; Morgan and Sayer 1988; Morris 1990).

In both areas there has had to be a painful diversification from heavy industry. Competition from cheap producers in less developed countries and higher-quality producers in the advanced countries has had its effect in steel. They also have industries (coalmining, shipbuilding) which have been in structural decline in Europe for the larger part of the postwar era. Thus restructuring has been closely tied to strategies of rationalization and technological change. In the 1980s and 1990s, however, an extra dimension of 'flexibility' has been added. Different aspects of industrial 'flexibilization' include: a tendency towards vertical disintegration through subcontracting; a reduction of semi- and unskilled workers and an increase in professionals and contract workers; investment in flexible auto-mation; and a new appreciation of the importance of quality and customer satisfaction.

The role of regional institutions in restructuring

Wales

Wales has experienced major state involvement in its economic life during the postwar years, and the epithet 'nationalized region' was being employed at the turn of the 1980s in an attempt to express this. By the late 1970s the proportion of the working population employed by the state directly, approximately 40 per cent, was considerably higher than elsewhere in Great Britain. This excluded inward investors enticed by regional incentives, and hill farming which survived through EEC subsidy, plus the 14–15 per cent of the workforce unemployed in 1984. Some of this state-dependence was accounted for by industrial structure, with substantial employment in nationalized industries such as coal and steel, rail transport, power generation and other public utilities.

Awareness of structural imbalance in the Welsh economy dates from the interwar years, when some of the earliest state interventions were made to provide employment in consumer goods industries for unemployed coal miners: the Treforest industrial estate, for example, was one of the first to be opened. Advance factory building was also a major vehicle of state intervention in the postwar era. In the 1960s this process continued apace, although the proportion of new plant openings in development areas received by Wales fell from 36 per cent in the active phase of regional policy between 1945 and 1951 to 24 per cent in the next active phase between 1960 and 1971.

The current relevant institutional framework operating in Wales dates largely from the 1970s. It comprises three main actors, the Welsh Development Agency (WDA), the Development Board for Rural Wales (DBRW) and the Welsh Office, although other agents such as the EEC, BSC Industry and British Coal Enterprise also play roles. The WDA and DBRW are the key development agencies and thus merit attention.

The Welsh Development Agency   The WDA was set up in 1976 to further economic development in Wales, promote international competitiveness, maintain or safeguard employment, and help to improve the Welsh environment. The principal innovation was that the agency could use its own finances to make loans or purchase stock in private companies, and it could set up new companies which were subsequently expected to be sold to the private sector. It was not charged with performing an economic planning function for Wales, a position reiterated publicly in 1977. Moreover the WDA was keen to counter the image that it represented 'creeping nationalization', a fear which was present amongst industrialists in Wales, given the rhetoric surrounding its sister agency, the National Enterprise Board. Rather, it sought to present itself as 'a fairly adventurous merchant bank', 'an industrial property developer', and a 'major land reclaimer'. The relative success of this presentation is shown by the fact that the WDA became a corporate member of the Confederation of British Industry within three years of its establishment. The agency itself portrays itself as 'in effect the economic arm of the Secretary of State for Wales' (Waterstone 1989, p. 1).

Between 1976 and 1981 the Welsh economy experienced a loss of 110,000 jobs in the primary and secondary sectors. The major response was a massive factory-building programme. At the height of the economic crisis £48 million of additional government aid was made available to the WDA for this purpose. It was claimed that by 1981 11,000 jobs had been helped into being. However, some of these were in buildings which pre-existed the WDA's formation. The number of jobs in new WDA factories in 1981 was 5,125, a more accurate measure of the achievements of the WDA's job-generation arm. Retrospectively, senior agency representatives have since cast doubt on this policy. As David Waterstone, current Chief Executive of the WDA, recently admitted,

> This was a fair achievement in terms of the management of the building process but the extent to which it was achieving results must be

questioned. By 1983, the Agency would admit to having something like 16% of its factory space vacant though in fact the figure was probably nearer 26%. (Waterstone 1989, p. 2)

In the 1980s the WDA has moved somewhat from being a 'state enterprise' form of agency, drawing its funds from the public sector, towards a more strongly 'entrepreneurial' style of activity. In 1982 £1 million (subsequently increased to £2 million) was placed in a new risk capital fund. This was set up expressly to supply investment capital to new-technology ventures and small businesses. The WDA changed direction somewhat, proposing to increase its investment activities. Hitherto, its property development programme had made the agency possibly the largest general property developer in Western Europe. Further diversification followed with the Financial Services Initiative in the late 1980s which led to overseas and City of London finance houses opening up 'back offices' in Cardiff and Newport.

In early 1985 it had been announced that the WDA was to collaborate with the Commercial Bank of Wales to establish a pension fund which would act as a source of industrial investment capital. This was a response to the Welsh Secretary of State's criticism of the City of London for stifling the prospects of industry in Wales through its unwillingness to stimulate investment in areas perceived to be 'remote' from its normal sphere of influence. The WDA also entered agreements with a small number of private pension funds and insurance companies to finance both property development and investment schemes.

A move away from building standardized advance factories towards the provision of a smaller number of 'bespoke' premises for known high-technology companies was accompanied by the establishment of two new bodies – WINvest (in April 1982) and WINtech (in May 1984). The former arose from the need, expressed by the House of Commons Select Committee on Expenditure in 1978, to overcome what was seen as confusion and waste caused by the proliferation of agencies engaged in attracting industry to Wales. WINvest co-ordinated the inward investment roles of the WDA and the Welsh Office Industry Department, rather as 'Locate in Scotland' did for the Scottish Development Agency. WINtech, by contrast, was a technology-transfer organization, linking industry with sources of scientific and technological expertise in universities and other centres of scientific research.

Neither of the two new bodies survived the 1980s. WINtech was unwound in 1989. Its functions were split four ways into inward investment, technology marketing, university liaison and a technology growth fund. WINtech's weakness lay in having to spread its limited expertise too thinly with insufficient technical or financial resources. WINvest, too, has now disappeared, transformed in 1989 into Welsh Development International. This organization has its own management board (including former directors of Shell and ICI) which reports direct to the chairman of the WDA and is charged with selling Wales in a more positive, integrated way than its predecessor did. The WDA's new physical planning role as an urban renewal agency is part of the more integrated package now being presented.

Despite these changes there has been employment growth, especially in electronics-related activity since the WDA was established. Moreover, the claim of the Secretary of State for Wales, echoed by the Press, is that in the two years 1982/3 and 1983/4, Wales was highly successful in winning around 25 per cent of all mobile investment projects in the United Kingdom. In the late 1980s the figure remained high at approximately 20 per cent.

New investment on this scale during a severe recession, and after the reductions in regional aid brought about by the redrawing of the Assisted Area map in 1979–82, suggests that the WDA is a reasonably effective means of augmenting inward investment. It also suggests that, with the erosion of Assisted Area status after 1984, the co-ordination and forward planning embodied in the WDA's Corporate Plan 1984–90, allied with a predictable level of government funding (set at £50 million per annum 1984/5 to 1986/7), have proved capable of sustaining private-sector interest. By 1988/9 the WDA's level of funding was £115 million per annum, of which 52 per cent was generated from private sources (including retained WDA profits). In 1989 the possibility was seriously raised that the WDA would become a private corporation, though thus far this has been denied. Perhaps public–private partnerships, as in the Welsh Venture Capital Fund or in property development, are now the more likely future trajectory, given the continuing difficulties in attracting solely private development capital from major financial centres such as the City of London.

The Development Board for Rural Wales   The DBRW, the second major institutional arm, was also established in 1976. The board is strongly geared towards factory provision, its 207 factories in 1982 providing '6,000 job opportunities', although the true figure lies somewhere between 1,000 and 6,000 jobs in these factories. Moreover, given the attractiveness of eastern Mid Wales, which is relatively close to the West Midlands, and the new town (at Newtown), a focus of the Board's 'mini-growth pole' policy, the impact of the DBRW's activities tends to be geographically concentrated, particularly in the Severn valley. This has been the subject of considerable criticism and has led the DBRW to pursue a more diffuse strategy, based on encouraging indigenous potential by providing more small factories and workshops often in relatively small village settings.

Besides the WDA and DBRW, the other main industrial policy actor is the Welsh Office. For example, inward investment is dealt with administratively and financially (grants etc.) by the Welsh Office, though it is increasingly procured by the WDA. The most important element of the grant package is Regional Selective Assistance (RSA). Hill (1989) has shown that inward investors are major beneficiaries of such assistance; between 1983 and 1987, for example, the share of RSA assistance going to foreign-owned firms averaged 47 per cent. This does not imply, however, that the indigenous sector has claimed the rest. A Wales TUC (1985) study concluded that the majority of the remainder was going to inward investors from elsewhere in the UK.

The major thrust of the Welsh 'model', at least until relatively recently, has been to concentrate on attracting inward investment projects. Allied to this has been a shift to a far more entrepreneurial mode. However, it is worth noting that the WDA has recently shifted its emphasis to the small firm sector, pointing amongst other things to the financial priority it gives to small and medium enterprises (SMEs), and the likely decline in inward investment to Wales, given the liberalization of eastern Europe (Waterstone 1989).

The Basque Country

In 1979 the Basque Country received limited self-government from the Spanish state. By contrast, in the same year the Welsh people voted decisively against being given fewer autonomous powers than the Basques were ultimately to receive. Key powers were the right to make laws and the right to raise income tax. Uniquely in the Spanish state's devolution exercise, the Basque country had these powers confirmed. Even the Catalan government, presiding over the stronger local economy and culture, lacks the powers to determine the size and nature of its own budget.

One of the most striking features of the government's concern for the problems of the Basque economy is the existence of not one but three separate ministries dealing with economic affairs. These are the Ministry of Economic Planning and Studies, the Ministry of Industry and Commerce and the Ministry of Budget.

In interview, the Minister for Economic and Planning Studies, Sra. Milagros Garcia Crespo, pointed out that the Basque Country has some of the worst unemployment figures in Europe, as can be seen in table 10.1 (Cooke *et al.* 1989). The ministry's task is to ensure that the plan for economic recovery is constantly updated in the light of changing circumstances by the interpretation of accurate and up-to-date statistical analyses of the Basque economy. One of their findings is that some 20 per cent of Basque gross domestic product is actually directly controlled by the government through its own investment in the public sector in the form of employment and expenditure on education, health and so forth. Thus the policies of the government can be tailored in such a way that local purchasing and employment favours those firms and individuals located in the Basque Country.

Table 10.1 Selected unemployment rates, 1984

	Total	Female	Youth (14–24)
Basque Country	22.3	27.4	54.1
Spain	20.3	22.7	46.2
Ireland	16.5	17.5	23.5
Belgium	11.9	18.3	25.2
Italy	9.8	16.0	32.4
UK	10.9	10.0	19.1
Wales	16.7	11.4	24.2

Source: Eurostat Panorama, 1987

Regular analysis of the nature of the Basque economy using input–output analysis has shown that the economy is a very open one, with indigenous consumption of Basque output measuring only 34 per cent of the total, compared to 60 per cent in Spain and 40 per cent in the EC as a whole. This is because of the Basque Country's traditional concentration on steel making, metal processing and shipbuilding, all requiring imports and resulting in high levels of exports. The crises of all these industries required special measures, some of which the Basque government was able to implement, though the Spanish government also has policies and greater resources to deploy. For example, Madrid has its own retraining programmes which operate in the area, but tend to relate to workers from large-scale industry, while the Basque government's strategy tends to apply smaller, innovative enterprises.

The small-business growth strategy   Because of the historic structure of the Basque economy, concentrated into very large corporations in declining heavy industry, the policy has been to leave assistance to such industry to the banks and the Spanish state, since otherwise the whole Basque annual budget of £1.5 billion could easily be swallowed up in just bailing out the steel industry. The focus has thus been upon small and medium-sized enterprises (SMEs). The main policies are directed at assistance in training, business advice and financial help to firms

Because of the openness of the economy, some 80 per cent of SMEs (defined as companies employing less than 200 people) export their output. The main industries are in machine tools — where the Basque Country has 80 per cent of the industry in Spain — metal manufacturing, electronics and consumer goods (refrigerators, washing machines etc.). In machine tools, which is a specialism, 60 per cent of output is exported. The ministry has been able to help the industry to move up-market, so that now 55 per cent of production embodies computer technology. Workers made redundant as the industry itself becomes more automated have been retrained. A part of the Basque machine tool industry is co-operatively owned as part of the Mondragon complex at Elgoibar, and there retraining has resulted in minimal overall job losses.

The business advice activity has concentrated on technology transfer through a programme to raise the level of technology in indigenous enterprise (compare this with the Welsh Development Agency approach, which has been weak on technology transfer into Welsh firms but has encouraged it by backing overseas firms to come to Wales). Thus the ministry gives financial aid to innovation by financing — over a three year period — 60 per cent of additional wage costs, 40 per cent of the cost of machinery, and 30 per cent of the costs of research and development. In addition, it has established Regional Technology Centres where industry can improve knowledge and use of available equipment, while joint efforts are made at product development between the firm and the technology centre.

Lastly, there is a programme of technological diffusion based on demonstrating new technologies, providing educational courses and creating a technology database easily accessible to potential users. One innovatory idea for acquiring the knowledge to disseminate amongst local firms involves the provision of scholarships to between ten and twenty-five students a year to study abroad and report back on what is the state-of-the-art technology in the industry and country in which they are studying. This has been a cheap and successful policy. A further innovation, one which predates the Basque government but is funded by it in part, is the network of five R and D centres. These assist industry by testing and certifying R and D applications, as well as developing new ones. They also act as agents for firms seeking access to EC programmes such as BRITE and RACE. One such centre, LABEIN, is currently involved in eleven such projects.

The financial aid to local industry is made up of 10 per cent-plus subventions to firms, depending on their industrial specialism and number of employees, along with grants to reduce by up to 3.5 per cent the interest rate paid to banks for investment capital. All in all, the Industry and Commerce Ministry had in 1988 a budget of 15 million annually to spend on these projects and programmes.

SPRI: Sociedad para la Promocion y Reconversion Industrial SPRI is the Basque equivalent of the WDA in some senses, except that it is much more involved in technological innovation and less concerned with inward investment than the WDA or the Welsh Office. It is a company rather than a government agency, though it is 70 per cent funded by the Basque government. The other 30 per cent comes from six savings banks. Its objectives are to aid in the reconversion or restructuring of existing companies and to assist with the development of new companies.

SPRI also has a budget of £15 million annually. It channels funds from the Industry and Commerce Ministry for reconversion, and uses its own funds for developing new companies. SPRI has Financial Programmes and Special Programmes aimed at setting up, through credits, loans and grants, innovative new companies. It builds workshops, and has established sixteen estates over the last four years. In addition SPRI has designed three Business Innovation Centres in Bilbao, Donostia (San Sebastian) and Vitoria, and has established a subsidiary company to run a Science and Technology Park (on which an aerospace factory will be the centre-piece).

SPRI has a corporate strategy to develop indigenous companies as leading exporters. This involves, amongst other things, enabling companies to use micro-electronics technologies, providing Open Tech centres where people can get access to videos and computer libraries, developing telematics (information made available through new telecommunications technologies), assisting firms to install computer-aided design and manufacturing systems, and generally encouraging a more outward-looking perspective in a traditionally introspective small-firm culture. Plans for the immediate future include developing management and marketing skills in the Basque small-firm economy.

In considering differences between the Basque Country experience and that of Wales, three things are of importance. First, because of the financial autonomy enjoyed by the Basque government, economic development priorities can be set in a manner sensitive to national culture and economic history. Priorities can also be changed through democratically applied pressure from the various interests in Basque society. Secondly, because the Basque Country, like Wales, is a country with a high valuation on community, the ministries and SPRI can pursue a policy of seeking to secure a future for indigenous private and co-operative industry, in accordance with democratic targets embodied in the economic strategy. Finally, instead of seeking development and linkages with the outside world mainly by inviting the outside world to come and set up shop in an EC cheap-labour zone, the Basque government encourages its smaller enterprises to become innovative and competitive on a global scale. As a consequence, political self-determination is underpinned by a growing economic independence as jobs in newer enterprises take the place of many lost in traditional industry.

Regenerating the Basque and Welsh economies: case studies of policy impact.

The Basque machine-tool industry

The Basque Country's machine tool industry is concentrated in an 'industrial district' centred upon Elgoibar with outliers in Urola and Logrono in Guipuzcoa province. There are in all about eighty small firms employing 4,000 in this area, some of them, especially in the Debako group of the Mondragon co-operative, functioning as advanced flexible productive systems. This means that one enterprise will focus on one aspect of the production process, passing on semi-finished parts or assemblies to the next co-operative, which specializes in the following production stage. The Basque Country has 80 per cent of the Spanish machine tool industry, of which it exports 60 per cent. Basque government and development agency assistance has enabled the industry to move up-market so that some 55 per cent of products are in the advanced computer numerically-controlled segment of the market. There was a 23 per cent increase in exports between 1986 and 1987 and a further 13 per cent increase in the first half of 1988, bringing about £140 million into the local economy from overseas on an annual basis. The main export markets are the USA and West Germany, two of the toughest international nuts to crack. Without government and development agency assistance, it is doubtful whether this industry could have performed so well in a hostile competitive climate and with tariff barriers with Europe in decline. The Basque machine-tool 'industrial district' is a good example of the success of a public–private partnership in assisting a depressed region to become a serious international competitor.[1]

One of the key factors in the development of these small independent firms during the 1970s and 1980s has been the formation of groups of companies. Two of the major groups are the Debako Group and Fatronic Systems. Debako was formed in 1983 from a previous group of independent co-operatives, Danobat, plus four other independent co-operatives. In 1984 Debako established an R and D unit called IDEKO to service the group, a process significantly assisted by the Basque government and SPRI in particular. Fatronic Systems consists of twenty private firms in a flexible production network, serviced by Fatronic Systems itself and Fatronic R and D. This grouping was also strongly promoted by SPRI in its machine tool industry restructuring plan. Financial aid was provided in exchange for inter-firm collaboration. The strategy had two objectives. The first of these was to establish a group capable of producing flexible manufacturing systems (FMS); this meant integrating different technical activities and divisions of labour using the service of Teknika, one of the government-sponsored R and D laboratories, to design the product as well as the production process. The second objective of Fatronic Systems was to acquire know-how indirectly or through technology transfer for the design and use of FMS. Teknika again played a key role in this regard.

The Basque machine tool industry is, therefore, a good illustration of the 'Basque' model of industrial regeneration. Having spurned a policy of attracting inward investment, local agencies have concentrated upon regenerating existing sectors, through research and development assistance, technology transfer, general financial assistance and the promotion of industrial reorganization.

The Welsh inward investment strategy

Unlike the Basque 'model', Wales has concentrated its strategy heavily on the attraction of mobile industrial capital, that is, on inward investment. While the WDA has maintained its commitment to small- and medium-sized enterprises, to technology transfer and to urban regeneration, the overall thrust of policy, including grant financing from the Welsh Office, has been towards companies wishing to locate in the region, either from elsewhere in the UK or from outside the UK.

By the late 1980s considerable success was being claimed for such a

---

1   For a longer description of the evolution of this industrial district, see Cooke (1990).

policy. By 1986/7 the Welsh share of the UK government's expenditure on Regional Preferential Assistance to industry was running at approximately 20 per cent, and in 1988 the Welsh share of inward investment jobs in Britain was 22 per cent (Hill 1989). The numbers employed in foreign-owned manufacturing companies in Wales actually increased between 1979 and 1988, against a backcloth of major overall manufacturing decline, and the percentage of Welsh manufacturing employment in foreign-owned companies consequently increased from 17.5 per cent to 24.9 per cent (Hill 1989).

The industrial sectors where inward investment predominated were electrical and electronic engineering and automotive components, and the majority of plants were US-owned. However, in the 1980s there has been a steady growth of investment from other sources, notably the EC and Japan, while investment from the US – measured by number of plants and employment – declined between 1981 and 1988.

Despite the success of the various institutions in Wales in attracting inward investment, there has been considerable disquiet as to the long-term implications of such an investment strategy. Typically, the impact of such investment has been characterized as producing large amounts of unskilled jobs, often filled by females, with little high-technology input through R and D and little impact on the local economy, as multipliers remain relatively low. The work of Morgan and Sayer (1988) and Morris (1987b) has shown this to be an oversimplification. There are a number of notable exceptions, with certain plants employing a large percentage of males, relatively high percentages of graduates and being relatively integrated into the local economy. Moreover in engineering there has been rapid growth of scientific, technical and professional grade jobs (EITB 1989). Overall, however, the stereotype probably applies, Wales is a low-wage peripheral country which has attracted a disproportionate amount of low-paid assembly jobs. This is, of course, a direct consequence of a *carte blanche* policy applied to inward investment.

Conclusion

The Basque and Welsh 'models' provide very different prescriptions for industrial regeneration in their countries. Thus in two fairly similar situations the key regional institutions have played a central role in shaping the form of industrial regeneration. In the former the relevant institutions have concentrated upon regenerating indigenous industry with financial or technical fixes allied to industrial reorganizations. The best illustration of this is the machine tool sector which has been revitalized to a level of competitiveness in the global market.

In Wales, by contrast, indigenous industry has largely been neglected, with the focus squarely placed upon the attraction of inward investment, which, it is argued, will introduce the new technologies and management practices needed to resuscitate the country's industry.

At a cursory level, the Basque model would be seen to have many advantages, as it maintains a degree of indigenous control and it ensures a level of technological development largely lacking in the Welsh case. However, the employment impact of the Basque case is not so persuasive. The Basque machine tool sector has actually lost employment in the reconversion process. This is set within a context of massive job loss in the country's two major industries — steel and shipbuilding — as a result of global changes in these industries, but also through policy changes, both from the central state in Spain and at an EC level. The inward investment strategy in Wales, by contrast, has resulted in a strengthening of the employment position in foreign-owned plants in Wales. Such comparisons are, perhaps, invidious, but unemployment rates in the Basque Country remain considerably above those of Wales. Perhaps the most ironic feature of recent developments is that they are on convergent policy paths. The opening up of eastern Europe to inward investment has placed a threat on Welsh capacity to attract it. This threat is comparable in effect to that suffered by the Basque economy from the activities of ETA. As the Basque development agencies were forced to make a virtue of necessity by going for an indigenous development programme, so the attentions of the WDA are increasingly being drawn towards SMEs in Wales as the prospects of large-scale inward investment recede into the distance.

Bibliography

Best, M. 1990. *The New Competition: Institutions of Industrial Restructuring*. Polity Press

Cooke, P. 1987. 'Wales' in P. Damesick and P. Woods (eds.), *Regional Problems, Problem Regions and Public Policy in the United Kingdom*. Clarendon Press

Cooke, P. 1990. 'From Spanish Armada to Flexible Specialisation' (paper presented to the International Sociological Association conference on 'Change and Quality Instead of Growth and Quantity', 5–9 May, Gilleleje, Denmark)

Cooke, P., G. Etxebarria, J. Morris and A. Rodrigues 1989.

Flexibility in the Periphery : Regional Restructuring in Wales and the Basque Country (Regional Industrial Research Report No. 3, UWCC)

Cooke, P. and K. Morgan, 1990. 'Learning through Networking: Regional Innovation and the Lessons of Baden-Württemberg' (Regional Industrial Report No. 5, UWCC)

EITB (Engineering Industry Training Board) 1989. *Economic Monitor,* No. 31 (November)

Etxebarria, G. and A. Rodrigues 1989. 'Industrial Change and Regional Restructuring Policy in the Basque Country' (paper presented at an ESRC symposium on 'Regulation, Innovation and Spatial Development', UWCC, September)

Frobel, F., J. Heinrich and O. Kraye 1980. *The New International Division of Labour.* Cambridge University Press

Hill, S. 1989, *An Analysis of Inward Investment* (report commissioned by BBC Wales, Cardiff Business School, UWCC)

Hymer, S. 1975. 'The Multinational Corporation and the Law of Uneven Development' in J. Bhagwati (ed.), *Economics and the World Order from the 1970's to the 1990's.* Macmillan (New York)

Massey, D. 1984. *Spatial Division of Labour: Social Structures and the Geography of Production.* Macmillan

Morgan, K. and A. Sayer 1988. *Microcircuits of Capital.* Polity

Morris, J. 1987a. *Japanese Manufacturing Investments in the EEC: the Effects of Integration* (report to DGI, EEC)

Morris, J. 1987b. 'Industrial Restructuring, Foreign Direct Investment of Uneven Development: the Case of Wales', *Environment and Planning A*, 19, pp. 205–24

Morris, J. 1990. 'Regional Profile: Wales' (paper presented to Regional Studies Association, 1988/9 Regional Review Panel)

Wales TUC 1985. *Employment Research: Progress Report of the Economic Committee.* Wales TUC

Waterstone, D. 1989. 'The Evolution of an Agency into a High Impact Force' (mimeo). Welsh Development Agency

Chapter 11

Restructuring the Periphery: State, Region and Locality in Northern Ireland

COLM RYAN AND LIAM O'DOWD

On the basis of evidence from Northern Ireland, this paper suggests that the state remains a crucial and integral element in economic restructuring particularly in peripheral regions. Furthermore, where ethnic-national divisions threaten the territorial integrity and legitimacy of the state, locality–state relationships are central to understanding the way in which the state manages economic and political change. This chapter draws on ongoing research into the political economy of Northern Ireland and on economic restructuring and state–locality relations in two urban centres: Craigavon and Newry.[1]

The centralization of state power

The scale of conflict over the state and the apparent political distinctiveness of Northern Ireland often obscure what the region shares with the rest of the UK. Firstly, it shares a common trend towards a centralization of state power. The trajectory of this centralization may have been somewhat different in Northern Ireland but the underlying pattern is clear. The process had its origins in the war effort between 1939 and 1945 and proceeded through the extension of the postwar welfare state. By the early 1960s, in common with other regions of the UK, the state formulated a more coherent regional strategy in encouraging multinational investment through

---

1 ESRC Research Grant: R000 23 1161, 'Local Responses to Industrial Change in Northern Ireland'.

infrastructural planning and state subsidies (O'Dowd *et al.* 1980; O'Dowd 1985).

The development of the welfare state since 1945 and the regional strategy of the 1960s were fundamentally to undermine the internal political status quo in Northern Ireland, however. The outbreak of the conflict did not disrupt the trend to centralization, in fact it accelerated it. The restructuring of local government including the removal of all major powers from local government, the abolition of Stormont and the imposition of Direct Rule under the aegis of a newly created Northern Ireland Office all contributed to the more centralized and bureaucratic management of the region.

Political and administrative centralization went hand in hand with major growth in the economic role of the state. The expansion of public-sector employment in the 1970s and the increasing reliance of the region's economy on public expenditure had rendered Northern Ireland a 'state-dependent' region by the early 1980s (O'Dowd 1986, 1989). The Thatcherite agenda of cutting back the role of the state limited further growth in public expenditure and state employment but did not reverse the overall state-dependency established in 1970s.

The increasing economic role of the state is also interwoven with the impact of global economic restructuring in Northern Ireland since 1945. It is, perhaps, misleading to designate Northern Ireland as either a 'core' or a 'peripheral' region of the United Kingdom. It contains elements of both — juxtaposing an advanced industrial economy with a relatively durable subsistence agriculture. Historically it has remained a low-wage region with high rates of female employment. Permanently a labour-surplus region, it has relatively high emigration and unemployment rates. These rates vary according to class, locality and communal affiliation within the region.

From the inception of Northern Ireland as a separate political unit in 1920 through to the 1960s, its manufacturing base in linen, shipbuilding and engineering had been in long-term relative decline. Production in this period was still largely under local control, but it was clear that local capitalists in general were failing to adapt to changing international markets, the end of empire, and the increasing dominance of multinational corporations.

From the outset the Northern Ireland government wished to diversify the industrial base of the province but its conservative *laissez-faire* ideology militated against state intervention to this end (Isles and Cuthbert 1957). Despite the reluctance of many of its supporters among local industrialists, it embraced the more active regional strategy established in the UK from the late 1950s onwards. The piecemeal attraction of external firms to Northern Ireland since

1945 now began to take place within a more formalized spatial strategy — the designation of growth centres, the new city in Craigavon, investment in industrial estates, roads, and harbour development. The strategy was much more heavily dependent on multinational investment than other UK regions — in this it was closer to the Irish Republic. The favourable climate of mobile international investment ushered in what Teague (1987) has termed the 'virtuous cycle' which ended in 1975.

In Northern Ireland terms, regional strategy was relatively successful in replacing jobs lost from the traditional manufacturing sector in the 1960s. Nevertheless regional unemployment remained the highest of all the UK regions, showing major variations within Northern Ireland across localities and the ethnic divide. Emigration also remained high, reaching a peak in the early 1970s (partly because of the political conflict). Although large numbers of new firms were established, there was little sectoral differentiation. Efforts to promote new high-technology industries had very limited success. Instead, the new firms remained relatively concentrated in traditional sectors: clothing and textiles, and engineering. Furthermore the internationalization of production left Northern Ireland's branch-plant economy even more vulnerable to international recession.

State economic strategy under Direct Rule

The mid 1970s saw the onset of prolonged global recession, deindustrialization and the restructuring of international capital. These factors, combined with the management of the political conflict in the province, profoundly altered the trajectory of the Northern Ireland economy, leaving it characterized by high unemployment and heavy dependence on the British state.

Dramatic contraction of manufacturing employment not only occurred in the remaining traditional industries but also in those which had located in the province since 1958. Conversely, there has been a major growth in service employment, especially in part-time jobs for women. Within the service sector, the state itself has assumed a crucial role as a direct employer. Public-sector employment in Northern Ireland has prevented major job loss and deterioration in unemployment rates. For example, employment in security services has become the major growth area for male employment in the province, while the expansion of employment in health, education and public administration has been a major source of (often part-time) employment for women.

Northern Ireland industry is also heavily subsidized by the British state. In 1987/8, direct per capita financial assistance in Northern Ireland industry was three times higher than in assisted areas of Scotland and seven times higher than in England. Compared with the average for all assisted areas in Britain, industrial assistance per capita in the province was almost five times higher. When account is taken of the levels of unemployment in the different areas of Britain, the degree of industrial assistance is greater still (NIEC 1990, pp. 16–17). Until very recently, only designated areas of Italy ranked above Northern Ireland within the EEC in terms of comparative levels of public expenditure on industrial development and the range of incentives available (NIEC 1990, p. 20).

Despite the level of state support for industry, the average duration of state-assisted jobs has fallen to between three and four years (NIEC 1985). Between 1982 and 1988 only 9,300 jobs assisted by the Industrial Development Board (IDB) were actually created (40 per cent of those claimed to have been 'promoted'). International investment from outside the British Isles accounted for only 1,200 of these jobs (NIEC 1990, p. 39). Most of the limited job creation came from expansions of indigenous firms and new local firms assisted by the Local Enterprise Development Unit (LEDU) — the region's other job-promotion body.

The overall result of state intervention and global economic restructuring has left Northern Ireland with an economy more dependent on the state than any other UK region (Rowthorn and Wayne 1988). Forty per cent of all employees are in the public sector. The provision of public and other services accounts for 36 per cent of GDP, compared with a United Kingdom average of 23 per cent. The combined effect of the different administrative arrangements in Northern Ireland, the greater incidence of public-sector housing and the exceptional demands of law-and-order provision means that per capita public expenditure is currently running at 42 per cent above that in Great Britain as a whole (NIEC 1989).

On one index of deindustrialization (loss of manufacturing employment) between 1973 and 1981, Northern Ireland ranked joint fourth of a total of ninety-six regions studied in the nine-member EEC (Wabe 1986). A further study of regions in the twelve-member EEC confirmed this poor employment performance for 1977–83. In this period, 20 per cent of manufacturing jobs were lost, compared to a loss of 3 per cent in the EEC periphery and 7.5 per cent in the EEC as a whole. Moreover the province lost 2 per cent of its total employment compared to a net gain of 7 per cent in the EEC periphery and 3 per cent in the EEC as a whole (Walker and Keeble 1987).

Walker and Keeble also found that Northern Ireland's unemployment rate was 70 per cent greater than the EEC average and 40 per cent greater than the EEC periphery. The current regional unemployment rate of 17 per cent is the highest in the UK, excluding the large numbers on state-sponsored training schemes. Long-term unemployment (three years or more) amongst males is currently much higher than in any other region of the United Kingdom (35.8 per cent, compared with a United Kingdom average of 23.9 per cent, and 23.5 per cent in the next-highest region — Scotland). Not surprisingly, social security benefits account for 19 per cent of total household income in Northern Ireland compared with 13 per cent in th United Kingdom (*Regional Trends* 1989).

Clearly then, any explanation of economic restructuring in Northern Ireland must take into account the central role of the state. Consideration of this role is even more urgent, given the fundamental conflict in Northern Ireland over the territorial integrity and legitimacy of the British state.

Explaining political and economic change

It is tempting to suggest, from a bird's-eye view of contemporary analyses of economic restructuring, that the role of the state has sunk without trace. It is as if the 1980s have rendered irrelevant those approaches which most emphasized the role of the state in the 1970s.[2] The neo-Marxist critique, for example, now seems much less compelling, given the failure of the crisis of the capitalist state to materialize. Moreover the political defeat of Keynesianism was accomplished not by the left but by the New Right.

In the 1980s analytical attention focused on 'production issues' — the restructuring of global production, industrial sectors and corporations. Discussions centred on 'regimes of accumulation' and on the long-waves and cycles of capitalist development.[3] In most of

2 In the 1960s and 1970s analyses of change in advanced capitalist studies devoted much attention to the role of the state. The still dominant Keynesian school and its many offshoots addressed the question of the state's managerial role with respect to the economy and social redistribution. The re-emerging neo-liberals were beginning to rearticulate their critique of the stultifying impact of the state's 'interference' with market forces. It was the neo-Marxists, however, who devoted most effort to developing a range of theories of the state. A whole literature developed around the instrumentalist approach of Milliband, the structuralism of Poulantzas, the legitimation theory of Habermas and Offe, the capital-logic approaches of the German school and Castell's work on the state as a reproducer of labour power.

3 For an excellent overview, see Martin (1989).

these analyses the national state was reduced to rather a shadowy presence. Nor was the state restored to its former place in the studies of the spatial effects of changing production practices and of the way in which the space economy operated. The focus was less on the state than on the rise and fall of regions and the changing urban and rural system. Advocates of regionalism and decentralization argued that transnational organizations, combined with the changing nature of capitalist production, would undermine the role of the nation-state.[4]

Empirical analyses of Northern Ireland recognized the degree to which the economy was supported by the British state but seldom linked this to an analysis of the way in which the same state institutionalized economic, political and cultural divisions within the province (O'Dowd 1989). Rowthorn and Wayne (1988) are exceptions but their main focus is the prospects of British withdrawal. Earlier analyses linking economic and political change in Northern Ireland also failed to deal adequately with the state. Hechter's (1975) application of dependency theory to the Celtic periphery failed to take sufficiently into account the impact of the state on the periphery of a metropolitan state — a factor which decisively distinguishes a metropolitan from a 'Third World' periphery. Likewise, the empirical evidence, on the economy at least, undermines Nairn's (1977) 'break-up of Britain' thesis, and in particular, his emphasis on an emergent Ulster Protestant nationalism.

In the 1980s, however, analyses of economic restructuring also turned to the locality as a counterpoint to the macro-scale analyses of economic restructuring. In Britain, from rather different starting-points, both major political parties stressed local economic development. Growing evidence of intra-regional differentiation and of the complex spatial manifestations of economic restructuring further encouraged locality studies. The latter were also seen as a means of examining in more detail the links between economic, political and cultural change and the capacity of local communities to influence the wider forces acting on them. The focus on the economic role of the central state, so important in the 1970s, became blurred.

In Northern Ireland, both policy and empirical research appeared to be focused on the options of the central state, especially through its newly created regional institutions, in mediating the impact of global economic restructuring. Although intra-regional differentiation was registered, localities were somewhat of a 'missing link' in the analysis. On the one hand, therefore, it seemed that Northern Ireland might prove a useful reminder of the continued importance of the central state on the 'periphery'. On the other hand, the general literature on

4   For an Irish example, see Kearney (1988).

economic restructuring as well as the experience of political conflict in Northern Ireland underlined the significance of locality and local consciousness.

State–locality relations and local consciousness

In undertaking our study of two (more accurately four)[5] Northern Ireland urban centres, we sought to develop a dynamic conceptualization of localities. Rather than see them as fixed demographic, physical and territorial entities, we saw locality formation as a dynamic process shaped by the interplay of the state, the international economy and local action. A locality can be constructed or reshaped in many ways. One example is the central state's redrawing of political and administrative boundaries. This was a major feature of state–locality relations in Northern Ireland since the mid-1960s. Similarly, as in Northern Ireland in the 1960s and 1970s, the state can sponsor multinational investment, infrastructural developments and public sector employment which can alter the social composition and spatial form of a locality.

Locality formation is complex and becomes fully visible only over an extended period of time. The particular type of interaction between the international economy, the state and local action varies over time and across localities. The local population forges a changing system of workplace and communal relationships linked in various ways to the state and the international economies. These relationships can affect the capacity of local communities to shape their own employment prospects.

Local collective consciousness is more highly developed in Northern Ireland than in Britain because of the intensity of inter-communal conflict. At one level, Northern Ireland is less a coherent region than a patchwork of interlocked Catholic and Protestant localities. The partition of Ireland had ensured that local boundaries

5   Craigavon is the result of a Stormont attempt to create a new city in the late 1960s as a counter-growth pole to Belfast. The plan was to link Lurgan and Portadown to form a linear city. The five miles between the two older centres were to be bridged by two new-build housing sectors and industrial zones. Only one of the housing sectors, Brownlow, was completed before development was abandoned. While Craigavon is officially recognized as an integrated city, its component parts (Lurgan, Portadown and Brownlow) have retained separate identites. Thus while our research was initially directed at two localities (Newry and Craigavon), the complex nature of Craigavon has forced us to take account of four.

had become proxies for national boundaries. In many parts of Northern Ireland even an occasional visitor is left in no doubt of the popular equation of local and national allegiance and of the degree to which local communities stake their claim to territory via marches, flags, arches, painted kerbstones and graffiti. Furthermore the history of the two decades of conflict had sharpened the sense of local consciousness. The province had threatened to disintegrate into its component parts with the emergence of 'no-go' areas, vigilante groups and a vast array of local community groups and tenants' organizations. The new regionalist structures under Direct Rule were a direct response to the local forces which had threatened to overwhelm the authority of the central state. The new arrangements had involved the removal of all major powers from local authorities in order to manage inter-communal conflict.

Inter-locality and locality–state relationships are contested in Northern Ireland to a degree unknown in Britain. The exchange of allegiance to the nation-state for citizenship rights continues to be problematical for locality–state relations in the province. Even the right to name localities, mentioned by Cooke (1989, p. 11) as one of the key attributes of sovereignty, is a major local issue in Northern Ireland.

Historically, the politics of exclusion, discrimination, national allegiance and communal segregation was expressed through more than seventy local authorities, many of which held power over housing, planning and education (Birrell and Murie 1980; Tomlinson 1980). Stormont's attempt to implement regional growth-centre strategy in the 1960s, although relatively successful in promoting jobs, greatly politicized locational decisions. It disrupted the power base of the unionist-dominated local authority system and simultaneously fuelled the emerging civil rights protests (O'Dowd *et al.* 1980).

The long-term outcome was twenty-six district council areas with exceedingly limited powers, the establishment of regional boards for health and social services and for education under the auspices of the relevant central government departments, with limited representation from local councillors and a single province-wide Housing Executive. With the suspension of Stormont in 1972 and the imposition of Direct Rule, the regional government began to act more as an arm of central government through the Northern Ireland Office. The Northern Ireland civil service expanded, further strengthening the process of centralization and bureaucratization.

In the postwar period, therefore, the steady progression of increasing central state control of Northern Ireland was influenced by a number of factors: the implementation of UK-wide welfare state measures, the pressure to rationalize local administration in order to facilitate multinational investment and economic modernization in the 1960s, and the attacks by the civil rights movement and the Northern Catholic minority on the system of patronage and political control exercised in the decentralized Stormont system. The new regionalist structures established under Direct Rule were a direct response to the localist forces which had threatened to overwhelm the authority of the central state.

However, given the flight of existing, and the low level of new, multinational enterprise and the government's opposition to direct state involvement in industry, there seems to be little alternative to its strategy of promoting small-scale indigenous enterprise at local level.[6] Yet the effectiveness of this strategy has been questioned in both Northern Ireland and Britain, especially in declining regions (Cooke 1989, p. 299; NIERC 1989, pp. 63–4).

The new strategy, directed at promoting local private enterprise and reducing state-dependency in localities, operates on an assumption that all localities possess an inherent entrepreneurial capacity that can be activated or reactivated given suitable conditions. In Northern Ireland, however, little account has been taken of the differential process of political, economic and social evolution across localities. Local consciousness and the capacity for local action (including economic development and political mobilization) shaped (and was shaped by) not only locality–state relationships but also the changing industrial base, the history of work, unemployment, workplace and inter-communal relationships within each locality.

Craigavon and Newry

Our current study of Newry and Craigavon is aimed at unpicking the linkages between economic restructuring, state economic strategy

6   LEDU (Local Economic Development Unit) is responsible for small business development in Northern Ireland — a regional organization with no direct parallel in Britain. Funded by the Department of Economic Development, it offers a range of advice and incentives to new and expanding firms with up to fifty employees. Since 1971, it claims to have spent £166 million in promoting 35,000 jobs (24,000 since 1981). Since 1983, in its Local Enterprise Programme, it has sought to involve local people in the economic regeneration of their own localities. It has spent £3 million encouraging people to establish up to thirty local enterprise centres throughout Northern Ireland providing business services to over 300 new business and involving 1,500 jobs (Viggers 1989).

and local action. While our selected areas can in no sense be considered representative of the diverse range of localities in Northern Ireland, they do offer contrasts in terms of their respective relationships to the state, their industrial histories and, ultimately, their capacity for local action in the face of current state policy.

The district council areas of Craigavon and Newry and Mourne had populations of 79,000 and 73,000 respectively in 1981. Craigavon's population was concentrated in three linked urban centres, Portadown (population 24,000), Lurgan (21,000) and Brownlow (11,000). Brownlow was built by the state in the 1960s and 1970s to link the other two long-established towns in an attempt to create a new regional city — Craigavon. Newry (population 20,000) is by far the biggest urban centre in its district council area. It quickly became clear from our research that each of the four urban areas retained a local identity in spite of being part of a wider local government unit.

Newry and Craigavon presented sharp political contrasts, the former predominantly Catholic and nationalist, the latter mainly Protestant and unionist, albeit with a large Catholic minority. In this sense, Craigavon was more representative of Northern Ireland as a whole. Newry, as a border nationalist town incorporated into Northern Ireland against the will of a local majority (Canavan 1989), was, along with Strabane, the only local authority to remain consistently in nationalist control under Stormont. Its nationalist politics were coloured by a strong local labourism. In contrast, Portadown and Lurgan, were historically unionist, with little labour influence on local politics. Both towns had strong political connections linking them to the Stormont regime.

Apart from Belfast and Derry, both areas are among the urban centres most affected by the conflict of the last twenty years. Newry was an early centre of the civil rights protests. Even though republicans have little formal political influence at local level, Newry has been the scene of several attacks on the security forces. Northern Ireland's communal divide is sharply expressed in Lurgan and Portadown, which rank as among the most segregated towns in Northern Ireland (Poole 1982), a segregation clearly reflected in the local borough council. At various periods since the 1960s, assassination, intimidation and discrimination have deepened sectarian divisions in the area.

Unemployment rates indicate most sharply, perhaps, the substantial differences in the economic fortunes of Newry and Craigavon. Throughout the three decades between 1950 and 1980, Newry's unemployment rate averaged 17.5 per cent, compared to 7.5 per cent for Northern Ireland as a whole. Craigavon's unemployment remained at or slightly under the Northern Ireland average throughout (although Lurgan has been affected by higher unemployment rates traditionally). In the 1980s Newry's average annual unemployment has been 27 per cent compared to 19 per cent in Northern Ireland as a whole and 18 per cent in Craigavon. Furthermore, throughout the twentieth century manufacturing employment in Craigavon has been proportionately larger than in Northern Ireland as a whole. In Newry it has been smaller than the regional average — a fact reflected today in Newry's heavier reliance on public service employment.

Both in terms of industrial structure and of unemployment experience, Craigavon reflected fairly closely the regional average (dominated by Belfast). Newry on the other hand, was closer to the experience in the western part of the region. In a sense, Newry was to Northern Ireland what Northern Ireland was to the rest of the UK — it was geographically peripheral, and it had a much higher unemployment average and a local economy, vulnerable to external forces, which failed to diversify.

Newry's twentieth-century history has been one of relative economic decline. Its economy has been marked by high unemployment, low wages and a dependence on declining or recession-prone industries such as linen, port and docks and construction industries. Historically its linen industry — centred on the Bessbrook Spinning Company — yielded largely female employment. The bulk of its non-manufacturing employment was dominated by its port-related activities and construction and by its role as a commercial and transport centre. Unlike Portadown and Lurgan, local employment was dominated by a relatively small number of mainly family-based concerns. By the 1980s the canal, railway links and port were closed, as were the linen mills and many of the small externally owned factories which had been set up in the town in the 1960s and 1970s.[7]

Newry's economy today remains heavily influenced by its history. Its adaptation to recent phases of economic restructuring and the growing economic centrality of the state has not altered its relative economic position within Northern Ireland. It remains one of the province's unemployment black spots with a small, if more stable, manufacturing base. By the 1980s it has become heavily dependent on public service employment and relies heavily on government training and work schemes.

Both Portadown and Lurgan suffered from the long-term decline of linen, although in each case there were compensating factors. In the

---

7   It is appropriate that one of the chapters in a recently published history of Newry is entitled 'Closure after closure' (Canavan 1989).

former, food and drink industries, carpets, engineering and canning replaced linen jobs. Portadown diversified even more successfully than Lurgan and also benefited from its position as a strong market town. In general, Lurgan has not performed as well as Portadown, with periodically high rates of mainly male unemployment (NIEC 1980, p. 85) and less durable employment in the large factories which supplanted the linen industry (*Belfast Telegraph*, 6 October 1958; *Newsletter*, 24 and 31 March 1975).

Our research to date suggests that of the four urban areas examined, Portadown stands out as the most economically successful. Its local labour market is buoyant,[8] it has managed to retain and diversify a relatively substantial manufacturing sector and it also has a strong retail and public services sector.

In contrast, the new area contiguous to Portadown, Brownlow, remains the poorest and most disadvantaged of the four areas, with mass unemployment and scarcely any locally based employment. Brownlow remains a collection of eighteen, largely public, housing estates, a reminder of the failure of the attempt to link Lurgan and Portadown into the integrated 'new city' of Craigavon.

The reasons for the differential local experience of economic restructuring are complex. What is clear, however, is that the legacy of previous capital investment and industrial history affects how each locality adapts to changing economic circumstances. In the case of the four localities being studied, however, the changing patterns of economic restructuring and state involvement since the 1960s do not seem to have altered the relative economic position of the three established towns — at least in so far as employment prospects and unemployment rates are concerned.

The four localities do bring out, however, the importance of local consciousness and of state–locality relationships in Northern Ireland. Local politics in Newry and Craigavon provide examples of contrasting attitudes, not just to the Northern Ireland/British state, but also to the role the state should play in improving the local economy.

Newry's nationalist and labourist politics reflect the mutual hostility between the town and Belfast administrations. Newry's anti-state politics was combined with recurrent campaigns to get state help to promote employment prospects locally. There was a strong local sense (which still survives) of the area being discriminated against in terms of government infrastructural and employment strategies. Newry gained relatively little from the phase of active regional strategy in the 1960s, for example, in stark contrast to Craigavon.

8 Interviews with local Job Market personnel.

Local coalitions involving business, trade union and professional interests frequently pressed for more active state involvement in the local economy but with relatively little success. The campaigning style of these coalitions, with popular fund-raising, unemployment marches and protests, approaches to Westminster and Dublin political parties as well as to Stormont, reflected the strength of local consciousness, but also its economic and poltical marginality within Northern Ireland.

Recent local employment initiatives in Newry have brought it into a more direct relationship with the regional state than heretofore. For example, the Newry and Mourne Enterprise Agency, the town's most enduring jobs promotion body, is heavily reliant on direct state funding and government work schemes such as 'Action for Community Employment' (for the adult unemployed). It also works closely with LEDU as an assessor and trainer of local small business and in advancing the government's policy of creating an 'enterprise culture'.

Craigavon provides an instructive contrast. Again the importance of local consciousness, as in Newry, is borne out, notably in the failure of the state to merge the identity of Lurgan and Portadown into the new city of Craigavon despite massive public expenditure and promotion. Unlike Newry, the dominant unionist politics of Portadown and Lurgan was basically suspicious of state intervention, even if they were militantly pro-unionist and therefore pro-Stormont. We have found little evidence of local coalitions overtly campaigning for local economic development.

Community activists in Brownlow have sought to add an employment campaign on to previous lobbying on housing and environmental issues but have been handicapped by the extent to which Brownlow is a recent state creation. A reassessment of managing the planning disaster in Brownlow has resulted in the Brownlow Initiative, a top-down attempt by government to mobilize local economic initiatives. However, the overwhelming state dependency of Brownlow, its lack of local resources and a coherent identity, the area's marginalization by Portadown and Lurgan, and the complexity of its administration by a plethora of government bodies mean that this project is operating in an area with perhaps the weakest entrepreneurial base in Northern Ireland.

We have also found little evidence of concerted local economic initiatives in Lurgan, perhaps because of the depth of divisions in a town split evenly between unionists and nationalists. The newly established New Enterprise Trust is making considerable efforts, however, to mobilize cross-communal support and to compete with Portadown for new industry and state resources (interviews).

Portadown's relative economic success seems to be linked in part to the successful efforts of a powerul business elite in the postwar period in attracting industry to the town prior to the initiation of a more formalized regional strategy in the 1960s. This elite was drawn from a large network of local industrial and commercial employers and loosely organised into a New Industries Council. It was influential enough in local and external political and economic circles to succeed in promoting substantial and durable inward investment. This was despite the fears of existing linen industrialists that such investment would increase competitiion for labour and force improved pay levels and working conditions locally.

These activities became more formalized from the 1960s when the Craigavon Development Commission, set up to initiate and manage the new city project, carried on the functions of the unofficial industrial promotion body. Although Craigavon has failed as an entity up to now, Portadown seems to have gained most in terms of employment from the new city initiative and the wider regional strategy surrounding it. In the 1980s, a Portadown-based Craigavon New Industries Council has re-emerged to take advantage of the government's local enterprise initiatives. However, in Portadown, as in Newry, the impact of such initiatives on local employment is vastly overshadowed by the importance of direct state employment — notably in health and social services and education.[9]

Overall, we have found little evidence of collective mobilization in the Craigavon area, unlike Newry. The lack of concerted local opposition to the long-drawn-out closure of the Goodyear plant between 1979 and 1983 illustrates this point.[10] This suggests that locality, class and sectarian divisions are not conducive to local mobilization. On the other hand, Portadown in particular

9   In 1981 the public sector accounted for 28 per cent of employees in employment in Newry and 20 per cent in Craigavon (compared to 22 per cent for Northern Ireland as a whole). The Southern Health and Social Services Board alone currently employs nearly 1,000 workers in Newry and Mourne, and nearly 2,000 in Craigavon. The largest manufacturing employer in Newry currently employs less than 300 workers, while the largest in Craigavon employs less than 900.

10   Goodyear was directed to Craigavon in 1967 at a cost of over £3.5 million to act as the industrial anchor of the new city project. It employed 850 when opened, and nearly 2,000 by 1977 and was by far the largest manufacturing employer in the area. From 1978 it began to experience difficulties, and between 1979 and 1983 its workforce was halved through redundancies despite substantial government assistance. It eventually closed in October 1983 with the loss of 770 remaining jobs.

demonstrates the effectiveness of elite lobbying when there are strong political and business links between a locality, the wider economy and the state.

Conclusions

The evidence presented in this paper clearly suggests the continuing importance of the state at both regional and locality level. Historically, the nature of the state's involvement in economic restructuring has altered from a *laissez-faire* stance to an active regional strategy to the recent emphasis on promoting local private enterprise. Current government strategy is heavily influenced by its attempt to negotiate the legacy of past policies. In fact the direct impact of local enterprise promotion appears relatively limited when juxtaposed with the fundamental importance of direct public-sector employment to Northern Ireland's economy.

Northern Ireland also demonstrates the key role the state plays in a declining peripheral region. Its problematic responses to global restructuring are interwoven with the nature of its management of localities. The form this management takes and its consequences depend not only on the state's economic power but also on inter- and intra-locality division.

At locality level, prospects for indigenous job creation are shaped by the past interaction of economic restructuring, state intervention and state–locality relations. The attempt to apply the UK-wide strategy of empowering local initiatives to Northern Ireland is proving problematical in practical terms. The aim of reducing state dependency and encouraging local private enterprise is limited by the continued preoccupation with exerting central control (i.e. regional) over a range of divisive and often disruptive local forces. The state seems unable to integrate its role as a major employer into a coherent territorial development strategy to combat local unemployment. If it were to do so explicitly, it would run the risk of exacerbating locality and community rivalry — a risk it has sought to minimize since 1972 by breaking the link between local authorities and real power over local resources.

Bibliography

Birrell, D. and A. Murie 1980. *Policy and Government in Northern Ireland: Lessons of Devolution*. Gill and Macmillan
Canavan, T. 1989. *Frontier Town: an Illustrated History of Newry*. Blackstaff Press
Cooke, P. (ed.) 1989. *Localities*. Unwin Hyman

Hechter, M. 1975. *Internal Colonialism*. Routledge & Kegan Paul

Isles, K. and N. Cuthbert 1957 *An Economic Survey of Northern Ireland*. HMSO (Belfast)

Kearney, R. 1988. *Across the Frontiers: Ireland in the 1990s*. Wolfhound Press

Martin, R. 1989. 'The Reorganisation of Regional Theory: Alternative Perspectives on the Changing Capitalist Space Economy', *Geoforum*, 20 (2)

Nairn, T. 1977. *The Break-up of Britain: Crisis and Neo-nationalism*. New Left Books

NIEC (Northern Ireland Economic Council) 1980. *Unemployment in Northern Ireland 1974–9*. NIEC (September)

NIEC 1985. *The Duration of Industrial Development Maintained Employment*. NIEC

NIEC 1989. *Economic Strategy: Overall Review*. NIEC

NIEC 1990. *The Industrial Development Board for Northern Ireland: Selective Financial Assistance and Economic Development Policy*. NIEC

NIERC (Northern Ireland Economic Research Centre) 1989. *Job Generation in Manufacturing Industry 1973-86: a Comparison of Northern Ireland with the Republic of Ireland and the English Midlands*. NIERC

O'Dowd, L. 1985. 'The Crisis of Regional Strategy: Ideology and the State in Northern Ireland' in G. Rees *et al.* (eds.), *Political Action and Social Identity: Class, Locality and Culture*. Macmillan

O'Dowd, L. 1986. 'Beyond Industrial Society' in P. Clancy *et al.* (eds.), *Ireland: a Sociological Profile*. Institute of Public Administration (Dublin)

O'Dowd, L. 1989. 'Ignoring the Communal Divide: the Implications for Social Research' in R. Jenkins (ed.), *Northern Ireland: Studies in Social and Economic Life*. Avebury

O'Dowd, L., B. Rolston and M. Tomlinson 1980. *Northern Ireland: between Civil Rights and Civil War*. CSE

Poole, M. 1982. 'Religious Residential Segregation in Urban Northern Ireland' in F. Boal and J. Douglas (eds.), *Integration and Division: Geographical Perspectives on the Northern Problem*. Academic Press

Regional Trends, 1989 edition. HMSO

Rowthorn, B. and N. Wayne 1988. *Northern Ireland: the Political Economy of Conflict*. Polity Press

Teague, P. 1987. 'Multinational Companies in the Northern Ireland Economy: an Outmoded Model of Industrial Development?' in P. Teague (ed.), *Beyond the Rhetoric: Politics, the Economy and Social*

Policy in Northern Ireland. Lawrence & Wishart

Tomlinson, M. 1980. 'Relegating Local Government' in O'Dowd, Rolston and Tomlinson

Viggers, P. 1989. 'Northern Ireland', *Initiative*, 3

Wabe, J. S. 1986. 'The Regional Impact of De-industrialisation in the European Community', *Regional Studies*, 20 (1)

Walker, S. and D. Keeble 1989. 'The European Regions and the Twelve-Member European Community: an Overview' (paper presented at British Association for the Advancement of Science, Annual Meeting, Belfast, August 1987)

Chapter 12

The Regeneration of Rural Wales: Prospects for the 1990s

GRAHAM DAY

On 20 February 1990 it was reported that production of Welsh mineral water from Brecon was to be doubled following the health scare which had temporarily halted world sales of Perrier water. The company concerned, which owned 5,000 acres of the Black Mountains, where the waters rose, was Belgian-owned. Next day, the same newspaper carried a story that the largest employer in Welshpool, Floform, was making seventy workers redundant because poor market conditions in the US car industry had hit the demand for electrodes (*Western Mail*, 21 February 1990).

These events illustrate how deeply rural Wales is entangled in processes which take place far beyond its borders, and how difficult it is to exert influence over them. Within the British Isles, rural Wales is among the most peripheral of regions; it contains large areas of 'extreme rurality' (Cloke and Edwards 1988), and has a history of considerable deprivation. But it has also been undergoing very profound transformations in its economic, social and cultural structures, which some see as marking a break with previous conditions, and setting the region on the road to prosperity. Writing in 1989, the head of one of the principal rural development agencies said, 'Many of the problems that [we] face . . . are the result of incoming prosperity and a new confidence in the area' (*Mid Wales News*, April 1989, p.1). In this chapter I want to examine a number of issues which arise from the effort to overcome peripherality and achieve the regeneration of rural Wales, and their likely consequences into the 1990s. To what extent can rural Wales participate in the (alleged) miracle of the contemporary Welsh economy?

Understanding rural society

Most of the area of Wales is 'rural', i.e. open countryside with sparse population. All Welsh counties have rural districts within them, but 'rural Wales' can be taken to refer mainly to the counties of Dyfed, Gwynedd and Powys, along with south-western Clwyd. This area contains no town with a population greater than 20,000; it holds only 27 per cent of the total Welsh population (*c.*760,000 people), and it is a region which has long been thought to show symptons of 'backwardness' and neglect. These had their most obvious expression in the prolonged experience of depopulation, a narrowing economic base, ageing population structure, and social and cultural decay.

A number of explanatory frameworks have been used to say why this should be so. The argument that, in common with most or all other rural areas, rural Wales simply suffered from its failure to 'modernize', and its excessive reliance on a declining industry (agriculture), thus being 'overtaken' by the more industrialized/ urbanized regions, was superseded during the 1970s by approaches which theorized the problem as one of dependency and under-development. These referred to processes whereby the rural areas of Wales, like most of the rest of Wales in fact, had been confined to particular, limited, functions within a broader division of labour, determined elsewhere, which served to benefit interests outside Wales (interests variously defined as ethnic/national, regional, or class interests) (see discussion in Lovering 1978; Day 1979).

More recently, changes in rural Wales have been situated within larger analyses of economic and social 'restructuring' which have sought to relate local transformations to basic alterations in the economic order of Western capitalism (Rees 1984; Day *et al.* 1989). This sort of analysis has the advantage of recognizing that not all 'rural' areas are alike: some now occupy positions at the forefront of economic and social development, whereas others find themselves unable to participate in the benefits of such progress. Depending where you look, you can get very different impressions of the 'rural' situation, as the following statements about rural America show:

> Post- or advanced industrialism is giving rise to new social conditions in rural America ... A new rurality is emerging that promises growth, new opportunities, integration with the rest of society, and new problems. (Bradshaw and Blakely 1979)

> Rural America is in trouble. It is losing jobs, it is losing people; it is losing its identity . . . rural America finds itself in crisis. A key to rescuing [*sic*] this crisis is developing and nurturing a more diversified industrial and economic structure. (Falk and Lyson, cited in Marsden and Murdoch 1990)

The former of these comments refers to California; the latter has a more general application. In Britain 'favoured' rural areas would include East Anglia, and much of the Home Counties; but it is obvious that what has been happening there is very different from what is going on in, say, Cumbria or rural Yorkshire. One implication of these contrasting paths of development is that the meaning of 'rural' or 'rurality' (never very straightforward) becomes highly contentious (Hoggart 1988; Cloke 1987). Largely as a result of the ESRC's 'Countryside Change' initiative, a good deal of work is now being done to elucidate the 'restructuring' approach (e.g. Marsden and Murdoch 1990).

Changes in the economic basis of rural communities

A brief summary of the more fundamental recent changes in the nature of rural economies is necessary to provide the context from which probable future changes can be judged. It also serves to highlight the rapidity and unpredictability of change: many of the developments which have altered rural life would have been difficult to predict on the basis of past expectations. Key alterations include the following:

The decline of agriculture and other primary industries (forestry, mineral extraction) as major sources of rural employment. This has been occurring for decades: in Wales, the agricultural labour force has fallen steadily since records began to be kept. In 1911 it stood at over 120,000 and is now down to around 66,000. The shift in the weight of the rural economy from land-based activities, and from an emphasis on natural resources, obviously involves changes in the meaning of 'rural' life.

The expansion of manufacturing through new firm formation and the relocation of manufacturing firms and plants from urban to rural settings. This has been conditional upon certain advantages which rural locations have afforded to particular employers (or 'capitals'), such as pools of underused labour (especially women), weak unionization, freedom from congestion costs, and 'quality of life' considerations that are attractive to technical and managerial staff.

Shifts within manufacturing which reflect, in part, national trends, e.g. the relative growth of electronics and electrical engineering; but also the differential impact of the types of conditions listed above on the various sectors and branches of production. There has been some development of 'high-tech' activity in certain rural areas.

The expansion of services as a whole, with growth concentrated among certain service sectors such as hotels and catering, rather than others, such as business services, finance etc. Services constitute by far the most significant component of the rural economy in employment terms.

The centralization of control in a variety of organizations and activities, particularly the public sector (health, welfare, local government, public and newly privatized utilities) which has tended to remove some of the key functions from rural localities, making them more dependent on the larger population centres. These processes are associated with the imposition of new forms of 'businesslike' management and corporate structures, which have spread out from business and industry into local government (Cockburn 1977), education, and welfare.

The combined effect of these processes has been to create much greater diversity in the rural labour force, and to reduce the general distinctiveness of rural economies since they are no longer dominated by 'traditionally' rural activity. This has played a part in the overall reduction of 'regional' variations. Rural areas continue however to show higher levels of part-time and casual employment. They also have lower female activity rates than are normally found in more urban or industrialized regions. Unemployment rates tend to be low, but to some extent this is because people in rural areas are less likely to register as unemployed when not in work, so that a pool of potential labour may be concealed from view. Rural wage levels, partly because of the lack of full-time job opportunities, lag behind.

At the same time as contrasts betwen erstwhile 'rural' regions have become more marked, they have also become internally more varied and 'disorganized'. Restructuring appears to have made local differences more important, largely because the particular form it has taken has echoed, and amplified, pre-existing social and economic conditions. There has also been scope for a variety of interventions which have served to channel and influence local outcomes.

A detailed examination of one part of rural Wales, the County of Dyfed, illustrates the internal diversity and the contrasting patterns of change. Roughly similar points could be made with reference to the other Welsh rural counties (e.g. Day 1989) although of course the range of contrasts across rural Wales as a whole would be still larger. Tables 12.1, 12.2 and 12.3 provide information on the eight Travel to Work Areas (TTWAs) which, with the addition of the urban centre of Llanelli, make up Dyfed: Aberystwyth, Lampeter and Aberaeron, Cardigan, Llandeilo, Carmarthen, Fishguard, Haverfordwest, South Pembrokeshire. TTWAs are arbitrarily defined geographical units, and would not correspond directly to people's perceptions of their 'localities', nor to the labour markets within which they move. Nevertheless they give some general impression of local variations.

Table 12.1 Changes of employees in employment by TTWA and broad industry group, Dyfed 1981–7 (percentages)

TTWA	1	2	3	4	5	6	7	8	%change 1981–7
Males									
Aberystwyth	11.96	22.01	14.58	−17.94	−9.89	−20.43	34.21	−28.75	−3.24
Cardigan	−0.69	−21.74	6.81	143.52	−27.83	14.74	−15.26	−11.76	−2.25
Carmarthen	1.24	−54.84	−28.55	62.76	5.30	−3.81	−0.69	14.88	−4.80
Fishguard	−3.77	−50.00	−10.53	−7.32	−7.37	8.62	−8.33	153.33	−0.35
Haverfordwest	−10.65	−46.31	−20.78	−14.36	−17.60	−8.37	−9.87	51.97	−15.16
Lampeter/ Aberaeron	1.70	−41.53	−28.10	−20.83	6.56	−27.33	−9.72	14.29	−8.63
Llandeilo	7.69	−37.04	12.99	−28.48	−31.98	−42.57	18.91	328.57	+8.91
South Pembs.	−15.35	49.06	−19.24	−68.20	−33.71	−18.39	−32.03	130.77	−28.26
Llanelli	−16.85	−6.50	−19.85	15.15	14.66	−14.08	−10.82	59.89	−8.16
Females									
Aberystwyth	58.62	61.11	15.91	−75.00	3.08	23.32	12.53	−0.49	+8.18
Cardigan	5.61	0.00.	20.96	420.00	−33.02	68.09	−10.46	69.57	+6.35
Carmarthen	−12.61	62.07	−54.27	26.09	11.58	112.41	9.26	55.51	+26.65
Fishguard	52.78	0.00	49.52	−100.00	19.38	3.55	−29.84	78.85	+23.02
Haverfordwest	−32.39	−50.56	38.23	−32.08	−16.59	20.86	−5.34	−2.83	−6.74
Lampeter/ Aberaeron	6.34	−53.85	−12.57	−57.14	77.60	62.99	−10.64	199.62	+74.26
Llandeilo	5.43	0.00	−51.26	−81.82	−14.71	9.03	26.47	147.22	+24.82
South Pembs.	−28.94	26.47	48.48	23.08	−0.96	35.90	−11.61	250.67	+39.77
Llanelli	−28.72	−28.13	−12.16	−16.08	11.76	−8.21	10.38	10.69	+1.21
All employees									
Aberystwyth	18.73	25.99	15.12	−21.50	−2.80	−6.52	22.27	−15.32	+1.78
Cardigan	0.47	−21.74	14.04	155.75	−30.33	27.84	−14.46	35.00	+0.51
Carmarthen	−1.17	−48.57	−37.15	60.67	8.89	24.27	4.33	43.04	+8.81
Fishguard	4.68	−50.00	24.31	−11.63	7.16	7.79	−13.09	88.24	+6.33
Haverfordwest	−18.91	−46.74	−3.14	−15.64	−17.10	0.49	−7.56	9.93	−11.51
Lampeter/ Aberaeron	2.59	−42.75	−22.41	−21.86	41.55	−0.73	−9.95	121.60	+19.30
Llandeilo	7.35	−37.04	−3.17	−31.48	−21.78	−28.26	20.82	206.23	+14.16
South Pembs.	−19.43	47.92	−9.44	−65.96	−16.00	−3.26	−27.04	210.70	−7.98
Llanelli	−19.71	7.28	−17.62	11.64	12.84	−12.46	0.00	23.52	−4.67

Note: 1. Agriculture, forestry and fishing; 2. Energy and water supply; 3. Manufacturing industries; 4. Construction; 5. Distribution, hotels/catering, repairs; 6. Transport/communication, banking, finance; 7. Public administration and defence; 8. Other service industries.
Source: NOMIS

Table 12.2 Employees in employment as percentage of total in broad industry groups by TTWA, Dyfed 1987

TTWA	1	2	3	4	5	6	7	8	Total
Aberystwyth	13.1	3.9	2.7	6.5	8.6	7.1	17.3	16.6	10.7
Cardigan	13.1	*	4.8	6.5	5.2	8.9	4.2	2.3	5.2
Carmarthen	15.5	11.8	4.8	13.0	14.4	24.8	29.0	22.3	18.2
Fishguard	6.0	*	2.1	2.2	2.9	8.0	2.6	1.1	3.1
Havefordwest	16.7	17.6	9.6	15.2	15.5	15.9	23.2	13.1	16.0
Lampeter/ Aberaeron	10.7	2.0	2.7	4.4	8.0	3.5	1.1	5.7	4.6
Llandeilo	7.1	*	3.4	2.2	2.3	3.5	1.6	5.7	3.4
South Pembs.	10.7	19.6	5.5	19.6	16.7	10.6	3.7	13.7	11.1
Llanelli	7.1	45.1	64.4	30.4	26.4	17.7	17.3	19.4	27.6
Dyfed (a)	8,400	5,100	14,600	4,600	17,400	11,300	19,000	17,500	97,600

Note: see note for table 12.1.
(a) Excludes a small area of Dinefwr located in Swansea TTWA
* Negligible
Source: NOMIS

The number of employees in employment exceeds 10,000 in only four of the eight rural TTWAs: Aberystwyth, Carmarthen, Haverfordwest, South Pembrokeshire. The largest workforce is that of the Carmarthen TTWA, which in 1987 totalled 17,800. Fishguard and Llandeilo have employed workforces of 3,000 and 3,300 respectively, while Lampeter/Aberaeron has 4,500, and Cardigan just over 5,000.

During the 1980s, at least up to 1987, the latest date for which figures are available, all TTWAs in rural Dyfed with the exception of Llandeilo witnessed losses of male employment (table 12.1). This was particularly severe in South Pembrokeshire (a loss of 28 per cent) and Haverfordwest (15 per cent). Partly because of these losses of male jobs, rural west Wales shared in the 'feminization' of the labour force which took place throughout Wales and the UK (Winkler 1987). Female employment grew in seven of the eight TTWAs, with substantial rates of growth in Lampeter/Aberaeron (almost 75 per cent), South Pembrokeshire (40 per cent), and Carmarthen, Fishguard, Llandeilo (roughly a quarter). Only in Haverfordwest was there a fall in the number of employed women. By 1987 female employment as a proportion of total employment was highest in Carmarthen (50 per cent), Lampeter/Aberaeron (48.9 per cent) and Aberystwyth (46.7 per cent). Female employment was around one third of total employment in Cardigan, Fishguard and Llandeilo, suggesting that these are areas with considerable reserves of untapped

Table 12.3 Distribution of employees in employment by TTWA and broad industry group, Dyfed 1987 (percentages)

TTWA	1	2	3	4	5	6	7	8	Total
Males									
Aberystwyth	16.1	3.6	3.6	3.6	12.4	8.9	28.6	23.2	5,600
Cardigan	27.1	*	9.1	9.1	15.2	21.2	18.2	3.0	3,300
Carmarthen	12.4	5.6	5.6	5.6	12.4	19.1	29.2	11.2	8,900
Fishguard	20.0	*	5.0	5.0	10.0	40.0	20.0	*	2,000
Haverfordwest	11.8	10.6	9.4	8.2	14.1	14.1	24.7	8.2	8,500
Lampeter/									
Aberaeron	30.4	4.3	8.7	8.7	21.7	8.7	4.3	8.7	2,300
Llandeilo	24.8	*	19.1	4.8	, 9.5	9.5	9.5	24.8	2,100
South Pembs.	10.2	17.0	10.2	13.6	17.0	11.9	8.5	10.2	5,900
Llanelli	3.1	14.1	39.9	8.0	11.0	9.2	8.6	6.7	16,300
Females									
Aberystwyth	4.1	*	4.1	*	18.4	6.1	34.6	32.7	4,900
Cardigan	11.8	0	23.5	*	23.5	17.7	5.9	17.7	1,700
Carmarthen	2.3	1.1	2.3	*	15.7	13.5	32.6	33.7	8,900
Fishguard	10.0	0	20.0	0	30.0	10.0	10.0	20.0	1,000
Haverfordwest	6.9	1.4	8.3	*	20.8	9.7	31.9	20.8	7,200
Lampeter/									
Aberaeron	9.1	*	9.1	*	40.9	9.1	*	36.4	2,200
Llandeilo	8.3	0	8.3	*	25.0	16.7	8.3	41.7	1,200
South Pembs.	4.1	*	4.1	2.0	38.8	10.2	4.1	36.7	4,900
Llanelli	0.9	0.9	27.4	0.9	26.4	4.7	17.0	20.7	10,600
All employees									
Aberystwyth	10.5	1.9	3.8	2.9	14.3	7.6	31.4	27.6	10,500
Cardigan	21.6	*	13.7	5.9	17.6	19.6	15.7	7.8	5,100
Carmarthen	7.3	3.4	3.9	3.4	14.0	15.7	30.1	21.9	17,800
Fishguard	16.7	*	6.7	3.4	16.7	30.0	16.7	6.7	3,000
Haverfordwest	8.9	5.7	8.9	4.5	17.2	11.5	28.0	14.6	15,700
Lampeter/									
Aberaeron	20.0	2.2	8.9	4.4	31.1	8.9	4.4	22.2	4,500
Llandeilo	18.2	*	15.2	3.0	12.1	12.1	9.1	30.3	3,300
South Pembs.	8.3	9.3	7.4	8.3	26.9	11.1	6.5	22.2	10,800
Llanelli	2.2	8.6	34.9	5.2	17.1	7.4	12.3	12.6	26,900

Note: see note for table 12.1.
* Negligible
Source: NOMIS

female labour. The industrial sectors within which female employment tends to be concentrated are manufacturing, retail and distribution, and other services. Part-time employment is a significant feature of women's working patterns.

Examination of the contribution which each TTWA makes to the total employment pattern of Dyfed, according to broad industry division, immediately shows the differences in TTWA make-up (table

12.2). Lampeter/Aberaeron and Cardigan remain strongly oriented to agriculture, forestry, and fishing, with Fishguard and Llandeilo also contributing disproportionately to this sector. These primary activities are much less significant within the local economies of South Pembrokeshire and Carmarthen. While the Aberystwyth TTWA has some strength in agricultural employment, the weight of its labour force is concentrated in public administration and other services. The same is true of Carmarthen, which also has strength in transport, communication, banking and finance. The fastest-growing TTWA was Lampeter/Aberaeron, where employees in employment grew by 19 per cent. Llandeilo saw a gain of 14 per cent. On the other hand, overall losses were recorded in Haverfordwest (11.5 per cent) and South Pembrokeshire (fractionally under 8 per cent).

Manufacturing plays only a minor role in rural Dyfed. Haverfordwest provides just under 10 per cent of the county's manufacturing jobs; South Pembrokeshire is the only other TTWA to contribute more than 5 per cent. With the exception of Llandeilo (19 per cent) and South Pembrokeshire (10.2 per cent), manufacturing employment elsewhere failed to account for as many as one in ten of male jobs. Among women there were much greater employment opportunities in manufacturing, with manufacturing jobs especially strongly represented among employed women in Cardigan (23.5 per cent) and Fishguard (20 per cent) (table 12.3).

It is services that dominate the employment situation: service growth, especially in the category 'other services', has been the main source of new employment in rural west Wales during the 1980s. The proportion they now contribute ranges from 60.6 per cent in Cardigan to no less than 82 per cent of employment in the Carmarthen TTWA.

Within just one part of rural Wales, therefore, we find distinctive local economic configurations. Aberystwyth and Carmarthen are labour markets which are heavily geared to service activity, within which there is relatively well-entrenched female employment, including areas of professional work like higher education and local government. This explains the relatively high socio-economic profiles they display. According to the 1986 Inter-Censal Survey, Carmarthen had 28.9 per cent of its workforce in the 'professional and managerial' category, with Aberystwyth close behind. Cardigan and Lampeter/ Aberaeron are much more 'traditionally' rural in their composition, with agriculture and services for tourism (distribution, catering, hotels) strongly represented. Haverfordwest and South Pembrokeshire are places with serious problems of job loss, and have relatively large numbers employed in energy and water, and transport. According to Champion and Green's (1988) scale of labour market performance, Pembroke fell between 1981 and 1987 from 198th position to 277th, while Cardigan went from 249th to 276th. Only three local labour markets in the entire UK were performing less well than these two parts of rural west Wales by 1987 (the worst performance was that of Holyhead, in Anglesey).

Future economic prospects for rural Wales

To summarize the key considerations for future prospects which emerge from the examination of Dyfed:

1   Agriculture is a declining industry and likely to remain so. Rural Wales will see continuing reduction of full-time employees, and substitution of family and part-time labour; current policies can only add to this trend. Farming will be pushed away from its past stress on production towards more conservation-oriented activity — Wales already benefits from assistance to 'Less Favoured' and 'Environmentally Sensitive' Areas (LFAs, ESAs). There will be emphasis on diversification and pluractivity, although research suggests that Welsh farmers find it hard to grasp what this might mean, other than minimal increments to income from farm tourism (Aitchison *et al.* 1989). The UK government has resisted the idea of direct payment of income support to farmers for 'stewardship' of the countryside, although this is implicitly what happens already. There is growing interest in the attempt to find market niches for organic and Welsh-labelled products, in which there has been some success, but rural Wales has no particular edge in these respects.

2   Manufacturing plays a larger part in other areas of rural Wales than the Dyfed figures might suggest; particularly in the eastern districts (e.g. Powys). Even so, it is not a major part of the rural Welsh economy, and there is little to suggest any enormous growth in the foreseeable future. A limited amount of manufacturing activity may trickle through from the extension of good-quality roads into south Dyfed (the M4) and along the North Wales coast (A55); past experience suggests that it does not locate very far from the road corridors — thus, whereas Clwyd attracted almost a third of inward investment to Wales between 1984 and 1987, less than 1 per cent went to Gwynedd. The impact of the single European market and the Channel Tunnel will be to drag manufacturing employment towards the south-east of England and to worsen the competitive position of rural Wales.

3   As at present, it will be from within the service sector that most of the key forces affecting future development in rural Wales will be generated. 'Service' activities are themselves diverse. So far as rural

Wales is concerned, there are three distinct sources of service employment.

The first relates to the provision of services for the local population: i.e. retailing, distribution, certain care activities, etc. These have always played an important part in rural economies, and often are provided by self-employed individuals or by small family businesses. Such provision is under pressure from processes of rationalization and centralization: e.g. rural post offices, village shops, doctors' surgeries etc. Retailing, for example, has seen the growth of the supermarket and the franchise chain, which tend to serve a relatively large area and can undercut or out-compete more local business (Aitchison *et al.* 1989).

Secondly there is employment in the public sector services such as health, education and welfare, local government and administration, which have formed a major element in economic activity, providing up to one-third of the jobs. The distribution of such functions according to principles of reasonable equity has probably ensured that peripheral populations had somewhat better provision here than their numbers alone might merit. However, these services have suffered severely from government cut-backs, from centralization and from threatened or actual privatization, which have tended to concentrate activity in fewer places, with consequent losses to many smaller rural centres and greater distancing of services from those they serve (Day and Hedger 1990), and to accord greater significance to issues of profitability or cost-efficiency.

Finally there is the servicing of people from outside the region: accommodation, tourism and recreation. Clearly this is already a vital activity: in 1984 it was estimated that in South Pembrokeshire and Preseli alone tourism contributed £120 million to the local economy; in 1986 North Wales accommodated some 4,000,000 visitors who spent around £216 million in the region. Almost half a million visitors a year visit Snowdonia. Tourism is a booming world industry (Urry 1990), and it is widely seen as the major growth area for the rural economy, which will provide the replacement for loss of more traditional activity. The Wales Tourist Board's *Strategy for Growth* (1988) presupposed that Wales was entering a new tourist era. Apart from the expansion of overseas demand, there are particular tendencies within Britain resulting in more frequent holidays, a longer tourist season and a more demanding (and free-spending) tourist market. Much of the new tourist demand originates in London and the south-east, among more affluent members of the 'service' class. Rural Wales has much that the modern visitor seems to want: outstanding environment and scenery, space and 'quality of life'. This is one sphere in which 'peripherality' seems an advantage, particularly if it is actually becoming more accessible by road.

Unfortunately Wales's tourist industry is not especially rewarding. There is at present a high proportion of self-catering (21 per cent) and caravan/tented accommodation (48 per cent); guest houses heavily outnumber quality hotels; the infrastructure for tourism is often lacking (all-weather centres, visitor sites etc.); and in any case, much of the employment arising from tourism continues to be part-time or casual, low-paid etc. Extensive efforts are under way to 'modernize' and upgrade the Welsh tourist sector; large investments of both private and public money are involved. As will be further considered below, they are highly significant in contributing to changing the meaning of rural places.

It will be noted that all the above services are 'consumer'- rather than 'producer'-oriented (Allen 1988). Rural Wales has not participated to any great degree in the most dynamic aspect of the contemporary economy, the expansion of services that are provided for organizations and businesses. These activities, such as financial services, insurance, banking, legal and accounting services, have a considerably greater potential for earnings, and for pulling in income from elsewhere. As is well known, they are heavily concentrated in the south-east, where they enable people to acquire the high incomes that can then be spent in places like rural Wales.

The above broad-brush comments have to be qualified in terms of what was previously said about the increasingly fragmented composition of rural Wales. Given the diversification that has already occurred, different places (and different sections of the population) are launched on quite different paths. Some seem quite well placed to benefit from given forms of development: e.g. the Newtown/ Welshpool area has been significantly industrialized, contains a population of relatively skilled and experienced labour and can reasonably expect some further manufacturing growth. Elsewhere there is the potential for service-oriented, even science-based, expansion: Aberystwyth, Bangor, Carmarthen. Many localities however are still over-dependent on agriculture, or on the least rewarding forms of tourism and recreation (caravan sites/chalets), or unable to attract the better sort of employment opportunities (e.g. Cardigan and the Teifi Valley).

Forms of intervention: institutions and agencies

Changes of the sort described do not, in any sense, happen automatically. They are the complex outcomes of a wide range of interventions, and numerous interests and organizations seek to shape them. The significance of the relationship between restructuring the 'place-specific action' (Marsden and Murdoch 1990, p. 28) can be amply demonstrated in the case of rural Wales. It is by no means the passive recipient of external change; indeed rural Wales suffers from a multiplicity of agencies and organizations which act at various levels to try to influence development. While an intellectual case for integrated rural development has become more widely accepted and is embedded in policy at the European level (EC 1988), changes in the policy framework and the institutional structure of the British state have tended to complicate, and disorganize, rather than make coherent the rural policy sphere (Murdoch 1988). The difficulties this creates have been a recurring theme at a variety of recent conferences and meetings within Wales.

Apart from the inconsistencies and gaps which occur between different organizational responsibilities, the region also suffers from a more deep-seated problem (by no means peculiar to it), in that a variety of policies and decisions by government, and quasi-governmental bodies, mostly taken outside Wales, affect it in ways that are largely unintended, and often unnoticed. With the privatization and 'hiving off' of various bits of the public sector, this problem is likely to increase. For example, agricultural decision-making continues to be separated from other key policy areas; shifts in the assumptions which underlie agricultural policy and funding, directed mainly at problems which arise elsewhere (overproduction, environmental damage etc.), have significant repercussions for rural Wales. The best-known recent example was the impact of the introduction of milk quotas on the dairy industry of Dyfed; as many as 2,000 jobs may have been lost. More recently changes in the European sheepmeat regime and threats to reduce the Hill Livestock Compensation Allowance (HLCA) place the future of upland farming in jeopardy. At the very least, they do not help to sustain the agricultural base of upland Wales. The farmers' unions and the Country Landowners' Association join in warning that there is the possibility that land may be left to revert to scrub. The Forestry Commission argues that major afforestation may be needed to substitute for the withdrawal of agriculture. Judging by past performance, forestry will not generate the number of jobs required to replace those lost in agriculture.

The main development agencies have only marginal powers to deal with agriculture (e.g. they can assist marketing and packaging of products, but not production itself). Other organizations, more traditionally concerned with agriculture, are having to broaden their range of activity in order to try to encourage 'diversification' on and off the farm (ADAS, the agricultural colleges etc.), but this means that their activities increasingly 'trespass' on to territory that is already occupied, and create further confusion rather than coherence.

Similarly changes in the balance between public- and private-sector provision — ranging from the bus deregulation to educational cutbacks — have far-reaching implications for economic and social provision in the area. The privatization of Britsh Telecom rendered it ineligible for grant aid from the European Commission. Without subsidy, Telecom concluded that it would be unprofitable to attempt to modernize the communications infrastructure of the rural Welsh counties (Rees 1990). Yet inadequate communication systems are often cited as a key disincentive to the business development which many seek to achieve.

Very often agenices charged with improving the situation in rural Wales find themselves having to run faster and faster to keep up with the harmful consequences of what is being done by other organizations. The left hand rarely seems entirely clear about what the right hand is doing. Inevitably, in a congested policy arena, there is competition for space, as agencies seek to defend, and possibly expand, their range of operation. This surfaces, for example, in the occasionally prickly relationship between the two major rural development organizations which are active within Wales. Certainly there are many who perceive them as competing rivals, rather than as partners.

The role of the development agencies

By historical accident, it has come about that rural Wales is fragmented into distinct development areas administered by separate agencies. Since 1957 there has been a more or less continuous effort to develop central, or Mid Wales, an area which consists of the old counties of Breconshire, Ceredigion, Merioneth, Montgomeryshire and Radnorshire. This originated with an agreement, reached at local authority level, for the five counties to co-operate. Shortly after, the work became the responsibility of an independent government body. While the agency concerned has gone through several changes of name, its approach has been quite consistent. Currently it goes by the name, adopted in 1977, of the Development Board for Rural Wales (DBRW). It has been equipped with powers for economic and industrial development, and also for social and community support.

The parts of rural Wales which were not within Mid Wales, so defined, often faced more or less the same problems and issues. They have been dealt with by the Welsh Development Agency (WDA), which was created primarily to deal with problems of industrial decline, rather than rural deprivation, in South and North Wales, but which has assumed responsibility for rural developments as well. It has therefore been active in what were formerly the counties of Anglesey, Carmarthenshire and Pembrokeshire, and in the rural parts of Clwyd and South Wales. One consequence of this rather rough-and-ready division of labour has been that the modern counties of Dyfed and Gwynedd, formed after local government reorganization in 1974, are split between the two agencies. Since the WDA does not have the social/community powers of DBRW, people in Anglessey (Ynys Mon) and south Dyfed tend to feel relatively neglected.

To complicate the picture further, all county and district councils exercise some development powers; for instance, they fund rural workshops and help local enterprise agencies. They also perform the planning role which permits them to grant or deny permission for developments which might be put forward by either the WDA or the DBRW. County councils draw up broad 'structure' plans; district councils put together local plans; and the development agencies nominate centres for growth. None of these sets of proposals need be consistent! In cases of dispute the Welsh Office may adjudicate.

There has been, however, some general similarity in the way the development agencies operate, and some evidence of recent convergence of views. Both the WDA and DBRW enter the 1990s under new leadership; their recently appointed chairmen are cut from a similar mould of 'dynamic' young men with a strong commitment to the culture of 'enterprise'. In the case of the WDA, the chairman is a self-made businessman who created and then sold his own computer company. The chairman of the DBRW has local roots in Mid Wales, is from a farming family and claims to be the only man from his cohort of 'bright' young pupils at Llanfair Caereinion school who remained in the area.

DBRW has adopted a new business plan for the 1990s, known as its Corporate Strategy. Recently the new chairman has stated that the overall aim of the Board is to create a self-sustaining market economy in Mid Wales (House of Lords Select Committee 7 March 1990), a formulation which represents a rather more explicit statement of economic objectives than did the former emphasis on the restoration of population to a depopulated area. Within this general aim, the core activities are to be

(1) ensuring an alternative employment sector to replace traditional rural activity
(2) building an enterprise culture
(3) maintaining quality of life.

The first of these objectives continues to be associated with the growth of 'light' industry in the region. The DBRW has consistently stressed the attraction and generation of manufacturing employment, through the provision of advance factories, grants and cheap rents; a vision of the industrialization of rural Wales remains at the heart of its effort, and it has done much to orchestrate manufacturing investment in its region. During 1989, the Board reported unprecedented demand for factory floor space with a record allocation during 1988–9 of over half a million square feet (*Mid Wales News*, April 1989). The firms involved were active in the following sectors (in descending order): electronics and electrical assembly; furniture and joinery; health care goods; metal fabrication and engineering; clothing and fibres; packaging; service and design. While these show a promising spread of activity, questions have been raised about the validity of some of the claims made for the number of jobs created, and also about their quality (Thomas and Drudy 1987; Day *et al.* 1990). As in other rural areas, there has been a preponderance of assembly jobs, often for female employees, some of which are part-time. The Board itself acknowledges that there is still a need to create a promotion ladder within Mid Wales which will help retain the more ambitious school-leavers, particularly in the face of increased competition for their labour from employers faced by skills shortages elsewhere. Survey data have shown that factory jobs are the most desired form of work among a sizeable proportion of the population (27 per cent); but an even larger group (34 per cent) rates them as least desirable; it is the only form of work which receives a negative balance of opinion (IOWA 1988).

The alleged shortfall in 'entrepreneurial' ability in the area — sometimes attributed to the tendency for more dynamic people to move away — is tackled through a battery of business advisory services, 'start-up' courses, and school projects. There is also a specific programme (Menter a Busnes) directed at Welsh-speakers, who are said to be particularly deficient in entrepreneurial drive; it is intended to 'ensure that the economic potential of Welsh speakers is not wasted and to develop enterprise and business as an integrated dimension of Welsh culture' (DBRW Annual Report, 1988/9). Survey evidence shows that despite the high levels of self-employment within the population, there is among inhabitants of rural Wales some support for the idea that local people are less 'go-ahead' and less likely to consider going into business than outsiders (IOWA 1988).

The social and community budget of the DBRW is used to maintain and raise the local quality of life: in practice this largely means help towards building and maintaining sports halls, community and leisure centres, and some support for the arts and entertainment. These activities can be seen both as improving amenities for local residents and also raising the area's profile for tourism, with events like the Festival of the Countryside and the Aberystwyth Festival mainly benefiting the visitors. Out of a net annual expenditure of about £12 million, only a small proportion goes on these 'social' items; in 1988/9, grant aid of rather more than £500,000 was distributed between 374 projects.

The Welsh Development Agency operates in a very similar way to the DBRW, and the two organizations also co-operate on various initiatives. Like the DBRW, the WDA provides advance factories and starter units, promotes business and science parks, and offers business advice. Most of its attention is given to industrial Wales, and its Rural Affairs Division is a relatively minor part of its activity: one estimate is that the WDA created 130 rural jobs in 1986/7, rising to 340 in 1989 (*Western Mail*, 11 February 1990). Out of a total of 1.5 million square feet of new factory development in 1988/9, only some 15 per cent was devoted to North Wales, and like previous WDA investment in the region, this was mostly intended for the more urbanized parts of Clwyd (Deeside, Wrexham, Flint etc.). Smaller factories and workshops were planned for more rural places (Caernarfon, Porthmadog, Bethesda). The WDA is increasingly looking to schemes involving partnerships with private developers. One of the larger projects, a 'hi-tech' business park in St Asaph (Clwyd), intended to provide 2,500 new jobs, incorporates land belonging to Pilkingtons, who will play a major part in the development along with the County Council.

The WDA places a considerable emphasis on 'hi-tech' and high-value , low-volume products as the basis for job creation that will 'improve the viability and vitality of rural Wales'. But realistically viewed, these are not likely to make a major impact; while there may be localized possibilities of success in this regard — Aberystwyth and Bangor are university centres with particular expertise in biological science and electronics around which spin-off activities could be developed — it would be naive to imagine that rural Wales can compete fully with rival locations where there are better communications, better social and cultural amenities, and, most important, key inter-firm linkages. In any case, high-tech production is not especially labour intensive; where it does stimulate jobs in any quantity, they tend to be low-skilled assembly-type (screwdriver) operations, not essentially different from other sorts of manufacturing. The impact of new technology upon rural Wales may well be felt in quite different ways: changes in the service sector could be extremely detrimental, if, for example, 'tele-shopping' and 'home-banking' really caught on (according to a recent report in the

Guardian, even university lecturing could be replaced by new forms of home computer). This underlines some of the anxieties expressed during the 1990 St David's Day debate on Welsh Affairs. The comments of the MP for Merthyr (Ted Rowlands) could be equally applicable to rural Wales:

> We are entitled to warn that if our new local economies are built on the shifting sands of the service sector, it could lead to as many difficulties as the dependence on the old traditional dirty industries of coal and steel. (Hansard, 1 March 1990)

Two recent policy adjustments within the development organizations have significance for the future; they involve greater efforts to promote indigenous business and industry, and a programme which is more spatially diffused. The former leads to more vigorous encouragement for a variety of local enterprise groups and agencies, and attempts to mobilize 'grassroots' development effort. The WDA has, for example, been enthusiastic in its support of the 'Local Jigsaw' package, originally conceived by the Welsh Office of the Countryside Commission, which promotes 'village appraisals'. Appraisals have been adopted as a tool within the programme of WDA 'Rural Initiatives' to stimulate community backing for economic development. So far as the WDA is concerned, Rural Enterprise Groups should seek to enable rural communities to act to secure their own future prosperity.

Under the Welsh Office 'DRIVE' (Development of Rural Initiative, Venture and Enterprise) programme, the WDA and DBRW jointly operate a programme of grants aimed especially at service, tourism, leisure and craft projects. The WDA has assisted a number of experimental projects such as the Taff-Cleddau Rural Initiative in Narberth and the Pentrefoelas initiative in Gwynedd. These are intended to enrol local people in the development effort, and combine making improvements in the landscape and local amenities with the supply of business services. A strong message is put forward about the value of local refurbishment as a means of raising confidence and stimulating 'enterprising communities'. In the same way, the DBRW helps enterprise organizations within its area — the latest being Antur Penllyn based in Bala.

The kind of activity involved can be illustrated by the example of the Pentrefoelas Initiative. Pentrefoelas is a former estate village near Betws-y-Coed, in an area of severe depopulation, and had been identified for development as a 'heritage village' by the local authority. Following the failure of a local business attempt, the WDA provided support for a project manager, and towards the creation of a business and tourist information centre. The agency contributes about £18,000 per year, matched by the local authorities. As a result, help has been given to a handful of new businesses; a self-help tourism group has also been formed. Job creation so far has been estimated at eighteen full-time, three part-time, and fifteen outworkers. The scale of what has been achieved is typical; it is relatively modest, and eventual targets of forty-two full-time, ten part-time and twenty-five outworkers are probably wildly optimistic (none of the businesses expects to fail). There has been some dissatisfaction with slow progress, and some opposition from within the community to developments which might bring potential competition. There is little sign that rural self-help of this sort will make major inroads into problems of rural employment.

The second change is the increased attention being paid to the 'deeper' rural areas, resulting in a westward shift of activity. Past efforts by the development agencies have tended to have a very uneven spatial impact. Within the DBRW area, this is shown by the relative success of Powys (where manufacturing employment now accounts for more than a fifth of all jobs), compared to what has been done in Dyfed or Gwynedd. This arises from the particular importance attached to the development of Newtown, but also reflects a general bias towards the eastern (less remote) areas (Day and Hedger 1990). Now that the target for growth in Newtown has been achieved, DBRW is withdrawing its help and trusting to the private sector to continue the progress that has been made. Instead, it has launched a 'Special Rural Action Programme' aimed at places like Machynlleth, Aberystwyth, Aberaeron, i.e. coastal towns in the far west. The WDA has also announced increased attention to rural developments, naming places like Newcastle Emlyn, Llandovery, Bethesda and Pwllheli as targets. These proposals may go some way to counter complaints from within rural Wales concerning the damage inflicted by earlier selective aid to 'growth centres'. In practice, they are likely to involve the proliferation of rural workshops for craft workers, although there are signs of increasing numbers of small businesses concerned with aspects of communications, printing, design and so on, some of which are using modern technologies.

Despite all these efforts, and more which it would be too time-consuming to describe, the gap between rural Wales and other more advantaged areas remains large. Dyfed has been said to have the lowest average male earnings of any county in Britain – a point contested in the House of Commons by an MP from Powys who thought that if records were available, Powys might do even worse. It is clear that many jobs, for both men and women, are still low-paid, often insecure, part-time etc. Incomes in farming are also poor: Welsh farmers' incomes have fallen by 18 per cent at a time when farmers elsewhere were seeing 16 per cent gains (Farmers' Union of Wales, 1 March 1990). As was noted at the start of this chapter, even if local agencies and quasi-governmental bodies have played a significant part in organizing the development of rural Wales, control all too often remains outside it, and the gains made are vulnerable to shifts in economic fortune which people in rural Wales can do little to avert. A recent example is the precarious state of the great success story of rural Wales, Laura Ashley, which hinges on a downturn in consumer spending and a change in middle-class tastes. Rural Wales also faces the task of finding 1,000 new jobs to replace those which will be lost when the nuclear power stations at Wylfa and Trawsfynydd go out of operation.

There is a further key dimension which must be considered. The changes that have taken place in the economy of rural Wales, and in the balance between activities, have reshaped the social structure of the area. The importance of the farming community has clearly been reduced, even though it is still powerfully represented within local government and politics. A new set of 'service' classes has been installed. There has been substantial migration into the region, and to a large degree this has been biased towards more affluent, better-educated individuals from higher socio-economic positions than are held by the indigenous population (Day 1989). Among the incomers are many who have the same kind of social values and requirements as the visitor population which provides the increased demand for tourism. A range of important social issues have become contested: the most obvious is housing, but there are also indications that access to employment, and particularly to the 'better' jobs, is among them (IOWA 1988). Socially, as well as economically, rural Wales has become fragmented, and that process seems bound to continue. Consequently the meanings which attach to life in rural Wales are becoming more varied, and more contentious – i.e. the way in which rural Wales is 'represented'. As noted by Marsden and Murdoch (1990), representations play a vital part in the way in which localities are constituted, and can be understood as 'social outcomes of the various struggles to "represent" particular spaces' (see also Day 1987).

Certain forms of advertising play a key role here. The annual reports of the DBRW themselves project some revealing messages: e.g. 'Mid Wales – a New Wales' (1985/6) or 'Landscape for Living' (1988/9). The remaking of rural Wales in the interests of the modern tourist seems to be gathering pace. There is, for instance, a proposal to invest £1 million in a 'Celtic Heritage' centre in Machynlleth, in the former stately home of Lord Londonderry; after a certain amount of debate and argument a plan for a £500,000 Coracle Centre in

Cilgerran was dropped, but a scaled-down version is to go ahead. The tourist appeal of the former slate town of Blaenau Ffestiniog is to be enhanced by the addition of an 'Energy Interpretation Centre'. There can be few villages and communities which are not active in producing their brochures for walks and 'trails' suitable for tourists. Perhaps the most deeply ironic of all these schemes is the intention of the *Development* Board for Rural Wales to make the former spa town of Llandrindod Wells into a 'Victorian experience', at a cost of £1 million. Already Victorian street furniture has been put in place, and the local shop fronts are to be Victorianized in their turn. The people of the town will then become the living props for a recreated (and sanitized) past to be consumed by visitors from elsewhere (the English Midlands?). Not so much regeneration as resurrectionism?

Bibliography

Aitchison, J., G. Day and J. Murdoch 1989. *Social and Economic Change in the Upper Ithon Valley*. Rural Surveys Research Unit, UCW, Aberystwyth

Allen, J. 1988. 'Service Industries: Uneven Development and Uneven Knowledge', *Area*, 20

Bradshaw, T. and E. Blakely 1979. *Rural Communities in Advanced Industrial Society*. Wiley

Champion, A. and A. Green 1988. *Local Prosperity and the North–South Divide*. Institute of Employment Research University of Warwick

Cloke, P. 1987. 'Rurality and Change: Some Cautionary Notes', *Journal of Rural Studies*, 3

Cloke, P. and G. Edwards 1986. 'Rurality in England and Wales 1981', *Regional Studies*, 20

Cockburn, C. 1977. *The Local State*. Pluto

Day, G. 1979. 'Sociology of Wales: Issues and Prospects', *Sociological Review*, 27

Day, G. 1987. 'The Reconstruction of Wales and Appalachia', *Contemporary Wales*, 1

Day, G. 1989. 'A Million on the Move', *Contemporary Wales*, 3

Day, G. and M. Hedger 1990. 'Mid Wales: Missing the Point?' *Urban Studies*, 25

Day, G., G. Rees and J. Murdoch 1989. 'Social Change, Rural Localities, and the State: the Restructuring of Rural Wales', *Journal of Rural Studies*, 5

EC 1988. *The Future of Rural Society*. Bulletin of the European Communities

Hoggart, K. 1988. 'Not a Definition of Rural', *Area*, 20

IOWA 1988. *Rural Wales: Population Changes and Current Attitudes.* Institute of Welsh Affairs

Lovering, J. 1978. 'The Theory of the Internal Colony and the Political Economy of Wales', *Review of Radical Political Economics*, 10

Marsden, T. and J. Murdoch 1990. 'Restructuring Rurality: Key Areas for Development in Assessing Rural Change'. ESRC Countryside Initiative, Working Paper 4

Murdoch, J. 1988. 'State Institutions and Rural Policy in Wales', *Contemporary Wales*, 2

Rees, G. 1984. 'Rural Regions in National and International Economies' in T. Bradley and P. Lowe (eds.), *Locality and Rurality*. Geobooks

Rees, I. B. 1990. 'Wales Today: Nation or Market?' *Planet*, 79

Thomas I. and P. Drudy 1987. 'The Impact of Factory Development on Growth Town Employment in Mid-Wales', *Urban Studies*, 24

Urry, J. 1990. *The Tourist Gaze*. Sage

Winkler, V. 1987. 'Women at Work in Wales', *Contemporary Wales*, 1

Part 4
Theorizing the Periphery

Chapter 13

Internal Colonialism? Colonization, Economic Development and Political Mobilization in Wales, Scotland and Ireland*

NEIL EVANS

Fifteen years after its publication Michael Hechter's *Internal Colonialism* remains a work to be reckoned with. As a stimulus for sociological writing about the Celtic countries it was an important contribution, and it remains the most comprehensive attempt to discuss the experience of the three countries over a long time span. Day (1989) has rebuked Welsh historians for their failure to confront it in a satisfactory way: they have remained content to sneer and to dismiss it in passing comments. This chapter responds to that challenge. My enthusiasm for its achievment is not necessarily any greater than that of my colleagues, but I do respect its range and ambition. If nothing else, it poses issues and provides an antagonist. And, if I may return Day's serve, sociologists have not provided a complete theoretical critique. Hechter's sins are as much in broad conception as in detail, and it is also vital to look again at his work in the light of the progress made in development theory and historical writing in the period since he wrote. This chapter starts with theoretical objections and proceeds through an examination of three key issues in the comparative history of Ireland, Scotland and Wales.

* I would like to thank Patrick Buckland and Ieuan Gwynedd Jones for comments on the first draft of this paper, and Rees Davies for detailed bibliographical advice on medieval Scotland. I also learned much from the other participants at Gregynog, especially Raymond Crotty, Graham Day, Liam O'Dowd, and David McCrone, and from presenting the paper to a joint Coleg Harlech/UCNW seminar where John Borland, Joe England and Dai Michael's comments were especially helpful. None of these people is responsible for the contents.

Comparison is employed as a means of highlighting differences between the three countries, and the varied trajectories of development are stressed.

Theoretical discussion

What are Hechter's key propositions? Internal colonies are areas in which fortuitous economic differences (caused by differing resource endowments) are crystallized into dependency because of the influence of a culturally dominant core. In the colony, development comes from chiefly exogenous sources, and dependency is cemented by a cultural division of labour. This has two major consequences: the fixing of colonial development in a dependent mode, and the persistence of colonial culture as a means of fighting back against cultural and economic exploitation. This survives even if the colonized periphery is incorporated into the territory of the core, and peripheries are ruled solely for instrumental ends. Racial ideologies are a buttress from the seventeenth century onwards. These are the themes of the early sections of the book. Here we are showered with colonial analogies.

In the concluding pages, the theory is set out more thoroughly, if with little regard to what has gone before. There is a need to distinguish colonies, internal colonies and dependent peripheries. All are dependent in the economic sense, but the three other dimensions of dependency can be distinguished. There are five variables:

(1) the degree of administrative integration;
(2) the extensiveness of citizenship;
(3) the prestige of the peripheral culture;
(4) geographical contiguity;
(5) length of association between core and periphery.

The polar types are colonies which are low on all variables and dependent peripheries which are high on all measures. *Internal colonies are simply dependent peripheries which have a shorter time span of association with the core and which have cultures which are viewed as being inferior.* In fact, the concept is remarkably thin. In addition, we might detect a working assuption which is not spelled out as clearly, but is nonetheless central to the book's method: Ireland, Scotland and Wales have essentially similar histories. Indeed, the picture that is built up is a composite one; evidence of racial hostility to the Irish is made to pass muster for all three countries.

Critics weighed in from the beginning. One theme was the stress on divisions within all four countries of which Hechter failed to take adequate account (Nairn 1981). England was not a uniform core, it contained dependent areas within it, and the Celtic countries were similarly divided. In Scotland, the role of the Lowlands in repressing the Highlands was emphasized, and Hechter (1985) has acknowledged the weight of this criticism. This problem helps undermine the existence of a cultural division of labour, something for which Hechter provides only sketchy evidence, yet it is central to his case (Day 1979). The uniformity of the four countries in Hechter's view extends to class structure. The Celtic countries are treated as if they contain simply workers, and the role of their elites is glossed over (Mughan 1977). This is strange in a book which thrives on imperial analogies, given the centrality of local elites in discussions of imperialism. Yet William Sloan (1979) argues that Hechter is not really concerned with imperialism, but with ethnicity, and that the result is 'self-mystification through a fantastic hunt for the ethnic snark'.

Another theme was the priority of the theory over the evidence; it was a Procrustean bed into which facts were fitted and inconvenient ones ignored. Subsequent work by Katherine O'Sullivan See (1986) drew on a similar body of theory (but now extended by a decade of research and argument) with much more open-ended results. Quebec and Northern Ireland were shown to have different trajectories of development, though each was illuminated both by the other and by the corpus of theoretical work. She, more successfully than Hechter, found the middle ground between abstract theorizing and the peculiarities of the individual case. Others objected to Hechter's rather cavalier discussion of theory and found that his characterization of the two approaches to development as assimilationist theory and internal colonialism was both too dismissive and blurred more important distinctions within the field. Parsons and Rokkan have been seen by others as not exclusively diffusionist. Hechter has no truck with the idea of acculturation in the Celtic fringe, but other users of the framework have found that to be one of the central characteristics of internal colonialism (Page 1977; Hind 1984). Theoretical work has now moved on, with modernization theory making an unexpected comeback, and some writers accepting the possibility of there being some development within a situation of dependency. A clearer understanding of the history of western societies is held to be necessary for progress in the area (Roxborough 1988).

A substantial body of writing bears upon Hechter's work, yet no one has tried to take it on in its full range. Bulpitt (1983) has hinted at overall weaknesses when he suggests that the book is better in detail than in overall conception. Certainly the two fail to marry happily. It has been observed that the main interest of the book is in the period 1850–1966 (Sloan 1979); indeed 1536–1850 are disposed of between pages 47 and 123, while the later period gets pages 127–340. It is a book about outcomes rather than process (Browett 1984). Internal colonialism is made to cover the history of three countries over 400 years with scant regard for the changes within them, and their changing political and economic relationships to the core. An idea which is so accommodating is in danger from the outset of being nebulous. Just when did territories become internal colonies? Hechter gives us no clue. Others offer varying dates for Ireland. Was it 1541 (Bottigheimer 1978) or 1801 (O'Sullivan See 1986)? By failing to confront this issue Hechter leaves the concept dangerously vague.

Bulpitt (1983) attempts to repair some of this damage by providing a more nuanced account of the formation of the United Kingdom, a process which he rightly observes has been neglected by historians; and his attempt is informed by close parallels with historical work on imperialism. The effectiveness of this will be considered later. Hechter's book is studded with parallels from Third World societies, yet towards the end we are told that the Celtic countries belong in the First World and that the colonial parallels are only analogies. Is this simply part of a well-worn tradition of the loose use of words like 'imperialism', 'colony', 'colonialism' and 'empire' (Finley 1976)? Hind (1984) is explicit about the whole tendency of the theoretical strand which Hechter represents: 'Theories of internal colonialism derive from analogies'; and it is an 'arguably artificial analogy'.

The issue becomes little clearer when the problem of the relationship of internal colonialism to dependent regions is considered. Hechter's views have been set out above. The cultural division of labour is the key determinant of economic backwardness; indeed, variations in economic development between the three countries are related to the degree of colonial relationship which exists. Sloan (1979) makes a related point when he says that it is imperialism that creates ethnic nationalism, and not (as Hechter would have it) the suppression of ethnic identity which defines imperialism. This presents a difficulty in comparing dependent regions with internal colonies. If the cultural division of labour is so important in explaining the economic state of internal colonies, what explains the dependency of non-colonial peripheries, where (by definition) a cultural division of labour cannot apply?

The second broad area of disagreement concerns Hechter's constant invocation of the *persistence* of Celtic cultures. Surely we all know about reproduction now! It is hardly a recent discovery. Historical work in Wales (mainly post-Hechter, to be fair) has explored that process (Morgan 1981; G. A. Williams 1985), and is beginning to run into the problem of explaining why people in Wales chose to define themselves as Welsh even if the content of that definition changed markedly through the ages. By contrast, Hechter's view is a late manifestation of the Celticism which characterized nineteenth-century writing designed to harry the English away from philistinism and barbarism, and against which R. T. Jenkins (1935) warned so eloquently:

> The adjective 'Celtic' indiscriminately applied to everything Welsh in the heyday of the Romantic revival, has led to much confusion . . . Irish and Welsh are cognate languages. But in trying to understand the history and culture of Wales during the last five hundred years (at least) it is even more important to forget this . . . in the realm of culture there has been the most trifling commerce. Attempts to explain this or that or the other thing in the recent history of Wales — political, social, even religious — by a wholly fictitious 'Celticity' are a mere waste of time.

Historians are beginning to explore the history of the British Isles in its cultural diversity and interactions (Robbins 1988; Kearney 1989). Debating with Hechter can play a role in this process. Three paths lead out from his work into the nature of those fascinating but very different Celtic societies of Britain. The first is the nature of colonialism and its impact on the three countries. The second is the impact of the political tie with England on economic development in the three areas. Thirdly, there is an exploration of the nature of political mobilization in the nineteenth and early twentieth centuries. The conclusion heads us back towards this theoretical starting point.

Colonization in the 'Celtic fringe'

About the time that Hechter wrote, some medieval historians also began to use the term 'colony' (Davies 1974; Frame 1981).Inattentive readers sometimes bracketed them with Hechter, yet the verbal similarity should not mislead. What they were saying was quite different. The key thing is that the word 'colony' was not qualified in any way; they were not using analogies, but a quite literal employment of the word. Hechter's internal colonialism seems mealy-mouthed by comparison. This colonialism was based on rule by an alien culture, a system of one law for the Welsh and another for the English, which is described as 'apartheid', and centrally as involving the process of colonization. This consisted of the cultivation of new land and the displacement of the native population (Davies 1974,

1974–5). It can be dated fairly precisely to the thirteenth century and the reign of Edward I in particular. It was then that sustained conquest displaced a looser domination which the English/Norman state had long exercised over the Celtic lands (Davies 1990). Government ambitions became greater as earlier schemes of conquest proved to be unsuccessful, and the looser sense of lordship gave way to the tighter conception of colony. This implied uniformity in law — or at least the hierarchical ordering of laws — and the purging of native laws of customs and practices which were held to be inimical to good Norman behaviour. Lordship was personal, took over the existing social structure and pattern of authority, and could tolerate racial differences and varying customs. Its key demand was subjection and not uniformity. By the thirteenth century, however, the English polity was more clearly defined, and along with it went a more precise sense of national identity. Different practices in the Celtic lands were held to lead to disloyalty. At the same time the doctrines of the Roman Church were imposed from Canterbury. Edward I was very hostile to Irish law and swore to root out all bad practices from his territory. Welsh law was reviewed in 1284, and Scottish in 1305. As colonial rule took over from the looser sense of lordship, so colonial resistance stiffened. In the year 1258 Ireland rediscovered its tradition of high kingship, and the princes of Gwynedd invented the idea of the Prince of Wales. In 1287 the Irish rejoiced in a rebellion of the Welsh (Davies 1984; Trevor-Roper 1982). Scotland which had long-established independent kingship, honed its consciouness and independence in a long series of wars to maintain its autonomy.

The origins of imperial rule in the Celtic countries can therefore be precisely defined and differentiated from an earlier view of lordship. Colonialism is least applicable to Scotland, where, while there was an early process of colonization, the settlers were quickly assimilated into Scottish society and ceased to look south for their identity and authority. Crucially, they were imported to bolster the power of the Scottish Crown — especially of David I in whose twenty-nine-year reign from 1124 the process began — rather than the Norman monarchy of England. He was bolstering his own feudal power by drawing on men who also held land from him in the Honour of Huntingdon. There was no extensive settlement by an alien peasantry, expropriation was limited and chiefly took place south of the Tay. The new elements were absorbed peacefully and transformed by the process of settlement. Unlike Wales and Ireland, an institutionalized form of racism failed to develop. A relatively lightly settled territory made incomers easy to absorb. In the High Middle Ages, there was a clear process of the formation of a Scottish territorial state, and incoming colonists contributed their mite to the process (Grant 1988; Duncan 1975; Barrow 1980, 1981).

In Wales, there was planting from the beginnings of contact with the Saxons in the seventh century, which rapidly accelerated after 1066. The marcher lordships had Englishries and Welshries, and Glamorgan and Pembrokeshire were the most affected areas; in some lowland areas, settlers were probably a majority of the population. The most extensive — and most culturally conscious of its Englishness — came after the conquest of Gwynedd in 1282. Large numbers of Welsh were displaced from fertile land — 5,000 acres of it — reserved for the new, exclusively English, boroughs and given equivalent acreages of inhospitable upland or burrows in exchange. It was not dynastic conquest so much as racial. English officials were harsh, and the Welsh gentry were kept from the higher echelons of power, though given enough of a taste of it at the lower levels so as to whet their appetites. Clearly the sense of separate consciousness was fostered by this situation. Tensions exploded in 1400 with the Glyndŵr revolt, which broader social dislocations turned into a national rebellion of sorts. The penalty was harsh discriminatory legislation against the Welsh (Davies 1968, 1974, 1974–5).

Yet this was only one side of the story. Welsh landowners assimilated themselves to the English law of primogeniture and built up estates. The older kin-based system of the *gwely* withered away in the face of a money economy and individualistic ownership (Pierce 1972). The princes of Gwynedd had tried to foster this in the first place as a central part of their strategy of state-building, and it continued silently under the rule of the Crown (Carr 1982). When the Tudors incorporated Wales in 1536, it was a process welcome to the local wielders of power, for they had come to depend on the English law, seeing enhanced opportunities within the new structure. The 'union' gave rights of representation and imposed uniformity in law and administration. Much of the discriminatory legislation had already gone by then and the rest would disappear within the century; the Welsh were not banned from high office, though the ability to speak English was a requirement (Rees 1948; Roberts 1972, 1972–3; W. O. Williams 1958). Culturally the process was eased by the tendency to see the Tudors as the fulfilment of the old prophecy that the Britons would regain their ancient land (G. Williams 1979). Gentry pedigrees were traced back to the Welsh princes.

The implication of all this is that colonial Wales ended with the union: indeed, it was already waning by the time of Glyndŵr's rising and would probably have disintegrated earlier had not the bitterness and destruction of that decade sustained it (Davies (1974–5). Incorporation ended the plurality of laws, and there was no hint of planting after the thirteenth century. The process was at worst not resisted, and at best welcomed because of a tendency towards social convergence between Wales and England. Some Welsh gentry had urged upon the government the need for union, and in the second incorporating Act of 1543 Welsh MPs took part in the deliberations. The marcher lords had been weakened by the Wars of the Roses, and, far from being Hechter's potential leaders of Welsh revolt, had sunk to the role of lesser gentry rather than the great barons they had once been — that is, if their land had not already been forfeit to the Crown. The acid test of incorporation was the Reformation, a cause of rebellion in northern England and Cornwall, but of scarcely a ripple in Wales. The requirement of speaking English for officials in the incorporating Acts has to be distinguished from earlier racially-based Acts. The Welsh were not debarred from office, even if monoglot Welsh speakers were. In practice, Welsh was to be a language of administration for a century and more because of the impossibility of applying the act of 1536 in a virtually monoglot society (W. O. Williams 1964). Cultural pluralism was accepted in the realms of religion, with the recognition of the use of Welsh in religious services. A well-connected clutch of Welsh intellectuals made the necessary political advances and provided the vital translations. Wales sat more easily in the transformed Tudor state than the north of England did. With Ireland there is no comparison.

The medieval conquest of Ireland had been partial, and by the early sixteenth century royal authority was confined to the narrow pale around Dublin. The Tudor state-building process was difficult, and complicated by an almost simultaneous occurrence of military conquest, colonization and Reformation. The first tightening of royal control in the 1530s challenged the long-established Kildare ascendancy (that is, the leading role of the Fitzgeralds in the colonial administration) and resulted in the rebellion of Silken Thomas in 1534. Opposition to the religious changes then being undertaken was used as a rallying cry, but the connection was not inevitable. It was the early seventeenth century before it was clear that the Reformation had failed to take root, and before Counter-Reformation Catholicism was established (Bradshaw 1978; Canny 1975, 1979; Bottigheimer 1985).

Military conquest and large-scale planting became a feature from the mid sixteenth century. The processes were complicated and their nature is still contested by Irish scholars, yet a few generalizations would seem to be valid. Firstly, the scale of plantation was huge — and very late — even if it was not as great in its impact as was intended. New landowners often failed to bring tenants with them and were forced to retain the local inhabitants in this role (Stewart 1989). Yet this was supplemented by a larger, non-colonial migration of Scots and West Country English to Ireland, overflowing from their own crowded countries into the nearest available space. More than 150,000 settlers came to Ireland between 1586 and 1700, roughly the same number that Spain and Portugal sent to Latin America in the period (Smyth 1978). Secondly, politics in Ireland was based on a struggle for superiority fought on ethnic lines. The descendants of the first colonists — the Old English — asserted their right to rule, and their superiorty over the Gaelic chiefs (despite a degree of inter-marriage and acculturation between the two groups). The New English — the colonists of the period *c.*1550–1640 — used the links between the existing two ruling groups to claim precedence for themselves, especially in view of the lukewarmness of the Gaels and Old English towards the Reformation. When those two groups fused in 1641 to rebel against the New English, the process of élite definition suddenly swung to being religiously based rather than based on ethnic origin (Clarke 1970, 1984). Ireland was the only part of Europe after the Peace of Augsburg (1555) where the religion of the rulers and the ruled did not coincide (Crotty 1986). The beneficiaries of the process were the new English, who prevented the even newer Cromwellian settlers from getting to the top of the tree of Irish society, with the aid of the sympathetic and conservative administration of Henry Cromwell in the 1650s (Barnard 1973). The Penal Laws of the period 1691–1778 completed the process of identification. Arguably, it was the seventeenth-century shift in landownership which was central. In 1641, Catholics still owned 59 per cent of the land, yet by 1688 it was only 22 per cent and by 1703 a mere 14 per cent. The land which remained in Catholic hands was mainly in the more barren western province of Connaught. Dispossession and exclusion were searing experiences. Polarities became a recognizable Catholic–Protestant divide rather than the earlier ethnic rifts (Simms 1984; Wall 1984).

Ireland then was colonized at the same time that it was more fully brought within the bounds of the Kingdom. Bottigheimer (1978) has argued that this makes it a clear case of internal colonialism, but in a precisely defined way which distinguishes his work from that of Hechter. It also greatly limits the use of the term to a very particular period. By this view Wales was not an internal colony in the early modern period. It was simply a part of the Kingdom, in which colonization and conquest had taken place in the remote past, but had now ceased to have any real political significance. Scotland was not a part of the Kingdom until 1603 and had never been colonized in any important way. Unlike Ireland, it had had a largely successful Calvinist Reformation based on localized reform traditions and a desire to end French domination and preferment; English military aid was vital in securing this liberation, and began to take Scotland out of the French orbit and into the English. Arguably, the Reformation was the first act in the process of union (Cowan 1978). The border between the two countries now stabilized — Berwick ceased to be the tennis ball of frontier politics — even if it would be some years before it became peaceful (Tuck 1979).

What is the process of development in the period 1200–1800? In all three countries the starting-point is similar, but the outcome very different. That starting-point is imperialism. Wales was conquered and a colonial society created. This then underwent long-term social changes which were an essential preliminary to its absorption into the Kingdom in 1536–42. The extent of that change made the process quite smooth. Wales moved from being a colony to being a part of the Kingdom. At no stage was it an internal colony. Ireland was only partly conquered in the Middle Ages, so that its absorption into the Kingdom was accompanied by colonization and religious changes. It makes some sense to call this internal colonialism, for reasons already discussed. Scotland was only lightly colonized by Normans and not conquered by the English until Cromwell did so. As it was an independent kingdom until 1603, and retained its own parliament until 1707, it makes no sense at all to call it an internal colony in the period. The path, then, is from colony to part of the Kingdom, but by varying routes. The emphasis of the medieval historians upon the colonial nature of thirteenth-century relationships implies a shift away from them in the longer run, and needs to be sharply differentiated from Hechter's timeless and largely undefined internal colonialism.

Bulpitt (1983) has produced a sophisticated set of variations on Hechter's themes in which there is much insight and subtlety. He uses the analogy of 'informal' empire to discuss Wales in the period 1282–1536, Ireland in the period 1603–1800 and Scotland from 1603 to 1707. What the periods have in common is that they are eras of regal union, when there was little Anglicization. He gives much attention to the motives of the centre (here over-narrowly defined as the Whitehall–Westminster axis, rather than Hechter's too broad England) and recognizes the pressures from the fringe and their contribution to the three unions. This is an important advance, for in using different periods he is confronting the issue of historical development and variation. He also emphasizes the dependence of the process on strategic and political concerns. This has the dual advantage of agreeing with the historical evidence and avoiding Hechter's entanglements with the cultural division of labour and its role in economic dependency. Yet he too ignores the historians' literal use of the term 'colonialism'. As each country is incorporated into the realm, so it becomes an instance of 'formal' rather than informal imperialism. The process is one of a move towards imperialism rather than away from it. Yet elsewhere he argues that union means that the same rules apply as in England: the territory becomes part of a dual polity. The centre needs local collaborators in its rule, and Parliament is the vital institution which mediates between centre and periphery. In fact he does not look at the era of formal imperialism in a very serious way, and the term is probably best seen as a not very profitable development from his real insights gained by the application of the idea of 'informal' empire. By contrast, it can be argued that the historical trajectory was quite the opposite: from a common starting-point there was divergent development; industrialization and political mobilization would only emphasize this.

Economic development

Much of the discussion of Hechter's work has focused on the inadequacy of his core–periphery model for explaining economic relationships within the British Isles. The essential starting-point is to narrow down his core from England to southern England — south of the Severn–Wash line — so that account can be taken of the position of what he calls dependent peripheries. The south of England was the core of English — and British — state-building, and rested upon both agricultural prosperity and the development of the woollen industry. The prominence of the Woolsack in Parliament symbolizes that economic basis of the state (Kearney 1989). Northern England was incorporated fully into the structure of government only under the Tudors. This was coincidental with the full incorporation of Wales and not prior to it, as a dependent region should be in Hechter's model.

The processes of economic development of the three Celtic countries and the English periphery need to be compared in a more sustained way. None of them could claim any clear comparative advantage in the pre-industrial period, as all produced commodities which could have as easily been produced in southern England. Their trade was based on England's ability to consume more meat, leather and coarse woollen cloth than it produced, and to pay for it with grain and manufactured products (Mitchison 1983). Industrialization modified this somewhat because it added a range of new commodities which the Celtic countries and northern England could produce in quantity — coal, iron and steel, linen, cotton and engineering manufactures. Many of these could not be produced in the English core, and presumably this gave the periphery some advantages relative to the past. Yet this was an uneven process within the periphery much of which was pastoralized by the regional specialization of the nineteenth-century industrial economy. The west of Ireland and the Highlands of Scotland were the most spectacular examples, but no less real (though much less severe) was the deindustrialization of large areas of North and Mid Wales in the nineteenth century, as they failed to sustain the 'fragile industrialization' of 1780–1820 (Richards 1988).

Perhaps the most surprising thing about long-term economic development in the three Celtic countries is the way in which Scotland and Ireland changed their relationships to each other in the course of the period 1600–1900 (Cullen and Smout 1977). In 1707 the population of Scotland was one-third of that of Ireland, a position which still obtained in 1841. By 1901, however, they were virtually equal, such was Scotland's growth and Ireland's decline. Such movement is difficult to explain within Hechter's framework. In 1600 both had underdeveloped economies with large elements of semi-subsistence in them. Edinburgh was at that time larger than Dublin, but would not remain so for long. By 1800 Dublin was twice the size of Edinburgh, though Scotland was already regaining the economic lead. Ireland had grown rapidly in the seventeenth century because of the hothouse atmosphere created by the imposition of a new ruling class, while Scotland had grown more slowly, and faltered at the end of the period. Ireland had prospered partly because it had attracted both people and capital from Scotland. Just when did Scotland establish its lead? Recent work is pushing it further into the past and further emphasizing that patterns of inequality are established *before* the onset of industrialization, and then fixed by that process, at least as far as differences in per capita income are concerned (Mitchison and Roebuck 1988).

It may have been that the Union was at the root of Scotland's long-run success. Many historians have thought so. The evidence is, however, far from clear-cut. Certainly Scotland altered its position in the world economy from peripheral in the late sixteenth century to joining the core by the early nineteenth century (Smout, 1980a and b). Wallerstein's (1980) objections to this are largely about the typicality of the process rather than the fact; he also registers a caveat about the experience of the Highlands, which was in many ways closer to that of the west of Ireland than to Lowland Scotland's. Overall Scotland's development had deeper roots than the Union, and its impact was a delayed one, though probably beneficial in the long run. Indigenous factors like entrepreneurship, agricultural progress and education also played a large part in the whole process of growth. Union seemed to go with the grain of economic development, but was not the crucial factor, one way or the other. It was partly neutralized by the protection afforded by the Act to the vulnerable salt and coal industries until well into the nineteenth century. Scotland had the kind of economy which was able to benefit from the British connection by means of complementary development (Devine 1985; Whately 1987, 1989).

Scotland's growth was more secure in the long run than was that of Ireland. The Anglo-Irish colonial elite did not form the basis of a successful capitalist landlord class. They were too far removed from their tenants to produce anything like the necessary cordial co-operation. The virtual exclusion of Catholics from landholding outside underdeveloped Connaught precluded much advance in this sphere. Furthermore Irish tenants had memories of partible inheritance, and landlords lacked the necessary power to prevent this from escalating. Scottish landlords in the Lowlands at least were of the same ethnic group as their tenants and had much tighter social control, which they used to improve agriculture. They also had larger farms and the ability to prevent their break-up. These advantages coexisted with the presence of large towns which formed markets for industrial and agricultural products, and trade linked in with the British colonies in the Atlantic world. It was a nexus of growth in which agriculture played a central role. As Cullen and Smout (1977, p. 10) observe: 'No country has ever been transformed into a modern economy without a successful agricultural revolution preceding or co-inciding with industrialization. Ireland could not be an exception to that rule.' Ireland went along the path of subdivision, sustained temporarily by the cruel ecological 'advantage' that made potatoes grow particularly well in its soil. Scotland also gained some advantages from its access to British colonial markets after the Union of 1707. Geographical position made two voyages a year to the Chesapeake possible, rather than the one from the Thames. Trade encouraged industrial growth and formed vital links to the Caribbean, which were to count for much in the rise of the cotton industry. Trade played its part in the creation of a benevolent circle of growth which was also composed of urban development and agricultural/industrial innovation. Partly this was because of the influence of returning exploiters of colonial opportunities, and the entrepreneurial skills they had acquired (Cullen 1977; Devine 1977; Devine and Dickson 1983).

Ireland, by contrast, suffered from its position in the empire. Its cattle trade was the victim of organized interests in the English Parliament on a number of occasions in the late seventeenth century. This encouraged the growth of a more labour-intensive provisioning trade for the colonies, from which the Navigation Acts did not exclude Ireland. The Woollen Act of 1699 likewise banned imports of a cloth in which Ireland was competitive, and had the long-term effect of switching production towards linen, which was not banned from the British market. The colonial system distorted the Irish economy in other ways too. The ban on direct trade with the British colonies meant that trade concentrated on Dublin, and hence looked inward to the British archipelago rather than out into the Atlantic, as Cork did. It developed financial markets suited to the needs of a rentier aristocracy, but not with the sophistication which international trading required. Dublin gathered too many of the urban eggs into one basket, and its size was not an indication of economic well-being. It was a bloated primate city, not a vigorous leader of the development process (Cullen and Smout 1977; Cullen 1977; Devine and Dickson 1983).

A number of things stand out in the economic history of Ireland and Scotland in the early modern period. One is the fact that Scotland had established its advantages well before the onset of the industrial revolution, so that physical resources are not the total explanation of the process. Secondly, Scotland's advantages at least in part derived from its position as part of the core of the British empire, while Ireland's disadvantages were partly the result of colonial status. Equally, this does not explain totally the underdevelopment of Ireland. That also rested upon subdivided holdings and the lack of the cultural advantages which literacy and the Enlightenment gave to Scotland.

Industrialization fixed these differences in aspic. Ireland had a rural population of some 3,000,000 who were at risk from famine, Scotland 100,000. In 1911 51 per cent of Ireland's population worked in agriculture, as compared with 11 per cent in Scotland. In 1907, 41 per cent of Scotland's output was from industry, compared with only 14 per cent in Ireland. The proof of the pudding was in GNP: Scotland reached 95 per cent of the British average, but Ireland only 62 per cent. Ireland's decline in the nineteenth century has often been ascribed to the Union, but this was only one factor amongst several. It is doubtful that an Irish parliament could have done much to alter the basic situation. Certainly the collapse of linen and wool in much of Ireland from the 1820s was related to the ending of protective tariffs, but it is likely that external economies would have given centralized English production the crucial advantages in the longer run anyway. Transport improvements, the late start of many Irish industries (Belfast's early start making it the exception which proves the rule) and failures in entrepreneurship provide a series of explanations which are largely economic in focus rather than political. Free trade exarcerbated what was bound to be a difficult situation, rather than determined it. Could an Irish parliament have offset the process in any significant way? It might have resolved the issues of landlordism and rural credit earlier and provided the basis for a healthier rural economy in so doing. It might also have provided finance banks on the Continental model, institutions more appropriate to a late-developing economy. The British link did, however, provide much of the impetus behind railway development — one of the chief beneficiaries of the greater degree of state intervention in Europe (Cullen and Smout 1977; Lee 1973; O'Malley 1981).

The Union clearly benefited one part of Ireland as much as it did Scotland and made separation or even a large degree of Home Rule unthinkable in both. For the rest of Ireland, the Union was a highly dubious advantage, and a convenient scapegoat for the ills of a distressed society. Crotty (1986) describes Ireland as an example of 'capitalist colonialism'. This is much more precise than Hechter's analysis and does not support it. He emphasizes the *uniqueness* of Ireland in the world economy. While racially and geographically it is part of the First World, it is part of the Third World in that it underdevelops rather than develops. Like the Third World, it suffered the imposition of an individualistic capitalist economy upon a pastoral and tribal society. English prosperity allowed high prices to be paid for cattle, a commodity which required declining inputs of labour. In the long run this meant a failure to provide a living for half its population, so that Ireland fulfils Crotty's first condition of undevelopment, that is, that there are fewer people as well off as formerly. None of this gives comfort to a notion of internal colonialism which is present, varying only in degree, throughout the Celtic fringe. Crotty is not using analogies any more than the medieval historians are; he is saying something much more specific and much more challenging than is Hechter. The outcome was what Crotty has graphically called 'coolie' labour. When Ireland joined the empire and its free trade network a century after Scotland, the effects were much more serious than they were in Scotland. Yet neither in Scotland nor in Ireland were purely political factors a total explanation of either prosperity or devastation.

It is hard to discuss Wales with the same degree of precision that Irish and Scottish historians have brought to their subjects. The markets provided for its cattle trade and woollen cloth were vital for survival, and South Wales benefited from the influence of the Bristol market (P. Jenkins 1983). Yet its late eighteenth-century leap forward would seem to be less well prepared for than was Scotland's, and to depend to a much greater extent upon natural resources. It was at a remove from Bristol, the city which sponsored much of its development, and did not interact with agricultural improvement in the way that Edinburgh and Glasgow did. Growth was much less balanced than it was in Scotland. But much more research on the period 1500–1750 will be necessary before we can link it closely to the changing fortunes of Ireland and Scotland.

The main objection that Welsh historians made to Hechter's book was to assert that in the period of industrialization Wales belonged to the economic core rather than the periphery (D. Smith 1980a, b and c; R. M. Jones 1980; G. A. Williams 1982). Southern Scotland and Northern Ireland could easily be added to this argument. Gourevitch (1979) generalizes the argument when he explains the distribution of ethnic nationalism in terms of a lack of fit between economic and political cores. The nineteenth century certainly saw a radical shift in the locus of power and influence in the British Isles. Briggs (1959, pp. 50–1) has found a north–south divide as significant as in the United States, and 'boosters' of northern industrial towns looked forward to the day when Liverpool and Manchester physically joined each other and became the capital (Kiernan 1972). The balance tilted to the north, where there existed a west–east string of almost contiguous industrial towns — none more than forty miles apart — from Liverpool to Manchester via Sheffield to Leeds. A detour could have been taken south from Sheffield to Nottingham (forty miles) and Birmingham (fifty). All these towns were at least 20,000 people strong in 1801 and 100,000 by 1911 (Banks 1973, pp. 105–8).

Perhaps just as significant was the collapse of the wool textile industry in East Anglia and its relocation in Yorkshire. The impoverishment of the southern farm labourer and London's chronic casual labour problem were expressions of the same restructuring (G. S. Jones 1971). Yet the old core was challenged rather than totally eclipsed. London retained its dominating role in many spheres (Barker 1989; Sheppard 1985). Perhaps (the point is currently being contested) the greatest individual fortunes were always made by commerce rather than industry anyway (Rubinstein 1977). The shift in the economic balance in the nineteenth century was relative, not absolute. This is some comfort to Hechter's analysis. He had anyway partly allowed for shifts in the location of the core by observing that natural advantages were the origin of the core–periphery distinction, but this could be modified by the later discovery of minerals.

The movement to the coalfields is a central element in this process, but not a total explanation of it. The differing spatial distribution of industrialization also depended on other variables, the most prominent of which were agricultural prosperity, proto-industrialization, urbanization and colonial trade. South Wales and the north-east of England shared many features by the nineteenth century, not least their prominence within Britain as export coalfields and their heavy industry. Both were indubitably part of Britain's industrial core. Yet this is not to say that there were not significant differences between them, and between their patterns of development. In the north-east a higher level of urbanization and agricultural prosperity, coupled with an earlier start in the coal trade built up a more diversified economy, and one more dependent on localized sources of capital than South Wales. The difference is not the result of ethnic discrimination, as Hechter would have us believe, but of a different place in changing regional divisions of labour over the centuries which gave the north-east economic advantages which South Wales lacked. Yet he was right to draw attention to issues of dependency and the narrowness of South Wales's industrial base. His answers were not adequate, but sustained comparison between Celtic and non-Celtic areas can provide better solutions to issues that he raised (Evans 1989b).

National mobilization

Mass political mobilization was something in which Ireland was a European pioneer and it grew out of a colonial heritage: it also reflected the crisis economy of the early and mid-nineteenth century.[1] The politics of discrimination lasted until the very eve of the era of mass politics, and then had the bitterness of the Famine years stirred in. A Catholic middle class had grown in the eighteenth century despite the Penal Laws, and began to win a niche for itself alongside the Protestant establishment in the late eighteenth century. After the Union, Daniel O'Connell thought in terms of Irish cross-religious alliances against the English, whereas the older generation of Irish Catholics saw England as a potential defender against the local Protestant elite; his charismatic leadership was a vital factor. The Union of 1801 had been undertaken with the intention of coupling it with Catholic Emancipation; the influence of Catholics would be diluted and therefore easier to contain within a larger state, it was thought. But Westminster and the king would not contemplate emancipation. The situation was worse because Ireland was grossly under-represented on the basis of population in the early nineteenth century.

Ireland remained in some ways a colony because it could not be governed by the normal means of nineteenth-century Britain. It had a Viceroy, a sub-state lacking the elements of autonomy which

---

1   The material in this section on Ireland derives from the following sources, unless otherwise specified: O'Tuathaigh (1972), Lee (1973), MacDonagh (1977; 1983), Boyce (1988a). To acknowledge individual points separately would overburden the text with references.

distinctive Scottish institutions gave. Government was highly centralized — the voluntary work of landlords, the norm of early
nineteenth-century administration, would not operate in Irish circumstances. Periodically the rights of assembly and *habeas corpus*
would be withdrawn. It is true that these withdrawals were temporary
and tempered by liberal traditions in Britain, but they existed none
the less. It is indicative of the problem of Irish government that the
British state managed to contain an often challenging working-class
movement without recourse to serious breaches of civil liberties after
1819, yet in Ireland such expedients were quite routine aspects of
government throughout the Union. The explosive mix was a blend of
religion and the land question — religion and potatoes as Disraeli
rather dismissively put it. As the century progressed, land tended to
steal the ascendancy from religion, but they were always entwined.
The Irish peasantry had a sense of dispossession, and communal
occupation of the land was carried down in folk memories of the
sixteenth- and seventeenth-century colonization, a feature largely
absent in Wales and Scotland.

O'Connell's new style of mass politics won the ending of the ban on
Catholics becoming MPs in 1829. Thereafter he turned his attention
and the popular movement towards a radical renegotiation of the
terms of the Union. There was a clear desire to restore Grattan's
parliament, but that implied autonomy within the British state rather
than the dismemberment of it. He argued for justice *or* repeal, so that
there was always room for compromise, yet he operated mainly
outside the structure of British party politics, which set Ireland apart
from Wales and Scotland. At O'Connell's death in 1847 his major
aims still had not been achieved — indeed, he had largely given up the
struggle in 1843 when it seemed likely to lead to violence. The more
romantic nationalism of Young Ireland, along with the immediate
problems of the Famine, tended to take the centre of the stage. There
was a lull in mass activity in the next generation, which the
conspiratorial and ideologically vague politics of the Fenians filled.
In the late 1870s popular nationalist politics was reborn, in
association with a resurgence of the land question in the face of the
international depression in agriculture. Irish issues came to block
'domestic' issues in Britain, and Gladstone attempted to cut the
Gordian knot by the expedient of Home Rule in 1886. The Liberal
Party talked itself out of effective power for a generation by taking
this course, and Ireland became a central aspect of British politics
until the era of the postwar settlement. Home Rule in Ireland made
Home Rule for the other Celtic countries a potential issue.

The exact relationship between politics in the three countries is
more difficult to specify. K. O. Morgan (1963, p. 305) has summed up

the differences between Wales and Ireland: 'The ideal of Wales was to be recognised as part of the British political and social structure: the ideal of Ireland was to be severed from it. The object of the one was equality: the aim of the other was exclusion. Home rule in Wales, unlike home rule in Ireland was indeed "killed by kindness".' This is incisive, but no longer an adequate summary of Irish historiography. Irish Home Rulers through to Redmond had no desire to leave the British empire, though they did want a radical renegotiation of the Union. Repeal had been a convenient rallying cry for O'Connell, but it was to be an inducement to take Britain to the negotiating table rather than a demand for total separation. Even Arthur Griffith and his Sinn Fein accepted the British monarchy, while wanting to create a dual polity on the model of the *Ausgleich* of 1867. Separation from Britain was the outcome of the Irish national revolution, but not the intention of most politicians until very late in the process, and even then it was possible to fight a bitter civil war over the degree of separation that was acceptable.

Revolution in Ireland came from a combination of forces, not the least of which, as Boyce (1988b) has recently argued, were counter-revolutionary ones (see also Garvin 1986). The dynamic of mass politics was the land question, but the long-term tendency of economic change after the Famine was to reduce the issue's significance as the congestion of the land declined. Yet Ireland's political potency was increased by its relative over-representation in the late nineteenth-century political system — it proved politically impossible to adjust its representation to the new realities of population levels after the Famine and in line with continued population growth on the larger island. The extension of the franchise helped make the land question a more prominent issue than it had been under O'Connell. Conservative policies tried to address this issue in order to save the Union. Between 1886 and 1916 they virtually abolished landlordism and instituted peasant proprietorship (with the aid of a state subsidy). In the process, one of the political props of the old system was taken away, and Irish aspirations which had once been for responsible landlordism, through the enforcement of tenant rights, shifted away from this communalism to individual ownership. This was the first influence of 'counter-revolution'; the second was the increasingly militant resistance of Unionists to any measure of Home Rule. It included armed struggle and tended to raise the stakes in the nationalist camp, increasing the likelihood of violence. The third force was a backward-looking intelligentsia which came to the fore in the European crisis of 1910–20, and gave separation its impetus. Redmondism was totally eclipsed, but only very late in the day.

Yet there was a clear difference in politics in Ireland, Scotland and

Wales, even if it was not what Morgan has specified. In Wales, political mobilization was much later than in Ireland and was confined to the British party political structure; there was no separate Welsh party. The aim of negotiating within the British s⁺ate was more frankly acknowledged than it was in Ireland. Land was clearly a less bitterly divisive issue, both in popular protest movements like anti-enclosure and Rebecca and in parliamentary politics. Occasionally agrarian redressers looked across to Ireland for their models, but their violence was usually more theatrical than real (D. Jones 1973). In the quarrying districts of North Wales there was a more serious land question, based on an almost Irish sense of dispossession. Quarry owners had enclosed great tracts of land almost within living memory and proceeded to make vast fortues out of them. It was here that Michael Davitt was most welcome (R. M. Jones 1981). Yet the dynamic of Welsh politics was not the land: industry and country towns were vital – and initiating – in the process of mobilization, unlike Ireland where rural areas led the market towns into politics (I. G. Jones 1981; Lee 1973). Industrialization tended to siphon off rural discontent. Liberal politics rested upon a range of social and economic bonds which tied Wales together effectively..

Scotland belongs somewhere down the scale from Wales, probably because it had a well-established place in the British political and social structure already. The loss of its parliament in 1707 was not much felt in the days of limited state involvement in society and the economy, and the existence of autonomous institutions in law, religion and education was of more consequence. Harvie (1987) has called these three sectors a Scottish system of estates, on the continental model. It was added to by the creation of a Scottish Secretary and Scottish Office in 1885, partly to relieve pressure on Westminster caused by Irish filibustering. Lord Rosebery was probably hoping to use this as part of a strategy to build up a territorial base for an assault on the centre, on the model of Chamberlain in Birmingham. Scottish liberals were often carpetbaggers and therefore pro-Union. There was little to propel them beyond this position. While Scotland had a well-established tradition of emigration, a significant component of it was professionals seeking opportunities within the British empire. As in Wales migration to industrial areas blunted rural discontent, and the smaller size of the rural population made land a less significant issue than in Ireland. The crofters put their issue on to the centre of the political stage in the 1880s, but the impact of the world depression in agriculture was weaker than it was in Ireland. Scotland failed to produce a Liberal leader of the political stature of Tom Ellis and Lloyd George, and after 1886 its Liberalism faded because of the movement of its adherents into Liberal Unionism. By 1902 it had a Unionist majority; four years later Wales would not return a single Unionist MP (Harvie 1977).

Scotland's failings were intellectual as much as anything. There was no adequate sense of history. Walter Scott had captured a sanitized version of the Scottish past, which was seen as both sentimentally touching and well buried. It was not romantic; he was seeking to provide a decent funeral rather than resurrection (Harvie 1977; Nairn 1981). The success was in marketing. The world beat a path to Scotland's door to see the sights that Scott, Ossian and others had imortalized. Tourism from England produced the illusion that assimilation was a two-way process (Harvie 1977). Welsh historiography was also integrationist, but it led to the future with its stress on the achievements of the current age of the people, and its desire to extend these within the structure of the British state (Evans 1989a). Its history was democratic in form, where Scotland's was aristocratic and feudal. Ireland's views were, by contrast with both, essentially static. History was a constant action-replay, in which oppression and resistance were the central players and the result always a high-scoring draw (MacDonagh 1983).

Ireland buried its Liberal Home Rule politics in the national revolution of 1916–22, in which there was a great deal of violence and a shift in state form, but no social revolution (Boyce 1988b). In Wales and Scotland, the break up of Liberalism led to (and was caused by) the emergence of class politics based on industrial discontent as surely as nineteenth-century Irish nationalism had been based on the land question (O'Leary 1982). The new issues were not landlordism and tenant right, but nationalization and workers' control. Class proved to be as potent a form of mobilization in Scotland and Wales as nationality had been. The difference is not that national consciousness was absent from Labour politics but that the centre of gravity of the political coalition shifted towards the industrial working class, and national issues tended to be expressed in the language of class. In this sense, there is less of a gap in the ethnic politics of Scotland and Wales than Hechter perceives. Labour was capable of expressing both a sense of Welshness and of Scottishness. In Scotland the Tories could also express Scottishness, winning a majority of votes and seats in 1955. In Wales, the prominence of Aneurin Bevan and Jim Griffiths in the Labour governments of 1945–51 helped Labour to make its breakthrough into rural areas, culminating in the election of 1966, when Labour won 32 out of the 36 Welsh seats – not quite equalling the Liberal whitewash of 1906, but certainly winning areas that would have been Tory had only class counted in politics (Stead 1985). Class certainly needs to be given a prominent role, even in the understanding of ethnic politics.

Conclusion

The above analysis does not lead to any all-embracing theoretical conclusion, but neither am I content to leave the matter with assertions of historical uniqueness. One of the virtues of historical sociology or comparative history is that it can lead to a fruitful occupation of the middle ground between these extremes (O'Sullivan See 1986). This chapter opened with a rather schematic summary of Hechter's assertions; it ought to close with an attempt to do the same with my own arguments. Perhaps some itemized points might do this most effectively and put matters starkly enough to promote debate.

1   All the Celtic countries were victims of Anglo-Norman imperialism in the thirteenth century, but thereafter their histories diverged.

2   The strongest and longest-lasting influence was in Ireland, where conquest was a late process and its memory survived long enough to influence the politics of mass mobilization in the nineteenth century. Even in the nineteenth century, under nominal union with Britain, it could not be ruled by 'normal' methods.

3   The direction of movement is away from imperialism strictly defined and towards integration into the polity. This may be another nail in the coffin of imperial analysis of contemporary Ireland. Crotty's position is distinctive, as he sees the government of the twenty-six counties as being based upon an imperialist legacy, whereas the normal modern use of the idea of imperialism in Ireland is for Northern Ireland.

4   The term 'internal colony' has a limited utility for Ireland in the period 1541–1800, when it was simultaneously a part of the realm (though without representation at Westminster), colonized and treated simply as a convenience of the British economy. The kind of colony it most resembled was a white settler colony like those on the Atlantic seaboard of America, rather than the West Indies or India. Crotty (1986) calls Ireland an example of 'capitalist colonialism' which puts it into the category of India rather than North America. His reasons are precise — in Ireland the native population was ruled over by a settler elite, rather than displaced or destroyed. Historians like Canny (1973) stress that the origins of colonial ideology came from Ireland and were transferred to North America. Often this was done by the same people. Crotty is right to point to differences also, yet his own argument that Ireland was spared the full rigours of its economic undevelopment because of the absorption of its 'surplus' population into the British labour market — and the lack of any real racial barrier to this — equally points to differences from the Indian model. All this only puts additional urgency on the more precise

specification of the nature of colonialisms, a process which Smyth (1978) has helpfully begun.

5   What survives after integration into the British state (and, of course existed beforehand) is a structure of values in which the culture of the core has a much higher prestige than any peripheral culture, or any culture of the non-property-owning classes. This was fixed in its modern form during the process of industrialization. Hechter's concept of 'internal colonialism' amounts to little more than this in practice, since he cannot show that systematic cultural discrimination impoverishes the Celtic periphery. I prefer to call it 'cultural imperialism' where the sense of analogy is much more open, and where there is less risk of confusion with the real varieties of colonial relationship that there have been in these islands.

6   Cultural imperialism is an important phenomenon in modern politics. The peoples of the Celtic countries have learned to remake constantly their cultures as a form of resistance to this metropolitan domination. Their cultures do not 'survive' in any simple way — they are all Anglicized to a greater or lesser degree. Their cultural heritage has proved to be an adaptable resource in the modern world.

7   Economic dependency exists within any capitalist economy, as does uneven development. Neil Smith (1986) has a helpful view of the process: 'Uneven development is not an extraneous process which swoops down on static geographical blocks; rather it is the continual struggle of opposed tendencies toward differentiation and equalisation.' This is sometimes influenced by political decisions, but rarely can they go completely against the grain of the distribution of economic power. Hechter puts too much emphasis on the role of the state, when this was often quite a limited actor in the historical process. Even in the contemporary world, the limited impact of regional policy as a countervailing force to the trends of capitalist development has been demonstrated repeatedly. This was emphatically more so in the past.

If I have any overall theoretical message, it is to stress the need to consider what Trotsky (1977) called 'combined development'. His way of putting it was fraught with dangers, as it was based on a stages theory of development, yet it also pointed away from that. He spoke of the drawing together of different stages of the journey: we may say rather that the elements of a social structure combine in different ways because of the differing historical contexts in which those structures are formed. Ireland differed from Wales to a large extent because its formative historical relations with Britain were created in a very different period and pattern from those of Wales. Smith uses the term conjuncture in a similar sense; even Trevor-Roper (1982, p. 12), a historian immune from accusations of Marxism, has a similar formulation.

Hechter was right to set the development of the Celtic countries against each other, but he would have learned far more if he had explored more fully the diversity of experiences and the different paths of development. Yet we should be grateful to him. A large hypothesis which is wrong can be more fruitful than a minor one which is correct. There are enough similarities between the three countries to make comparison worthwhile and illuminating. Hechter examined the Celtic periphery when it was unusual for an outsider to do so. The study of those societies is still too often confined to people who know only their own part of the periphery. This volume has the aim of exploring the comparisons, and one reason that we have undertaken this is the stimulus (and the irritation) that Michael Hechter provided. Whether we regard it as the pearl or the speck of grit, we have reason to acknowledge the influence of *Internal Colonialism*.

Bibliography

Banks, J. A. 1973. 'The Contagion of Numbers' in H. J. Dyos and M. Wolff (eds.), *The Victorian City: Images and Reality*. Routledge & Kegan Paul

Barker, T. C. 1989. 'Business as Usual? London and the Industrial Revolution', *History Today* (February)

Barnard, T. C. 1973. 'Planters and Policies in Cromwellian Ireland', *Past and Present*, 61 (November)

Barrow, G. W. S. 1980. *The Anglo-Norman Era in Scottish History*. Oxford University Press

Barrow, G. W. S. 1981. *Kingship and Unity: Scotland 1100–1306*. Edward Arnold

Bottigheimer, K. S. 1978. 'Kingdom and Colony: Ireland in the Westward Enterprise, 1536–1660' in K. R. Andrews *et al.* (eds.), *The Westward Enterprise: English Activities in Ireland, the Atlantic and America, 1480–1650*. Liverpool University Press

Bottigheimer, K. S. 1985. 'Why the Reformation Failed in Ireland: *une question bien posée*', *Journal of Ecclesiastical History*, 36 (2)

Boyce, D. G. 1988a. *The Irish Question and British Politics, 1868–1986*. Macmillan

Boyce, D. G. (ed.) 1988b. *The Revolution in Ireland, 1879–1923*. Macmillan

Bradshaw, B. 1978. 'Sword, Word and Strategy in the Reformation in Ireland', *Historical Journal*, 21 (3)

Briggs, A. 1959. *The Age of Improvement*. Longmans

Browett, J. 1984. 'On the Necessity and Inevitability of Uneven

Spatial Development under Capitalism', *International Journal of Urban and Regional Research*, 8 (2)

Bulpitt, J. 1983. *Territory and Power in the United Kingdom: an Interpretation.* Manchester University Press

Canny, N. P. 1973. 'The Ideology of English Colonisation: from Ireland to America', *William and Mary Quarterly*, 30 (4)

Canny, N. P. 1975. *The Formation of the Old English Elite in Ireland.* O'Donnell Lecture, National University of Ireland

Canny, N. P. 1979. 'Why the Reformation Failed in Ireland: *une question mal posée', Journal of Ecclesiastical History*, 30 (4)

Carr, A. D. 1982. *Llewelyn ap Gruffydd, ?–1282.* University of Wales Press

Clarke, A. 1970. 'Ireland and the General Crisis', *Past and Present*, 48 (August)

Clarke, A. 1984. 'The Colonisation of Ulster and the Rebellion of 1641' in Moody and Martin

Cosgrave, A. 1984. 'The Gaelic Resurgence and the Geraldine Supremacy (*c*.1400–1534)' in Moody and Martin

Cowan, I. B. 1978. *Regional Aspects of the Scottish Reformation.* Historical Association (London)

Craig, C. 1982. 'Myths against History: Tartanry and Kailyard in 19th Century Scottish Literature' in Colin MacArthur (ed.), *Scotch Reels: Scotland in Cinema and Television.* British Film Institute

Crotty, R. 1986. *Ireland in Crisis: a Study in Capitalist Colonial Development.* Brandon Press

Crotty, R. 1987. *A Radical's Response.* Poolbeg Press

Cullen, L. M. 1977. 'Merchant Communities Overseas, the Navigation Acts and Irish and Scottish Responses' in Cullen and Smout

Cullen, L. M. and T. C. Smout (1977). 'Economic Growth in Scotland and Ireland' in Cullen and Smout (eds.), *Comparative Aspects of Scottish and Irish Economic and Social History, 1600–1900.* John Donald

Davies, R. R. 1968. 'Owain Glyndwr and the Welsh Squirearchy', *Transactions of the Honourable Society of Cymmrodorion*

Davies, R. R. 1974. 'Colonial Wales', *Past and Present*, 65 (November)

Davies, R. R. 1974–5. 'Race Relations in Post-Conquest Wales: Confrontation and Compromise', *Transactions of the Honourable Society of Cymmrodorion*

Davies, R. R. 1984. 'Lordship or Colony?' in J. F. Lydon (ed.), *The English in Medieval Ireland.* Royal Irish Academy

Davies, R. R. 1990. *Domination and Conquest: the Experience of Ireland, Scotland and Wales, 1100–1300.* Cambridge University Press

Day, G. 1978. 'Underdeveloped Wales', *Planet*, 33/4

Day, G. 1979. 'Key Issues in the Sociology of Wales', *Sociological Review*, 27

Day, G. 1980. 'Wales, the Regional Problem and Underdevelopment' in Gareth and Teresa L. Rees (eds.), *Poverty and Social Inequality in Wales*. Croom Helm

Day, G. 1989. 'Whatever Happened to the Sociology of Wales?' *Planet*, 77 (October–November)

Devine, T. M. 1977. 'Colonial Commerce and the Scottish Economy *c*.1730–1815' in Cullen and Smout

Devine, T. M. 1983. 'The English Connection and Irish and Scottish Development in the Eighteenth Century' in Devine and Dickson

Devine, T. M. 1985. 'The Union of 1707 and Scottish Economic Development', *Scottish Economic and Social History*, 5

Devine T. M. and T. Dickson 1983. 'In Pursuit of Comparative Aspects of Irish and Scottish Development: a Review of the Symposium' in Devine and Dickson (eds.) *Ireland and Scotland 1600–1850*. J. Donald

Duncan, A. A. M. 1975. *Scotland: the Making of the Kingdom*. Oliver and Boyd

Durkacz, V. E. 1983. *The Decline of the Celtic Languages: a Study of Linguistic and Cultural Conflict in Scotland, Wales and Ireland from the Reformation to the Twentieth Century*. John Donald

Evans, N. 1989a. 'Gogs, Cardis and Hwntws: Regions, Nation and State in Wales, 1840–1940' in Evans (ed.), *National Identity in the British Isles* (Coleg Harlech Occasional Papers in Welsh Studies, no. 3)

Evans, N. 1989b. 'Two Paths to Economic Development: Wales and the North-east of England' in Pat Hudson (ed.), *Regions and Industries: a Perspective on the Industrial Revolution in Britain*. Cambridge University Press

Finley, M. I. 1976. 'Colonies: an Attempt at a Typology', *Transactions of the Royal Historical Society*, 5th Ser., 26

Frame, R. 1981. *Colonial Ireland, 1169–1369*. Helicon Press

Garvin, T. 1986. 'Anatomy of a Nationalist Revolution: Ireland, 1858–1928', *Comparative Studies in Society and History*, 28 (3)

Gourevitch, P. A. 1979. 'The Re-emergence of "Peripheral Nationalisms": Some Comparative Speculations on the Spatial Distribution of Political Leadership and Economic Growth', *Comparative Studies in Society and History*, 21 (3)

Grant, A. 1988. 'Scotland's Celtic Fringe in the Late Middle Ages: the MacDonald Lords of the Isles and the Kingdom of Scotland' in R. R. Davies (ed.), *The British Isles, 1100–1500: Comparisons, Contrasts and Connections*. John Donald

Harvie, C. 1977. *Scotland and Nationalism: Scottish Society and Politics, 1707–1977.* Allen & Unwin

Harvie, C. 1987. 'Grasping the Thistle' in Kenneth Cargill (ed.), *Scotland 2000: Eight Views on the State of the Nation.* BBC Scotland

Hayes-McCoy, G. A. H. 1984. 'The Tudor Conquest (1534–1603)' in Moody and Martin

Hechter, M. 1975. *Internal Colonialism: the Celtic Fringe in British National Development 1536–1966.* Routledge & Kegan Paul

Hechter, M. 1979. 'On Separatism and Ethnicity: a Response to Sloan's "Ethnicity or Imperialism?" ', *Comparative Studies in Society and History*, 21 (1)

Hechter, M. 1985. 'Internal Colonialism Revisited' in Edward A. Tiryakin and Ronald Rogowski (eds.), *New Nationalisms of the Developed West.* Allen & Unwin

Hind, R. J. 1984. 'The Internal Colonial Concept', *Comparative Studies in Society and History*, 23 (3)

Jenkins, P. 1983. *The Making of a Ruling Class: the Glamorgan Gentry, 1640–1790.* Cambridge University Press

Jenkins, R. T. 1935. 'The Development of Nationalism in Wales', *Sociological Review*, 27

Jones, D. 1973. *Before Rebecca: Studies in Popular Protest in Wales, 1790–1835.* Allen Lane

Jones, G. S. 1971. *Outcast London: a Study in the Relationship between the Classes in Victorian Society.* Oxford University Press

Jones, I. G. 1981. *Explorations and Explanations: Essays in the Social History of Victorian Wales.* Gwasg Gomer

Jones, R. M. 1980. 'Notes from the Margin: Class and Society in Nineteenth-Century Gwynedd' in D. Smith (1980a)

Jones, R. M. 1981. *The North Wales Quarrymen, 1874–1922.* University of Wales Press

Kearney, H. F. 1989. *The British Isles: a History of Four Nations.* Cambridge University Press

Kiernan, V. G. 1972. 'Victorian London: Unending Purgatory', *New Left Review*, 76 (November–December)

Lee, J. 1973. *The Modernisation of Irish Society, 1848–1918.* Gill and Macmillan

MacDonagh, O. 1977. *Ireland: the Union and its Aftermath* (2nd edn). Allen & Unwin

MacDonagh, O. 1983. *States of Mind: a Study of Anglo-Irish Conflict, 1780–1980.* Allen & Unwin

MacDonagh, O. 1988. *The Hereditary Bondsman: Daniel O'Connell, 1775–1829.* Weidenfeld & Nicolson

Minchinton, W. E. 1954. 'Bristol: the Metropolis of the West', *Transactions of the Royal Historical Society*, 5th Ser., 4

Mitchison, R. 1983. 'Ireland and Scotland: the Seventeenth Century Legacies compared' in Devine and Dickson

Mitchison, R. and P. Roebuck 1988. 'Introduction' in R. Mitchison and P. Roebuck (eds.), *Economy and Society in Scotland and Ireland, 1500–1939*. John Donald

Moody, T. W. and F. X. Martin (eds.) 1984. *The Course of Irish History* (2nd edn). Mercier Press/Radio Telefis Eireann

Morgan, K. O. 1963. *Wales in British Politics, 1868–1922*. University of Wales Press

Morgan, P. 1981. *The Eighteenth-century Renaissance*. Christopher Davies

Mughan, A 1977. 'Modernisation, Deprivation and the Distribution of Power Resources: Towards a Theory of Ethnic Conflict', *New Community*, 7 (4)

Nairn, T. 1981. *The Break-up of Britain: Crisis and Neo-nationalism* (2nd edn). New Left Books

O'Leary, C. 1982. *Celtic Nationalism*. Queen's University, Belfast, Inaugural Lecture

O'Malley, E. 1981. 'The Decline of Irish Industry in the Nineteenth Century', *Economic and Social Review*, 13 (1)

O'Sullivan See, K. 1986. *First World Nationalisms: Class and Ethnic Politics in Northern Ireland and Quebec*. University of Chicago Press

O'Tuathaigh, G. 1972. *Ireland before the Famine, 1798–1848*. Gill and Macmillan

Page, E. 1977. *Michael Hechter's Internal Colonial Thesis: Some Theoretical and Methodological Problems*. University of Strathclyde: Studies in Public Policy, 9

Pierce, T. J. 1972. *Medieval Welsh Society: Collected Essays,* ed. J. B. Smith. University of Wales Press

Rees, W. 1948. *The Union of England and Wales*. University of Wales Press

Richards, E. 1988. 'Regional Imbalance and Poverty in Early Nineteenth-Century Britain' in Mitchison and Roebuck

Robbins, K. 1988. *Nineteenth-Century Britain: Integration and Diversity*. Oxford University Press

Roberts, P. R. 1972. 'The Union with England and the Identity of "Anglican" Wales', *Transactions of the Royal Historical Society*, 5th ser., 22

Roberts, P. R. 1972–3. 'The "Act of Union" in Welsh History', *Transactions of the Honourable Society of Cymmrodorion*

Roxborough, I. 1988. 'Modernisation Theory Revisited: a Review Article', *Comparative Studies in Society and History*, 28 (3)

Rubinstein, W. D. 1977. 'Wealth, Elites and the Class Structure of Modern Britain', *Past and Present*, 25

Sheppard, F. 1985. 'London and the Nation in the Nineteenth Century', *Transactions of the Royal Historical Society*, 5th Ser., 35

Simms, J. G. 1984. 'The Restoration and the Jacobite War (1660–91)' in Moody and Martin

Sloan, W. N. 1979. 'Ethnicity or Imperialism? A Review Article', *Comparative Studies in Society and History*, 21 (1)

Smith, D. (ed.) 1980a. *A People and a Proletariat: Essays in the History of Wales, 1780–1980*. Pluto Press/Llafur

Smith, D. 1980b. 'Wales through the Looking Glass' in D. Smith (1980a)

Smith, D. 1980c. 'Tonypandy 1910: Definitions of Community', *Past and Present*, 87

Smith, N. 1986. 'On the Necessity of Uneven Development', *International Journal of Urban and Regional Research*, 10 (1)

Smout, T. C. 1980a. 'Scotland and England: Is Dependency a Symptom or a Cause of Underdevelopment?' *Review*, 3 (4)

Smout, T. C. 1980b. 'Centre and Periphery in History, with Some Thoughts on Scotland as a Case Study', *Journal of Common Market Studies*, 18 (8)

Smyth, W. J. 1978. 'The Western Isle of Ireland and the Eastern Seaboard of America: England's First Frontiers', *Irish Geography*, 11

Stead, P. 1985. 'The Labour Party and the Claims of Wales' in John Osmond (ed.), *The National Question Again*. Gwasg Gomer

Stewart, A. T. Q. 1989. *The Narrow Ground: the Roots of Conflict in Ulster* (2nd edn). Faber & Faber

Trevor-Roper, H. 1982. 'The Unity of the Kingdom: War and Peace with Wales, Scotland and Ireland' in Robert Blake (ed.), *The English World: History, Character and People*. Thames & Hudson

Trotsky, L. 1977. *A History of the Russian Revolution*. Pluto Press

Tuck, A. 1979. *Border Warfare: a History of Conflict on the Anglo-Scottish Border*. HMSO

Wall, M. 1984. 'The Age of the Penal Laws (1691–1778)' in Moody and Martin

Wallerstein, I. 1980. 'One Man's Meat: the Scottish Great Leap Forward', *Review*, 3 (4)

Whately, C. A. 1987. 'Salt, Coal and the Union of 1707: a Revision Article', *Scottish Historical Review*, 66, (1)

Whately, C. A. 1989. 'Economic Causes and Consequences of the Union of 1707: a Survey', *Scottish Historical Review*, 68 (2)

Williams, G. 1979. *Religion, Language and Nationality in Wales*. University of Wales Press

Williams, G. A. 1982. 'Imperial South Wales', in his *The Welsh in their History*. Croom Helm

Williams, G. A. 1985. *When Was Wales? A History of the Welsh.* Pelican

Williams, W. O. 1958. *Tudor Gwynedd.* Caernarfonshire Historical Society

Williams, W. O. 1964. 'The Survival of the Welsh Language: the First Phase, 1536–1642', *Welsh History Review*, 2 (1)

Chapter 14

Ireland: A Case of Peripheral Underdevelopment or Capitalist Colonial Undevelopment?

RAYMOND CROTTY

Introduction

The periphery is a question-begging concept. Peripheral to where? When? London, a couple of thousand years ago, was peripheral to Athens and Rome. Last century it was the core of the largest and wealthiest empire in history. Yesterday's periphery is tomorrow's core, and vice versa. But core or periphery, what light does the status cast on socio-economic conditions? Of the six countries in Europe with the highest GNP per person, four are located in the Arctic periphery: Iceland, Norway, Sweden and Finland; and two are at the continental heartland: Austria and Switzerland. There are many examples within EC countries and within the USA of regions that have in the past been regarded as peripheral, now having above average rates of economic growth (Commission of the European Communities 1989, pp. 82–4). The wealthiest countries in Asia — Japan, Korea, Taiwan, Hong Kong and Singapore — are all located on the continent's geographical periphery. Their great wealth has suggested a new perspective: that of a Pacific-basin economy, with these five countries comprising an important segment of the circumference — not the core!

If the geographical concept of the periphery is nebulous, unstable and of limited explanatory usefulness, the frequently associated concept of socio-economic underdevelopment is hardly more conducive to clear thinking. Underdeveloped in relation to what? By Swiss standards, West Germany, where incomes are only 84 per cent as high, is 'underdeveloped'; and by West German standards, Britain, where incomes are only 92 per cent as high as German, is also 'underdeveloped'.

The concepts of 'developing' and 'undeveloping' seem to be analytically more useful than 'developed' and 'underdeveloped'. A society can be said to be developing when, in a realistic sense, it is better off now than it was in the past; while it can be said to be undeveloping, or retrogressing, if it is worse off now than before. It is suggested, as an operational concept, that a society can be taken to be better off if it fulfils two conditions: (1) it now has more people who are better off than it formerly had; and (2) it now has fewer people who are as badly off as it formerly had. By corollary, a society can be said to be worse off, undeveloping or retrogressing, if either or both of these conditions do not obtain.

Britain and its constituent parts are, according to this definition, developing, though it may be doing so less rapidly than Germany or Switzerland. There are in Britain today many more people with higher real incomes than fifty or even twenty years ago. Though poverty and squalor cannot be said to have been eliminated, they are much less acute and less prevalent than in the past. The same can be said of all the countries of continental Europe, not even excluding Romania. It can also be said for the countries northwards of the Rio Grande in North America, for Oceania and for 'the five tigers of the East', as Japan, Korea, Taiwan, Hong Kong and Singapore have been termed. With rather less confidence, it can be said that mainland China, with its one-fifth of the world's population, is developing.

The situation elsewhere is different. There are now more people who are better off than formerly in most of the countries of Africa, Asia and Latin America; most of them have expanding numbers of elites who participate, to a greater or less extent, in the good life of the modern world. All of these countries, however, have expanding masses of people whose standards of living decline ever closer towards a subsistence level, which itself is continuously lowered as modern medical science makes it possible for people to survive at nutritional levels where survival would have been impossible in the past. These countries, which comprise the Third World, while complying with the first, fail to comply with the second condition of developing and so are categorized as undeveloping, or retrogressing.

There is another country, closer to home, which, while complying with the second, fails to comply with the first condition for developing. That is Ireland, or more specifically, the twenty-six counties which comprise the Republic of Ireland. There are, thankfully, in the Republic now many fewer people who are as badly off as formerly. But there are also fewer who are as well off as formerly. In the Republic today, 7 per cent fewer people get a livelihood than ten years ago; 13 per cent fewer do so than when the state was established seventy years ago. In 1821, or 170 years ago, the area now known as the Republic of Ireland had a population which was almost twice as large as the combined populations of Scotland and Wales. Now Scotland's and Wales's combined population is more than twice the Republic's. Because of much lower dependency rates in Scotland and Wales, the excess of the number of people getting a livelihood in Scotland and Wales is even greater.

There has been in Ireland the same failure to mobilize resources to meet effectively the needs of society as obtains in the Third World. That failure 150 years ago reduced Irish living standards ever closer towards a subsistence level, in the same way as obtains now over most of Africa and extensively in Asia and Latin America. Ireland's Great Famine of the 1840s had most of the hallmarks of the megafamine that now threatens Africa. Following the trauma of the Famine and the opening wide of the channels of emigration, Irish living standards ceased to depend on the government of Ireland. The failure to mobilize resources, which is common to Ireland and to the countries of the Third World, no longer affects Irish incomes. Instead, it determines the number of Irish who remain in Ireland at living standards that are exogenously determined by those in Britain and the other countries to which the Irish emigrate and by the willingness of the Irish to emigrate. Over the long haul, since the 1840s, almost half those born in Ireland have emigrated. In 1989, when 53,000 were born there, there was net emigration of 46,000 from it.

It is implausible in the extreme to ascribe the socio-economic undevelopment, or retrogression, of a Third World that contains about half the world's total population to peripheralization, or to any conceivable adaptation of the concept. It is equally implausible to attribute Ireland's undevelopment over several centuries to the same cause. Recollect that in the last century, when Britain was the wealthy hub of the greatest empire that the world has seen, Ireland was closer to it than every other country, except France and Belgium; yet Ireland undeveloped, while more distant Denmark developed, as did also the much more distant New Zealand.

It is not merely possible, but perhaps too easy, to posit a whole series of explanations for particular countries, on particular occasions, retrogressing rather than progressing, as is the normal experience of countries which contain about half the world's population. A good example of this procedure is provided by Lee (1989). Sooner or later this approach must wear thin, however, and the persistent inquirer must look for a more general, more fundamental explanation. Why do some countries develop while others

undevelop? Is there anything that systematically distinguishes the
developing from the undeveloping countries?

Capitalist colonial undevelopment

One such distinguishing feature is capitalist colonization. All the
countries that have been capitalist colonized, including Ireland,
undevelop. All the countries that have not been capitalist colonized,
including Scotland and Wales, develop. Capitalist colonization may
be defined as the colonization, within the past 500 years, of countries
in which food production was limited by the natural resource-base
rather than by a capitalist stock, by one or other of the nine countries
which, along with Greece, Luxemburg and Ireland, now comprise the
EC. This argument requires expansion.

The Indo-European pastoralists who moved from the steppes of
Eurasia into the deciduous forest of central western Europe were
forced to adopt a new form of production by a new environment,
which also, however, made that new form of production uniquely
possible. The pastoralists of central western Europe were forced by
their environment, as no other pastoralists were, to preserve fodder in
the summer season of abundance to keep alive during the winter
season of dearth the cattle on which they were absolutely dependent.
They could do so only by growing crops; and in that cold, northern
environment, crop production needed, relative to output, vastly more
inputs like seed, ground preparation, crop tending and harvesting
than anywhere else where crops were grown. It needed, in a word,
capital, or the surplus which individuals save from what they produce
and which they use for further production.

A unique need for, and a unique capacity to amass, capital
distinguished central western Europe from the non-European world.
The non-European world was peopled either by those who hunted
and gathered food, or by those who produced food with little
or no capital. The cultivators, who were almost entirely restricted
to the warm, watered, alluvial river valleys of the tropics and
semi-tropics, were able to cultivate to the margin of the arable
land with little more than a hoe and a handful of seed. The output of the remaining food producers, who were pastoralists,
depended completely on the naturally determined carrying capacity
of their communally grazed pastures, which invariably tended
to be overstocked during the critical dormant season. In the non-
European world, therefore, output was determined, for hunter
gatherers and food producers alike, by the quantity and quality of
land available. It was natural-resource-based. In Europe, however, it

was determined by the amount of capital available. It was capital-based.

Ireland was the only part of Europe, from the Eurasian steppes to the Atlantic, where a society of natural-resource-based producers evolved. Ireland's location gave it a maritime climate which made it possible for cattle to survive the winter season without fodder. Ireland was thus the only country in central western Europe where, up to 1000 years ago, hay was not made. Its insular location also for a long time insulated Ireland from the political, economic and social forces operating elsewhere in Europe and allowed society there, more so than in Scotland or Wales where environmental conditions were otherwise not dissimilar, to evolve along lines determined by its own environment and independently of the rest of Europe. That environment, which in major respects was similar to that of sub-Sahelian Africa, gave rise in Ireland to a form of social organization that persisted till 100 years ago and that had more in common with sub-Sahelian Africa's than with mainland Europe's.

Three distinctive features are peculiar to countries that have been capitalist colonized. The first, as already noted, is that, in a socio-economic sense, they undevelop, while all other countries develop. The second is that they use as their *lingua franca* the language imposed on them by their capitalist colonizers, while other countries use their indigenous, national language. There is, for example, less Irish used in the Republic now, seventy years after independence, than there is Welsh in Wales. The third distinguishing feature of countries that have been capitalist colonized is that they all exist within boundaries imposed on them by the colonizers rather than ones determined by the interaction of neighbouring peoples. This is the case obviously in Latin America and Africa. It is also the case in Ireland, where the border between the Republic and Northern Ireland was settled by the colonial power.

It is understandable that colonies should have retrogressed socially and economically during the colonial era. It was the purpose of the colonial powers to 'squeeze' the colonized peoples for metropolitan profit. In doing so, they imposed on the colonized peoples socio-economic institutions that had evolved in European capitalist society and they applied capitalist European technology. The criterion in every case was profit for the metropolitan power. The impact on the indigenes was immaterial. For, to quote an observer of the Irish scene:

> Did insurrection break forth in Ireland? The aristocracy of the country never stirred; it was English artillery that subdued the

insurgents; and when everything was restored to order, the aristocracy continued to receive the revenue of its land as before.

Contrast that mode of spreading western institutions and technology with its spread first to eastern Europe 1000 years ago, and then to eastern Asia a little over a century ago. Sovereignty was never conceded by Russia or Japan, which were thus able to adopt eclectically from the West while retaining what they wished of their own. Whatever institutions or technology were borrowed had to pass the acid test of being broadly consistent with the well-being of the borrowing society; for, in their case, 'did insurrection break forth', there was no English, or other colonial, artillery to subdue the insurgents.

It was, to repeat, understandable that colonies retrogressed under colonialism. But, with the possible exceptions of Northern Ireland and South Africa, capitalist colonialism is dead; yet everywhere capitalist colonial undevelopment lives on. All the former capitalist colonies, and they alone, undevelop, use as their *lingua franca* the language of the colonial power, and all live within the boundaries imposed on them by the colonial powers. Seeking for a general explanation of the universal persistence of the capitalist colonial heritage of socio-economic retrogression and cultural and territorial frustration, one turns to the nature of capitalism, first as it evolved within its central western European heartland and then as it was superimposed elsewhere through the process of capitalist colonization.

The society that evolved in central western Europe was the product of decisions made by myriads of individuals. These were individuals who, in the first place, decided to break from the Golden Hordes on the steppe and to infiltrate into the forest. Even before that, the Golden Hordes were themselves the descendants of anonymous hunters who, instead of slaughtering and eating a feral goat or sheep, decided to breed it with a view to producing a future stream of goats or sheep. Within the deciduous forest of central western Europe, the *quondam* pastoralists took decisions about production, saving and investment. The outcome of those decisions transformed feudal lords into absolute monarchs; and absolute monarchs into representative governments. All the time, the impetus for change came from below, from the nation mass, the same source from which change now comes dramatically, in non-capitalist colonized eastern Europe.

Transposed out of its European homeland and imposed forcibly, for metropolitan profit, on nations which produced with little or no capital, capitalism has never rooted in the soils and cultures of these countries. The colonized nations were outside the decision-making process, from the beginning of capitalist colonialism. Decisions and the initiation of change were the prerogative of the colonizers and of their agents and collaborators in the colonies, to which the colonized nations could merely react. Investment decisions were not made, as in the forests of central western Europe, by the masses with a view to complementing their labour and expanding their product. These decisions were instead made by elites, the agents or collaborators of the colonizing power. They were invariably motivated by metropolitan or elite profit. Profit could best be secured by increasing exports to the metropoles, normally directly, but indirectly in the case of the eighteenth-century Irish provision trade with the West Indies. Investment was frequently of a labour-substituting rather than output-increasing nature, as was investment in livestock in seventeenth- and nineteenth-century Ireland. This type of investment allowed the elite decision-makers to take a larger share, with the nation mass taking a smaller share, of a reduced total product.

Capitalist colonialism invariably reduced the living standards of the colonized nations. The effect of this during the first 250 years was normally to cause population decline, almost to extinction in some cases, as in Latin America, the enslaved populations of the Caribbean and Cromwellian Ireland. The mortality-reducing influences of capitalist colonialism outweighed the effects of reduced living standards during the second 250-year period. Those influences included institutional factors, like the maintenance of western law and order, and technological factors like the application of the basic principles of medical science. The net effect was a decline in death rates and an increase in population.

The impotence of the capitalist colonized nations persisted though everything else changed. Change was unceasing in response to the saving, capital formation and technological change that were initiated by the myriad individual producers where capitalism was rooted. The impotence of the colonized nation masses persisted when their elites, who were the agents and collaborators of the colonizing powers, in the process of unceasing capitalist evolution, secured control of the colonial administration. Thereafter in the former capitalist colonies, the elites have squabbled among themselves for control of the administration taken over from colonial masters, and for the privilege which accompanies that control. Otherwise, like all elites, they favour the status quo and resist change. The disinherited nations meanwhile have undeveloped at least as rapidly under the new flags and emblems of independence as they did under colonial rule. The essential, enduring feature of capitalist colonialism is that it has rendered the colonized nations incapable of that generation of change from below which, from the beginning, has been the source of all human progress.

The impotence of the formerly capitalist colonized nations in most cases in the post-colonial era stems from the perpetuation of the impoverishment that was initiated by colonialism. The rapid growth of poor populations, which results from the application out of context of western institutions and technology, perpetuates the poverty of those populations. Their ever-worsening impoverishment and the impotence to which it gives rise make them incapable of changing a social order that was imposed originally to squeeze the colonized nations for metropolitan profit. Their poverty and impotence ensure the perpetuation of the heritage of capitalist colonialism.

The capitalist colonial legacy in Ireland

The Irish experience was in line with the general Third World pattern up to around 150 years ago. Then the ability of the Irish, who are the only capitalist colonized nation of the same Caucasian racial origin as the colonizers, to blend easily with metropolitan populations, facilitated emigration. Since then, though Irish incomes have risen in line with those of the West, the less contented half of every successive generation has found it easier to change its country of residence than to change the imposed socio-economic order of their native country.

It is important, when considering the outlying parts of the archipelago commonly known as the British Isles, to recognize the wide gulf of historical experience and the persistent disparities between the socio-economic order of Ireland, on the one hand, and that of Scotland and Wales on the other. These disparities persist despite the veneer nowadays of a common North Atlantic popular culture. The disparities are exemplified, for example, by the fact that, while there was virtually zero net migration into or out of Scotland and Wales in 1989, in the Republic, where 53,000 people were born, there was net emigration of 46,000. Ireland now has more in common with the Third World than it has with Scotland, Wales and the rest of Europe, just as 1000 years ago, it had more in common with sub-Sahelian Africa.

But while there should be no illusion about the fundamental differences, it is right that the other outlying parts of the British Isles archipelago should have a common concern about the perpetuation in Ireland of the heritage of capitalist colonialism. Putting the matter at no higher level: that perpetuation will mean the continuation and likely exacerbation of the violence associated with the partition of Ireland; the continued diversion of substantial British public funds towards containing that violence; and the continued irritation of a cancer of malorder within the British body politic.

At a higher level: Ireland is a close-to-hand microcosm of the vast, continuing and worsening problem of capitalist colonial undevelopment. Europe, and more specifically the nine capitalist colonizing countries which, with Greece, Luxemburg and Ireland, comprise the EC, bequeathed that problem, along with most of what is good in the modern world. From whatever mix of guilt, self-interest and altruism, western Europe now spends large sums trying to undo the enduring harm it did to the Third World through the original act of capitalist colonization; not, it should be added, through the latter-day withdrawal of interest and profit. But these efforts to aid the former capitalist colonies themselves do more harm than good. They are a major factor in perpetuating the disastrous regimes of elite privilege and national disability which were established by capitalist colonialism. The one useful service that Europe might now perform for the Third World, as some atonement for the vast harm it has done to it, is to help in giving to the Third World a precedent, an example, of a former capitalist colony throwing off its own heritage of capitalist colonialism. For in the long, worldwide history of capitalist colonialism, there has been no precedent of a nation that has been capitalist colonized ever subsequently developing economically, or restoring to pre-eminence its national language and culture, or integrating its national territory. The former capitalist colonies, in the absence of that precedent, seem bound to continue to flounder in an ever-broadening, ever-deepening morass of Third World poverty. They will continue to apply to their totally different circumstances measures and methods that have benefited the developing world, but that exacerbate the undevelopment of the former capitalist colonies.

However, although the pathology of capitalist colonialism has never been reversed, it is surely not irreversible. People, and the nations which people form, are more than patterns of atoms, slaves to the laws that guide them. People and nations are free to shape their lives, to seek truth, love and beauty. There are occasions, if rare in history, when people can and do act freely; and can and do defy precedent. Such an occasion seems to exist now in Ireland.

The realization of that opportunity to bring about desirable change depends on understanding the situation in question. That understanding can best be secured through the quintessentially European method of scientific study. For that reason, the scientific interest of fellow Celts in Scotland and Wales in the phenomenon of Irish capitalist colonial undevelopment would be highly desirable.

It is right to emphasize that what is not needed is maudlin sentimentality. An excess of the latter has caused the injection of vast material resources into Ireland and into the other former capitalist colonies which comprise the Third World. So far from those inputs relieving the situation, they have, for very understandable reasons, gravely exacerbated the heritage of capitalist colonialism. Cold, objective, scientific, Scottish and Welsh inquiry into the nature and causes of, and possible solutions to, the continuing undevelopment of their fellow Celts in Ireland would, on the other hand, be very positive.

Bibliography

Commission of the European Communities 1989. *Report on Economic and Monetary Union in the European Community.* Brussels
Lee, J. J. 1989. *Ireland 1912–1985.* Cambridge University Press

Index